WITHDRAWN

Library
Middle Tennessee State University
Murfreesboro, Tennessee

ILLUSTRATIONS

OF

Old English Literature.

EDITED BY

J. PAYNE COLLIER.

VOL. II.

Benjamin Blom
New York

Library
Middle Tennessee State University
Murfreesboro, Tennessee

First Published London 1866
Reissued 1966, by
Benjamin Blom, Inc., New York 10452
Library of Congress Catalog Card No. 65-16233

Printed in U.S.A. by
NOBLE OFFSET PRINTERS, INC.
NEW YORK 3, N. Y.

CONTENTS OF VOL. II.

1. PANCHARIS, by HUGH HOLLAND. 1603.
2. HORESTES, AN INTERLUDE. 1567.
3. PRESERVATION OF HENRY VII. 1599.
4. REFORMATION OF REBELLION, and SHORE'S WIFE, by THOMAS CHURCHYARD.
5. SEVEN DEADLY SINS OF LONDON, by T. DEKKER. 1606.
6. LOVE'S COURT OF CONSCIENCE, by H. CROWCH. 1637.
7. WILLIAM LONGBEARD, by THOMAS LODGE. 1593.
8. TRIUMPH OF TRUTH, by T. PROCTER.

INTRODUCTION.

HUGH HOLLAND, the author of the ensuing poem, was also the writer of fourteen lines, such as were then considered a sonnet, on the death of Shakespeare, and on the publication of the folio, 1623. They are conceited, and have little merit.

Nearly the same criticism may be offered upon the succeeding poem, though it certainly displays more talent and cleverness, but the whole fabric is violent and unnatural; and reading the prefixed eulogium by Ben Jonson (unknown to the editors of his works, and never republished by himself) we wonder at the manner in which, even in the partiality of friendship, he brought himself to speak so extravagantly of Holland's powers: Ben Jonson only terms Shakespeare the " sweet swan of Avon"; but Holland, according to him, was the "sweet swan" of nearly every river in Europe: and we almost wonder that, in the excess of his hyperbole, he did not carry him over the Atlantic to the Amazons and the Orinoco. We surmise that Holland was rich, and we know that Ben Jonson was poor, and we recollect no earlier effort of the kind by the learned and "inspired bricklayer." In its way it is admirable.

The best point about "Pancharis" is unquestionably the versification in the Italian *terza rima*, a form of composition then unusual in our language. The construction of the plot, so to call it, is little short of ridiculous, when we find the author bringing down Diana and Venus to hob-nob with Queen Katharine out of a cup formerly belonging to Edward the Confessor, while Cupid is represented as the chief agent in her amour. The court revel, according to the manner of the time, is, however, well and clearly described; but the best feature in it, the discussion between the Maid, Wife, and Widow, was borrowed from Sir John Davys, as printed in 1602 in the first edition of "The Poetical Rhapsody."

The date of the publication of Holland's poem is 1603, but he professes that it had been penned before the death of Elizabeth; and his letter to Sir Robert Cotton, at the close, is a sort of imitation of the method pursued by Spenser, when in 1590 he appended his exposition of the "Faery Queen" addressed to Sir Walter Raleigh. The Richard Martin to whom Holland addressed his rhyming Latin lines, near the end, was the man who had had so violent a quarrel with Sir John Davys shortly after 1596, and who was Recorder of London when James I. came to the throne.

Notwithstanding its many defects, and in consequence of some of its peculiarities, the production is worth preserving; and, as there is but a single copy of it in existence, we have reprinted it as a remarkable and curious relic by a friend of Shakespeare, Ben Jonson, and of other poets of their day. If Holland ever wrote or printed a continuation of this his "first book", it has not come down to us.

J. P. C.

PANCHARIS:
The first Booke.

CONTAINING

The Preparation of the Love betweene Owen Tudyr, and the Queene, long since intended to her Maiden Majestie:

And now dedicated

TO

THE INVINCIBLE JAMES,

Second and greater Monarch of Great *Britaine*, King of *England, Scotland, France* and *Ireland*, with the *Islands* adjacent.

Mar. Valerius *Martialis*
Victurus Genium debet habere liber.

Printed at London by V. S. for Clement Knight.
CIƆ IƆC III.

TO MY LORD THE KING.

SONET ACROSTICKE.

IMAGE of God; firſt as a man, and then
    As king, by moſt deſert, and onely right:
Man is the king of creatures, and thy might
Exceedes this too, for thou art king of men.
Sunne of our ſphære, may never clowde up pen
    So radiant beames from thy poore ſubjects ſight:
That ſtill our eyes may ſee their happy light,
    Ev'n as their heate did warme our boſoms, when
Unſeene they ſhone beneath the fixed ſtar.
    Up, noble minde, to thy fift empirie,
    And ſoare yet higher then thy fortunes ar:
Reſemble Heav'n in all but levitie,
    Take after earth in nothing more or leſſe,
    Except an irremooved ſtayedneſſe.

TO THE BRIGHT QUEENE ANNE,

HIS DEERE WIFE, AND OUR DREAD LADY.

1. What is ſhe that like ſilver *Cynthia* ſhoeth
    Amidſt the hoaſt of heaven,
    But fairer threetimes ſeaven?
It is the Queene of Love! ſee where ſhe goeth:
The Queene of Love and Beauty, (lo) together
With her faire ſon the Prince of Love comes hether.

2. The Southpole that in our horizon shined,
    And made the earth to wonder,
    Gone is that earth all under,
And to the Northpole hath her roome resigned:
On whom to waite our eyes and harts persever,
And may they cease, ô never, never, never!

3. Thou, in whose zodiak of white armes enchained,
    Our sunne so oft hath shined,
    In whose wombe was confined
What in this isle scornes to be long contained;
Live thou and he, and maist thou see him rather
Copartner, then successor to his Father.

TO MY LORD THE PRINCE

SONET ACROSTICKE.

Heire of thy Sires foure realmes, and (which I more
  Esteeme) foure vertues, that unto a fift,
  No doubt, will thee (o slowly, slowly) lift;
Receive this ryme of thine old aunceftore,
Yong Prince of *Wales*, and pardon me therefore.
So may glad VICTORY be one day swift
To crowne thy sacred head (that art a grift
Extracted hence) with holy bayes, before
(Unvanquish'd or unhurt by sea or land)
Upon thy brow the wreath of *England* fit:
And I with crowned head, but armed hand,
Ride by thy lordly side, and, after it,
Turne from thy Grandsires loves to sing thy wars,
Exchanging *Venus* mole for *Marses* skars.

Pancharis.

ILLUSTRISSIMÆ DOMINÆ
ARBELLÆ STUARTÆ.
SONULUS ELEGEIACUS ACROSTICHUS.

Auricomum alterius mundi jubar altera virgo,
  Regia cui stirps est, meus neque stirpe minor ;
Bis imperfectum facili cape fronte poema :
  Est quia perfectus qui tibi mittit amor.
Lactea nec Venus est illic, nec vena, nec unquàm
  Lætus amor Musæ novit adesse meæ.
Attamen Eugenii sacros cantillat amores,
  Sensit amans socium queis Catherina jugum.
Tandem orata Venus sic ambos juvit amantes,
  Unde genus tantis regibus, atque tibi.
Atque mihi scribenti utinam sic æqua fuisset :
  Ritè ego si colui, dum sub Amore fui.
Tu tamen (horridulæ faveas licet ipsa Dianæ)
  Alma veni, Musis et Venus esto meis.

Clarissimo et candidissimo ingenio Præceptori olim, semper
  Amico GULIELMO CAMDENO, Armorum Regi
    nulli secundo, poëmation hoc censendum et
      emendandum mitto.

Nanus Musæi cupit in quacunque locari
  Parte liber, magnum nec capit ille locum.
Sed neque se magnis studet immiscere Poetis
  Quales Meonides maximus, atque Maro.
Cernuus hic veterum lambat vestigia vatum,
  Atque pio sanctos basiet ore pedes.
Cum Nasone tamen ponas (hic namque libellus

Sanctior, ut multis doctior ille modis)
Vel cum Chaucero (nec enim mihi fidus amator
Eſt minùs, et multo Nympha pudica magis.)
Plus quoque quam tetigiſſe pedes fortaſſe meretur,
Quando tuas meritus ſit tetigiſſe manus.

ANDREAS DOWNES GRÆCUS PROFESSOR REGIUS CANTABRIGIÆ.

Antiquos memorat vatum chorus omnis amores,
   Sed plerumque quibus non Venus æqua fuit ;
Fœlices HOLLANDE *canis fœliciter igneis*
   Tu veterum, quibus haud abnuit alma Venus.
Et REGINA *fuit memorabilis, et* THEODORUS:
   Illam qui meruit, carmine dignus erat.
Nec tantùm furor ambobus fuit ille ſecundus,
   Nec blandum hoc modo tum invit utrumque jugum :
Sed populos domuit ſævos genteſque feroceis
   Hic tandem placidè conciliavit amor.
Cujus nunc volvenda dies fructum attulit vitro,
   Et majore beat munere longa dies.
Namque tribus populis diſcordibus inſula dives
   Ante colebatur, bellaque crebra movet.
Verùm exhinc mox læta duos concordia junxit,
   Firmus et hic ſtabili fœdere vinxit amor.
Tertia magnanimis reſtabant regna Britannis,
   Hæc quoque magnifico ſub duce nunc coeunt.
Hac etenim de ſtirpe venit rex inclytus, atque
   Clara recens ſoboles, et nova progenies.
Quæ penitus toto ſecluſos orbe Britannos

Æternâ reget in pace, favente Deo.
Et majoribus auspiciis dominabitur oræ,
   Circumquaque ingens quà fluit Oceanus :
Sceptra tenens, diadema gerens, JACOBI *age honores,*
   Aggredere ô magnos, maxime, lœtus ovans.
Horridulâ genitum in regione Eremanthidos, Arcti,
   Sol regem vidit, te simul atque hominem.
Creverunt animi pariter crescentibus annis,
   Sors tandem œqua animis cedere regna jubet.
Finibus exiguis arctari magna recusant,
   Virtuti campum fata dedêre parem.
Mollior horrifero Boreœ superadditus Auster,
   Una est virtutis facta palœstra tibi.
Quàm sapiens fuit Empedocles, qui fœdere amoris,
   Et cœlo et terrâ cuncta coire facit !
I nunc ô vates et Theseas atque Ariadnes
   Medeasque truces dic et Amazonidas :
Materiam noster novit sibi sumere dignam,
   Dignos et versus pangere materiâ.

NICOLAI HILLI CARMEN TESTAMENTALE ET VIATICUM.

Nunc migro, nec patrios forsan rediturus ad agros
   Urget, et officii debita cura premit.
Quid prohibebit enim quin veri testis honestem,
   Quem studii paritas lustraque multa probant ?
Raptim et discedens verbo quod sentio dicam,
   Totius gregis est gloria, nemo gregis.
Ornat et egregiis Catharinam millibus effert :
   Ut canit ille suam, sic canit illa suum.

E. B.

Anacreontickes.

Scarfe 'till now hath ENGLAND feen
A Poëm, but of verfes ftore;
Here an unenforced green
Hath native flowres, which heretofore
Had, at moft, well painted been,
As was the feafon which them bore:
Arts each *Venus* that doth fhine
In ancient Poëfie, heer more.
HOLLAND, this firft birth of thine
Put forth imperfect, ftands before
The finifhed, and fhall in fine
Somewhat be new for worlds t'adore:
CYNTHIUS (as we divine)
And the MUSES, and the GRACES,
And their QUEENE, by thee refine
Baftard fongs, whofe common bafes
Were but words, that KATHARINE
Beautie equall to her faces
Might enjoy. Here then unhard
A princely Love, and learned Bard.

BEN : JOHNSON.

Ode ἀλληγορικὴ.

Who faith our times nor have, nor can
    Produce us a blacke fwan?
    Behold, where one doth fwim,
      Whofe note and hue

Pancharis.

Besides the other swannes admiring him,
    Betray it true :
    A gentler bird then this
Did never dint the breast of *Tamisis*.

Marke, marke, but when his wing he takes,
    How faire a flight he makes !
    How upward and direct !
    Whil'st pleas'd Apollo
Smiles in his sphære, to see the rest affect
    In vaine to follow.
    This swanne is onely his,
And *Phœbus* love cause of his blackenesse is.

He shew'd him first the hoofe-cleft spring,
    Neere which the *Thespiads* sing ;
    The cleare *Dircœan* fount
    Where *Pindar* swamme ;
The pale *Pyrene*, and the forked *Mount :*
    And, when they came
    To brookes, and broader streames,
From *Zephyr's* rape would close him with his beames.

This chang'd his downe, till this, as white
    As the whole beard in sight,
    And still is in the brest :
    That part nor winde,
Nor sunne could make to vary from the rest,
    Or alter kinde ;
    So much doth virtue hate,
For stile of rarenesse, to degenerate.

Be then both rare and good ; and long
    Continue thy sweete song.
    Nor let one river boast
      Thy tunes alone ;
But prove the aire, and saile from coast to coast :
    Salute old *Mône*.
    But first to *Cluid* stoope low,
The vale that bred thee pure, as her hills snow.

From thence display thy wing againe
    Over Iêrna maine,
    To the *Eugenian* dale ;
      There charme the rout
With thy soft notes, and hold them within pale
    That late were out.
    Musicke hath power to draw,
Where neither force can bend, nor feare can awe.

Be proofe, the glory of his hand,
    (Charles *Montjoy*) whose command
    Hath all beene harmony :
      And more hath wonne
Upon the *Kerne*, and wildest *Irishry*,
    Then time hath donne,
    Whose strength is above strength,
And conquers all things ; yea it selfe, at length.

Who ever sipt at *Baphyre* river,
    That heard but spight deliver
    His farre-admired acts,
      And is not rap't

With entheate rage to publifh their bright tracts?
    (But this more apt
  When him alone we fing)
Now muft we plie our ayme, our fwan 's on wing.

Who (fee) already hath ore-flowne
    The *Hebrid* Ifles, and knowne
    The fcatter'd *Orcades*;
      From thence is gon
To utmoft *Thule*: whence he backes the feas
    To *Caledon*,
  And over *Grampius* mountaine,
To *Loumond* lake, and *Twedes* blacke-fpringing fountaine.

Hafte, hafte, fweete finger! nor to *Tine*,
    Humber, or *Owfe*, decline;
    But over land to *Trent*:
      There coole thy plumes,
And up againe, in fkies and aire to vent
    Their reeking fumes;
  Till thou at *Tames* alight,
From whofe prowde bofome thou began'ft thy flight.

Tames, prowde of thee, and of his fate
    In entertaining late
    The clloife of *Europes* pride,
      The nimble *French*,
The *Dutch* whom wealth (not hatred) doth divide,
    The *Danes* that drench
  Their cares in wine; with fure
Though flower *Spaine*, and *Italy* mature.

All which, when they but heare a ſtraine
    Of thine, ſhall thinke the *Maine*
    Hath ſent her *Mermaides* in,
      To hold them here:
Yet, looking in thy face, they ſhall begin
    To looſe that feare;
    And (in the place) envie
So blacke a bird ſo bright a qualitie.

But ſhould they know (as I) that this
    Who warbleth PANCHARIS,
    Were *Cycnus*, once high flying
      With Cupids wing;
Though, now by *Love* transform'd, and dayly dying:
    (Which makes him ſing
    With more delight, and grace)
Or thought they *Leda's* white adult'rers place

Among the ſtarres ſhould be reſign'd
    To him, and he there ſhrin'd;
    Or *Tames* be rap't from us
      To dimme and drowne
In heav'n the ſigne of old *Eridanus*:
    How they would frowne!
    But theſe are myſteries
Conceal'd from all but cleare propheticke eyes.

It is inough, their griefe ſhall know
    At their returne, nor *Po,*
    Iberus, Tagus, Rheine,
      Scheldt, nor the *Maas,*

Slow *Arar*, nor swift *Rhone*, the *Loyre*, nor *Seine*,
    With all the race
  Of *Europes* waters can
Set out alike, or second to our swan.

TO MY MAYDEN MUSE.

Goe, Virgin Muse, to her divinity,
That is the Vesta of Virginity:
For unto whom shouldst thou goe rather
So bound to her, and to her father?
Be gonne, and when thou com'st before her,
Upon thy knee, see thou adore her.
For thou mayst gather by her feature,
She is more then an earthly creature;
In whom no elements are combined,
But a sift essence, well refined
Above the vulgar grosse confections
Of any of the fower complexions,
Flegme, Sanguine, Melancholy, Coler.
  Tell her that once I was her scholer,
And how in grammer I was grounded
In the best schoole she ever founded,
By two great clerkes (two greater wasters
Of oyle then houres) that were my Masters:
Where I liv'd partly of her larges,
And partly of my parents charges.
Thence was I had, to learne more knolledge
To *Cambridge*, and her fathers colledge,
Of him whose fame is flowne ALL-OVER,
As well beyond as this side *Dover*.

On *Ariſtotle* oft I pored,
And here and there him over-ſkored:
Where poetrie too I found defined,
To which by birth I was enclined.
Yet heard I worthy DOWNES in *Homer*,
And every day I glean'd my gomer.
　　Thus having there for *Lea* ſerved,
(Though ſome ſaide *Rachel* I deſerved)
Some thonght the houſe could ſtand without me.
　　I then began to looke about me,
And forthwith deſperately did ventre
The wide world, in whoſe little centre
My friends (of whom death hath bereft me)
My loving friends ſome living left me:
Enough (if God the grace but lend me)
From cold and hunger to defend me,
That I may ſtudy ſtill by leaſure,
Without all paine, and at my pleaſure.
　　Now the blacke doune began to cover
My pale cheekes (for I was a lover)
And ſung acroſticke ſonets ſweetely;
For (if that ſome can judge diſcreetely)
I neede not feare that daintie DAVIES,
Though he ſing ſweeter then the Mavis.
And of my love they were. But, ſtay thee;
No more of that, my Muſe, I pray thee.
For either it muſt ſhow my folly,
Or elſe renew my melancholly:
Yet was ſhe faire, and honourable,
And vertuous (had ſhe beene more ſtable).
　　Though ſhe, perhaps, did but forget her,

Pancharis.

And now likes maydenhead the better:
Whereof she is the richest border,
Next CYNTHIA, soveraigne of that Order.
   When *Love* my bosome thus had fired,
Me for his prophet he inspired,
That every line, and every letter
Of my devise might passe the better:
Yet of this legend but the writer
Was I, and he the sole inditer.
   For how, alas! can it be other?
I am not I the Muses brother.
My lips I never yet have sowsed
In Hippocrene, nor carowsed
The lusty liquor thence distilling,
The braine with holly fury filling.
   The climat where I was begotten
Of father *Phœbus* is forgotten:
No Parnasse there (though mountaines many)
No Muse (though Nymphs as faire as any).
God wote it is too farre removed
From her, to be of them beloved.
Apollo, they and all the *Graees*,
Attend her onely in all places.
   This, in effect, when thou hast told her,
Thou must be yet a little bolder,
And beg that thou mayst waite upon her,
Among her many Maydes of Honor;
A modest maide with chaste variety,
To lull asleepe that sweete society;
Who may, as well as any other,
Reade every line before the Mother,

So shamefac'd are they, and so holly,
Voide of all looseneffe, and light folly :
Elfe had it beene too much impiety,
To vow them to fo great a Deity.
   This done, againe on knee lowe bended,
And hands as high to heaven extended,
Afcribe me of this golden ftory
Onely the paine, and her the glory :
Praying fhe would but reade the proem,
And fo breath life into my Poëm.

———o———

PANCHARIS:
The First Booke.

I SING Queene *Katharine*, and my countryman.
  O Love! if I before thy altare spread,
Blacke though I be, have oft lookt pale and wan,
And as white turtles there have offered,
(As are those that thy whiter mother drawe)
Draw neere; and with her myrtle deckt the head
Of me thy priest, that am too rudely rawe,
Nor once have bin baptized in the spring
Of *Helicon*, which yet I never saw,
A pinion plucke me out of thine owne wing;
And let thy godhead more propitious be
Unto my thoughts whiles others loves I sing,
Then in mine owne it hath beene unto me.
  And thou, O second sea-borne Queene of Love!
In whose faire forehead love and majestie
Still kisse each other (as the turtle-dove
Doth her beloved) thou whose frowne, whose smile
Presenteth both, who doth inspire and move
This lesser continent, this greatest ile,
Let smiling Love, when Majesty would frowne,
Infuse like life and motion to my stile.
I treate not I here of the awfull crowne,

(Though somewhat of the Court) my legend is
Compos'de of Love and Beautie up and downe.
Where if I aught have saide that sounds amisse,
Immortall Maid, thou pardon me that crime,
Sith thy white hand which (lord!) I long to kisse
May crosse out all, and rectifie my rime.
So shall the amorous readers seeme as those
That have seene thee full oft and many a time;
Yet seeing thee againe, anone suppose
They somewhat see they never saw before,
Such spangling objects thou dost still disclose,
As all desire to see thee more and more.

   From *London* westward doth a Castle stand
Along the Thames, which of the winding shore
Is called *Windsore*, knowne by sea and land,
For the rich Guarter and the holy *George*,
There founded first by the victorious hand
Of warlike *Edward*, he that was the scorge
And second hammer of the haughty Scot.
As the lame God in his Trinacrian forge,
Striv'd first to blow the stubborne yron hot,
And after laide about him like a Lord,
Till he thereof the upper hand had got;
So English *Edward* did with fire and sword,
Lighten and thunder in that northerne clime,
And never respite did his foe afford,
(No, nor himselfe almost) untill the time
As hardy *David* grac'd faire *Windsores* court.
Where also *John* of *France*, who long'd to clime
The wheele of Fortune in the selfe same sort,
A captive king was after shortly seene.

Pancharis.

 Yet neither this, nor that, so much report
The fame of *Windsore*, as faire *Katherine;*
She that hath yet (save her great neece) no other,
Daughter of *France*, of *England* Mother-Queene,
The sixt *Charles* daughter, the sixt *Henries* mother,
And (which is chiefest) the sift *Henries* wife.
 Here the sad Queene ful many a sigh did smother,
Resolved still to leade a widdowes life.
So chaste was she, though faire, and rich, and yong,
That yong and olde to praise her were at strife:
Of her high honour all musitians sung,
And thereto each sweet poet tun'd his pen,
That therewith *England* and all *Europe* rung.
She was the wonder of all mortall men,
Few queenes came neere her, and none went above
In grace and goodnesse, since, before, or then.
 Might once no minion dare to kisse her glove,
(Much lesse her hand) or mistresse her miss-call;
As men are wont when they for fashion love.
So modest was she, and so meeke withall,
That all good folkes might to her presence come,
No lesse then to some councellors common hall.
More doth the suter then the gaudy roome
Set out a monarchs majestie, by ods,
When life or death he lookes for as his doome.
 Not they that grav'd the gold did make the gods,
But such as did before them bow to begge,
All were they made of clay, but only clods:
Nor they the prince that still provoke and egge,
(That only they may golden idolls be
To which the subject bends his servile legge)

The sacred and anointed majestie
To robbe the realme, to gaine the subjects wealth,
To loose their hearts: but such as on the knee
Importune grace with happinesse and health,
Not posted off to those extreame delayes
Of bribing favorites, which is worse then stealth,
And scarce was heard of in those happy dayes.

    Her selfe, a widdow, would for widowes pleade
With much compassion, and at al assayes;
But as for orphanes bills, them would she reade,
And then shut in her princely orphans hand,
Whereby along with her she would him leade
Unto his uncle that did rule the land:
Hard were the heart, that in so just a cause,
With two such suters upon tearmes could stand,
And not dispence a little with the lawes.

    Thus with her great delight in doing good
She wanne such fame and popular applause,
That on a time the goddesse of the wood,
Diana, sorely longed once to see
This abstract model of all womanhoode,
And next her selfe the flowre of chastitie.
Wherefore (the sunne now scorching in the skull
Of *Leo*) foorth a hunting needes would shee
To *Windesore* forrest, which she found as ful
Of deere, as trees; yet trees so many ar
As there the darts of Phœbus are too dull,
And pierce no more then doth the meanest starre.
There was the lawrell that was glad to hide
Her greene head from the face of *Phœbus* farre,
The lordly oake that scorn'd not by his side

The bragging brier, and with wilde yvie was
Like great God *Bacchus* crownd: there was, beside
The smooth skinn'd beech, all kerved as did passe,
In curious knotts that did the names enshrine
Of many a lover, and of many a lasse.
There was the elme that underprops the vine,
And box, wherof poore shepherds frame their pipes,
The gentle woodbind, and sweete eglantine,
Each other clipping with their amorous gripes.
The budded hawthorn, and our *London* dames
Holy-reformers: the birch lacing stripes
On lasie truands; with such like, whose names
I know not, save the willow that did guirde
The bankes forsaken of the slippry Thames.

On every tree did sit a severall bird,
And every bird did sing his severall note:
This to the base a fift, that sung a third,
Each one according to his aery throate,
A summers day, me thinkes, were nothing long
With the rare musicke which they made by rote:
Phœbe her selfe with all her nymphs did throng
To heare it, as she had not heavenly beene;
And this was all the burden of their song,
Long live *Diana* and faire *Katherine!*

Wearied with toile, but never with the noyse,
High time she thought to goe and see the Queene;
For her declining brother, that enjoyes
One part in one of her three-formed realmes,
Bade her breake up those sports and earthly joyes,
Sith he must never quench his thirsty beames,
Till she to heaven returne and take his place,

To governe there the ſtarres, and here the ſtreames.
  She therefore to the Caſtle gan to pace,
That bounteouſly was built of faire free-ſtone,
Whoſe guilded inſide, for the greater grace,
Was all ſet out with many a precious one,
And they with one that yet more precious was:
The criſtall windowes round about it ſhone,
That, as ſhe ſtood therein, the very glaſſe
Seem'd rather to let out the luſty light.
  On did the goddeſſe with her meany paſſe,
Till they came to a roome all richly dight,
Of heavenly bliſſe and happineſſe the bowre,
Where each of other had this happy ſight.
The place was after calld the Maydens towre,
But of *Diana* and her maydes, no doubt,
So called was, and is unto this howre.
  Much the amazed goddeſſe look't about,
But moſt aſtoned at the Queene ſhee ſtood,
That ready word she could bring hardly out,
Before the lovely Queene (who could more good
Then halfe a world) did ſilence ſoftly breake,
Each Lilly blending with a Roſe of blood.
Madame (ſhe ſayde), my tongue can hardly ſpeake
That world of worth which I in you admire;
Then, all that I can doe is farre too weake
To anſwere your deſert and my deſire:
For ſince my Lord, my life, (God his ſoule ſave)
Was laide (as well may witneſſe my attire)
My better halfe ſince he was laide in grave,
I never yet came foorth in companie,
But in my chamber my ſelfe buried have.

Wherefore, if perfon here, or aught there be,
That unto you may breede the leaft offence,
God knowes it is without my privitie:
But did I knowe, I foone fhould rid him hence,
That of this action is not humbly glad.
And therewithall, they both lowe reverence
Did one another. Up the while was had
A banquet to a by rome as did paffe,
Bifket-bread, fucket, marchpane, marmalad,
Candids, conferves, and all that dainty was:
It haild downe comfects, and through every fpoute
The fugar-caftles powrd out hypocras;
Walk'd up and downe the boles, fo as I doubt
If I may call them ftanding cups or no.
    And as the wine, fo went the day about.
Diana rofe, and ready was to goe,
When, in another cup of maffie golde,
They crownd her wine that fparkled to and fro.
    It was the king Conffefors cup of old,
Who liv'd a maried man, and died a maide.
She kift the cup, where grav'n, fhe might behold
Actæons death, and downe it quickly laid;
Then turn'd a little to her maydes afide,
Rebuk't their want of fecrecie, and faide.
    Could ye no better your owne counfailes hide,
But over *England* too it muft be blaz'd?
Lo! heere, *Actæon* in his horned hide,
While on our fhame and nakedneffe he gaz'd.
Therewith fhe pauz'd, but they no word could fay,
So were they at that lively mappe amaz'd.
And fure the cup did all fo wel difplay,

As if it white wine were that therein ſtoode.
Then would ye ſweare *Dianaes* ſelfe there lay,
Nakedly clothed with the criſtall flood :
And were it redde, there lay, then would ye ſweare,
Actæon bathing him in his owne blood.
At laſt, as ſhe that halfe abaſhed were,
Unto the Queene ſhe turn'd and uttred this.

   Alacke, alacke! if his owne hownds did teare
This fond *Actæon*, yet the fault was his,
And mine the griefe : we gods are no leſſe ſory
For mortalls puniſhments, then for their amiſſe,
Though we, by this, and that, declare our glory,
And our owne juſtice in them both exalte.
Yet ſome will ſay (and they too peremptory)
That this his fortune was, and not his fault :
Was 't not his fault ſo to prophane a place,
That hallowed was with franckincenſe and ſalt ?
Were 't not his fault that ſhould ſurpriſe your grace
Here in your chamber, ſkare you or your traine,
And from your ſide your ſureſt ſervants race ?
Abortive fanſies ſwimme about his braine,
And faile him when himſelfe he moſt aſſures :
Runne all his plots and purpoſes in vaine,
That ſhall the like attempes on you or yours.

   Thus ended ſhe, and with this ſpeach the day.
On ſtole the night that parting ſtil procures,
As though it came to bid her come away.
Then tooke ſhe leave, and in her coach did clime
The eaſterne hill with horſes yron gray,
Where in flowe minutes ſhe muſt tell the time,
And ſerve the uſe of man.   God bade her ſo.

When neither cocke doth crow, nor clocke doth chime,
Whether we fee her filver face or no,
Yet there fhe walkes as wel by day as night,
And ftill about her criftall orbe doth goe.
 But (lord) with what a longing and delight
To *Windfor* ward fhe downe woulde caft her looke,
And guild the wide *Thames* with hir trembling light!
An other heaven ye would have thought the brooke
With moone and ftars, and here and there a cloude:
But in high heav'n what way fo e're fhe tooke,
Queene *Katharines* praifes there fhe rung aloude,
Set to the tune of her well tempred fpheare,
Much more harmonious then is harp and croud.
 Hermes, that all the ghofts belowe can reare,
And gently ufher with his fnaky rod,
To this new caroll gave attentive eare:
And (as he is a very prating god)
To the bright *Venus* hath it told anone,
From the firft point to the laft period.
When fhe in all the hafte would needes be gone,
To fee below what all had heard above,
Of Englands Queene and peereleffe paragon:
Her coach was drawne by many a turtle-dove,
And driven by a coachman of great worth,
Her little fonne, the mighty God of Love.
 So long he guided on his courfe by north,
When, having paft the feaventh and utmoft clime,
Out of the fea he might fee peeping foorth
A fpot of Earth as white any lime;
To which he thought it beft his courfe to hold.
 Now was the Earth, for it was paft the prime

That had unmask'd her of her tawny old,
Revested with a flowry diadem,
And new greene velvet, spangled all with gold:
Thus were the fields enameld all of them,
Along the silver Thames, that did embrace
The golden meades in wanton armes, and hem
Their looser skirts like an indented lace.
Acrosse, and up and downe the river swame
Her sacred swannes, who when they saw her grace,
Unto her coach to doe their homage came:
And from the land came turtles many a paire,
Unto her deity who did the same.
 Then *Citherea*, seeing them to repaire,
Bespake: Sir boy, we sure be gone amisse:
(But yet, the best is this, the way was faire)
Nay, doubtlesse, that no way to *Windsore* is,
But to our palace in mount *Citheron*.
And *Cupid* he was sore afraide by this
Lest it were so indeede; when (having gone
A little further) he might plainely see
Where with his eye a castle met anone,
High on a hill (as though it scorn'd to be
Built on the baser earth) and towr'd above
The lofty clowds, with such a majestie,
As saide it could not be the Court of Love.
Howe often have you seene together dwell
The lordly eagle and the lowely dove,
Of love and majesty concording well!
 By this they to the castle-gate be come,
That was shut in by warning of a bell.
In every roome yet stirring heard they some,

Pancharis.

Which made them loudly call, and loudly knocke;
Yet none, no more then if they had bin dombe,
Would anfwer them : a long houre by the clocke,
They waited there; now he, now fhe, now both.
Cupid at laft did peepe in at the locke,
Yet no man came; then *Venus* waxed wroth,
And fince of force fhe muft her purpofe miffe
To be reveng'd fhe tooke a folemne othe,
And faide, Much worfhip have we won, iwis,
If thus one filly woman may abufe
Two fuch great godheads : if we fuffer this,
What wretch, I pray you, may not well refufe
To burne on our high altars his perfumes,
And by this prefident the fact excufe?
Whether fhe on our gentleneffe prefumes,
Or her own greatneffe, all is one for that;
I fhall ere long fo pull her peacockes plumes,
That (though fhe now be yong and faire and fat)
She fhall no fooner looke upon a glaffe,
But fhe fhall greeve and fore repine thereat,
And fay, *That now is hay was fometimes graffe.*
Thinkes fhe to fcape our hands fo franke and free,
That fhee forfooth of *France* the daughter was,
Englands frefh bride, and thereby chaunc'd to be
Mother to him that now is king of both?
Alas! what's all this to a Deitie?
No more but titles and meere toies in troth.
As then fhe hath deferv'd, fo fhall fhe have,
Divine revenge comes fure, though late and loth,
Belike thefe giddie *French* thincke they may brave
My fonne and me at pleafure, leave undone

What at their hands moſt lawfully we crave,
Or do all lawleſſe outrage under ſunne.
They make but ev'n a woman and a childe
Of me and thee, and thereby thinke to ſhunne
Our vengeance: this it is to be ſo milde
To malefactors, that for very ſpight
Our temples and our altars have defilde,
Left unprophaned no religious rite,
But havocke made of holy maiden-head,
As if the charge we had renounced quite
That appertaineth to the bridall bed:
Wherein the lawfull heire begotten is,
Whom, after nine months fully finiſhed,
The ſhame-fac't father ſhall not feare to kiſſe,
At midnight to him by the midwife borne:
Yea, he himſelfe will ſweare it to be his,
When *Lucifer* lets foorth the bluſhy morne.
But if they ſtill my patience thus ſhall wrong,
By S. *Adonis* here, loe! have I ſworne,
And will not faile, I ſhall, ere it be long,
A plague ſend on them that will quickly tame
Their pride, and teach them ſing another ſong.
It ſhall feede in their marow like a flame,
And rage through ev'ry corner of the land,
That of the nation it ſhall take the name.
But to the point that now we have in hand:
Which to effect with more ſucceſsful ſpeede,
Sonne Cupid, you awhile my friend muſt ſtand.
  Mother (quoth he) to feare you ſhal not neede,
For I have ſtill beene your obſequious ſonne,
And ſtill will be, in thought, and word, and deed.

Pancharis.

Yet hold I not this dame fo much a nunne
By nature, as by vertue of the clime
Is far removed northward from the funne;
For she hath lov'd, and fo may do in time.
The bird that, having once efcap't the net,
Defies the fowler, may be caught by lime
Or other engines that for him be fet;
And fo may she by fome more quaint devife
(But what that is my felfe knows fkarcely yet)
Maugre her heart, all were it made of yce.

 Gramercie, fonne, quoth fhe, why then no doubt,
(Though she were ten times more then she is nice)
This act we shall bring well inough about.
But that I feare me which you lately tolde
About the climat all this ifle throughout,
Is all the let that ever happen could;
For though the Sunne now in the Lion raigne,
And his meridian, yet an uncouth cold,
Me thinks, doth hit me now through every vaine.
In *Affricke* if the lyon lift to rage,
Who fhall him from his ladyes fide reftrayne?
Yet heere he fleepeth out his idle age,
And dreames not once of Natures kindely fport.
Were it not this, what grate or yron cage
Could coope him from his pleafure? To be fhort,
The vine, that with the fcorching funne by noone
Growes quickely ripe in *France*, if you tranfport
Into this country, ripeneth not fo foone.
Yet is the foyle as thankful heere as there:
Yea, th' elements, all underneath the moone,
Remov'd from their owne place, fome otherwhere

Take new impreffions to them; for the fire
That only fhines in his celeftiall fphere
Here burnes moft violent. And with defire,
Said *Cupid*, fhall this faint, this *Katharine*
In *Windfhore* burne whom he did fo admire,
The man of *Monmouth*, when fhe did but fhine
In *France* at *Melaws*, like a blazing ftarre,
Whofe faire afpect, and influence divine,
Did ftoppe the hoarfe and open throate of warre.
As there great *Henry* fel in love with her,
Heere of another fhall fhe dote as farre,
Except my cunning, or this hand doe erre;
And that rich dowre, yea were it ten times moe,
Upon a fubject fhall I foone conferre.
 What! on a Saxon, Cupid, will yee fo?
Now by this mole (quoth fhe) upon my cheeke,
I rather had this high revenge forgoe,
Which I on her fo thirftingly do feeke,
Then any flinty Saxon fhould fucceede
A Prince fo mighty, and a Prince fo meeke.
Thefe Saxons cleane have wafh'd away my feede,
Swallowing the fat foyle like another flood:
Thofe fturdy Saxons, whom the ftones did breede,
Which *Pyrrha* (when yet all the earth was mudde)
By divelifh divination backeward threw
To take the forme of flefh, and bones, and blood,
Thefe men, thefe ftones, at an advantage flew
Of thy poore kindred thoufands with the fword,
And all the wofull remnant did purfue
To the bare mountaines, that could fcarce afford
Food for themfeves, or fafety from the foe,

Fowly intreating them in deede and word.
Long were they torne and tofft thus to and fro,
Now foiling, and then foild, till, at the laft,
Edward the firft (their fates ordaining fo)
To make them fubject to his crowne did caft.
His tender babe to be their Prince they tooke,
To whofe fucceeding heires they ftucke fo faft,
As none of them their faith as yet forfooke;
Save onely one, *Owen*, firnam'd *Glyndoore*,
Who became rebell againft *Bollinbrooke*,
And by his pride made all his country poore.
Ah *Harry!* why fhouldft thou, a civill Prince,
For one mans fault and fury play the Moore
Or Tartar thus, and tax a whole province
With fuch uncourteous and barbarian lawes
As never heard were of before, or fince?
If *Jove*, alas! as oft as men give caufe
Did every time but hurle a fiery ball,
A little time then fhould he have to paufe,
And in a while himfelfe leave none at all.
For all yet that betide them could, or can,
Here lives one ftill, and ftil I hope he fhall,
A gallant and refolved gentleman,
Faire *Owen Tudyr:* fire thou hir in love
With him, my boy. Mother (faid he) your fwanne
Shall not exceede this eagle, nor your dove:
Hereafter fhall fhe ftoope fo to the lure,
Though now awhile the clowds fhe toure above;
For her pure bofome with a brand as pure
I wil fo kindle, yet before the funne
Get out of *Libra*, that none may recure

Her heart, but onely *Owen*. Well faide, fonne!
(Him anfwered fhe) why fhould I then defpaire?
But (as one *Owen* hath us all undone)
Another *Owen* may thofe harmes repaire.
For who doth know, but that in time to come,
There may fpring from this wel conforted paire
(I will fo bleffe and fructifie her wombe)
H. 7., that feaven times happy man, who one day may
Sit on this throne, and thence with mercy doome
His and my people? O! when will that day
Shine from the eaft upon this northerne clime?
Then, then may well both Welch and Englifh fay,
That they were borne in a moft bleffed time.

   Mother, quoth he, thereof mine be the care,
And if I faile therein, mine be the crime;
But fith the court of heaven can hardly fpare
Us both at once, this caufe to me referre:
Perhaps the gods in no fuch bufines are,
Yet mortalles are. How fhall the mariner
That long in the wide ocean toffed is,
And nothing fees fave fea and heav'n, but er[r]e
When your propitious ftarre he there doth miffe?
How fhall the fhepheard doe, that to the hill
Leades forth his flocke, and home againe by this?
How fhall the ftrugling bride againft her will,
With her impatient love this night conceave,
Unles your gratious influence doe fill
Her fruitfull lap? God[s] muft not therefore leave
To helpe and comfort mortall men, becaufe
Of their due honor they the Gods bereave.

   This faid, he ftayd, and with this only claufe

She condefcended that all fhould be done,
As that her felfe therto her beft applaufe
Should give, and that as foone, too, as the funne
A judge betweene the night and day became.
  O filly Queene! thefe fnares how canft thou fhun?
And how, O *Venus* (hadft thou any fhame?)
Canft thou but blufh, what have ye reap't by this?
Thou and thy fonne, what great and glorious name,
When by Gods beguyld one woman is?
  A month and more, to make the Queene his flave,
He fought by all fuch traines and trickes of his
As knowe ye lovers (God from them me fave!)
By dreames and fanfies whilft abed fhe lay:
So wifely though herfelfe fhe did behave,
That once he thought it beft to runne away.
  By this the golden eye of heav'n, the funne,
From that difaftrous and midnight of day
Wherin his clewe of life was cleane out fpunne,
Henry, the firft in fame, in name the fift,
About the filver fkarfe of heav'n had runne:
Whofe firy courfers (howfoever fwift
To fome glad harts) feeme to the fory flow,
And dull as lead, then firft the Queene did lift
Her drooping ey-liddes from the earth belowe.
As one that having horded up his cheefe,
His only treafure, ftill his eye doth throwe
Backe to the place as to his beft releefe;
So was the Queene and all the court to glofe,
The more with her did flatter this her griefe:
For like the prince the people them compofe.
  Moov'd for their fakes, God wot, more then her owne,

The dowager Queene (like to the virgin rofe
That, all night is bedew'd, and newly blowne
Unto the morning funne for comfort feekes)
Thofe purer rofes wiping, that were fowne
Among the lillies in her lovely cheekes,
And with her teares bedewed day and night,
By the full fpace of two and fiftie weekes,
Refolv'd at laft to come by candle-light
Into the prefence chamber, and to glad
Her heart a little with the peoples fight;
Who to fee her againe were nothing fad:
For all the lufty courtiers did devife
(So foone as notice of her minde was had)
To entertaine her with fome ftrange difguife,
Done by *Dan Lidgate*, a great learned munke,
Who then in poefie bare away the prife;
For after *Chaucer* had he deepely drunke
Of *Helicon*, as few befides have yet.

   Now, when the funne into the fea was funcke,
They all together in the wardrobe met,
And them among (though farre above them all)
The gentle *Owen* was: a man well fet;
Broad were his fhoulders, thogh his wafte but fmal;
Straight was his backe, and even was his breaft,
Which no leffe feemely made him fhew then tall.
Such as *Achilles* feem'd among the reft
Of all his army clad in mighty braffe:
Among them fuch (though all they of the beft)
The man of Mone, magnifique *Owen*, was.
He feem'd an other oake among the breers;
And as in ftature, fo did he furpas

In wit, and active feates, his other peeres.
He nimbly could difcourfe, and nimbly daunce,
And ag'd he was about fome thirty yeeres:
But armed had ye feene him go to *France*,
Ye would have faide, that few on foote or horfe
Could have fo tofs'd a pike, or couch'd a lance,
Wherewith to ground he brought full many a corfe;
That oft alone when I recount the fame,
My tender heart cannot but have remorfe:
To write it then, alas! I were too blame.
Of onely Love, and of his armes, I fing:
Thy warres (O *Mars!*) I meane not once to name;
Yet hardly could I fpare that haughty ftring,
Did not the boy mine eare pull now and then,
Beyond my bounds for feare I chance to fling,
The fame and fplendor of my countrymen
Invite me fo. What is he that can holde
In his rude fingers fuch a flaggy pen,
If aught by chance of *Agincourt* be tolde,
But into teares his eies would quickely thawe,
Infteade of inke, to write the manifolde
And goodly flaughters which our men did drawe
That day in blood? But O! thou mighty ghoft
Of *Henry Monmouth*, who yet holdes in awe
My bolder ditty, that fo longs to boaft
Thofe olde *Heroës*, crown'd with holie bayes,
That under him did ufe to leade his hofte;
Beauforts, Veres, Nevills, Talbots, Cliffords, Grayes!
O! pardon thou, and they, that I leave out
Th'immortall mortall fights and blody frayes
By force of armes there fairely brought about.

And thou, *John Huntington*, whose acts I more
Admire than all, before whose face the rout
Of fearefull *Normans*, when thou cam'st ashore
From the triumphed ocean fled away,
As heartlesse hares the greyhounds doe before:
Redoubted Earle, of pardon I thee pray.
God wot I would, yet halfe so great a taske
I dare not undertake; and sooth to say,
That argument a lowder trump doth aske,
To sound a march too slender is my reede;
Inough is it to tune a courtly maske:
Then, to high purpose and the point procede.

    While they made ready there, ye might have seen,
One or an other, in a masking weede,
Go friske about upon the rushes greene,
And wish, if aught he chanced well to do,
That all were done no worse before the Queene.
    Some one the God of Love did pray unto,
With his milde mother, so to stand his friend,
As he thereby his ladies love might woe,
To whose sweete praise his paines he did commend:
Another, that he might good honors make,
As ev'ry measure did beginne or end,
Whereof his mistris might due notice take:
One that the dropping linkes defilde him not
For his white suite of costly sattensake:
An other that his impreafe, or his mot,
Or aught of his the princesse minde might please.

    Full many a suite in broken sighes, God wot,
Was offered there; yet all could not appease
His kindled ire, who by this easie baite

Thought now or never on the Queene to feafe,
That had fo often made him found retraite.
   It fell that foure and twenty pages were
Appoynted on the revelers to waite,
Who, two by two, before each paire fhould beare
The linkes aloft; and for the greater fhowe,
Like fuites to them and vizards alfo weare.
   The wily god, that all this did foreknow,
By putting on the perfon of a page,
Made up the compt, his quiver and his bowe
To buy a vifard which he layd to gage;
But turned into a blazing torch his brand:
A pretty ftripling, much about the age
Of fourteene yeares he feem'd, when he did ftand
Among the reft. Now was it time to fup:
So coftly nothing was by fea or land
But it was had, while ftill the frothy cup
Did hafte to deale about the lufty wine.
   When all was ended, and the boord was up,
In heav'n above the ftarres began to fhine;
Where alfo burned *Cithere* the bright,
To *Cupid* nodding, who knewe well the figne:
And, like an other heav'n, with ftarry light
Adorn'd was all the prefence round about,
That into day againe did turne the night,
Although the cheefeft light was yet without.
   With this the trumpets, lo! began to found,
And eke the multitude aloude to fhout,
(That all the roome did ev'n againe rebound,
Reechoing no particle amis)
God fave your Grace, and God your foes confound!

To fome her hand of fnowe fhe gave to kis,
She talk'd with other, and gave thanks to all
Along the chamber, as the manner is.
   Behold! how many fiery fparkles fmall,
The moone about her filver orbe doth fpend,
When *Hefperus* the evening foorth doth call:
So many glorious ladies, glad to tend
Upon the Queene unto her princely ftate,
Downe to the ground before her Grace did bend.
   As there in Majefty awhile fhe fate,
With fhamefac'd lookes lowe fix'd upon the ground,
Loe! three faire damfels fal'ne at foule debate,
And them before a trumpet hard to found.
The damfells, dreaft in white and blew and blacke,
Were afked, whence they were, and whither bound?
Whom they did looke for? or what they did lacke?
   Awhile they paus'd, and oft they changed hew,
The one ftill to the other looking backe,
Till fhe, that all appareld was in blew,
Stept foorth at laft, and making curt'fy low,
Beganne aloud. Moft mightie Queene, to you
In humble manner we prefent this fhowe:
A filly maide, a widow, and a wife,
As by our habits you may partly know.
Alate betwene us hapned heavy ftrife,
Whether the wife, the widow, or the maide,
Lives the moft happy and contented life?
All what we could, we three therin have faid,
And women (as men clatter) want no words.
Yet heere (alas!) the matter hath not ftaide;
For acted it muft needs be by the fwords

Of martialists ; but your majeſtike hand,
That unto miſers mercy ſtill affoords,
The ſame by your authority withſtand :
Which is ſo ſoveraigne, and doth carry weight
With all the mighty ſpirites of the land,
That ended all this ſturre will heere be ſtreight.
Eight hardy ſquiers doe holde of maidenhead
(Whereof is *Owen Tudyr* chiefe), and eight
Maintaine that it much better is to wed :
The laſt eight by like arguments approve
The life ſequeſtred from the nuptiall bed.
Renouned Empreſſe, then let pitty move
Your royall breaſt to ſave them from the ſpoile.
What heart of yron hath ſhe, that doth love
To ſee one man in fight an other foile,
Or once abide to ſee the blood to ſtreame
That in the manly boſome wonts to boile ?

   Heereat, as one awak'd out of a dreame,
The ſoftly ſighing Queene upſtarted ſoone,
Guilding the world with ſuch a glorious beame
As doth the ſunne this hemiſpheare by noone,
With morning ſhowrs though ſomewhat overſpred :
Or, as when in ſome miſty night, the moone
Breaks through the clouds, and ſhews her ſilver head.

   And thus ſhe ſpake. Ye vertuous maid and wife,
(For ſuch ye ſeeme) and thou whoſe halfe is dead,
Whoſe other halfe reſolves to leade the life
That alſo doth thy Queene : not all this ile
A fitter one could yeeld to ſtint your ſtrife,
Extended out though it lie many a mile,
And, but the ſea, abides not any bound ;

For all three courfes have I knowne awhile.
A very maide of me King *Henry* found,
(Whofe foule God pardon, and to mercie take)
To whom my love my faith kept ever found,
That all the world my honour might not fhake,
Ne wracke my fame againft fo foule a fhelfe.
As unto him, fo for his onely fake
I will remaine no leffe true to my felfe;
For *Henries* wife and widow will I die.
Honours, vaine pleafures, tranfitory pelfe,
I force not of fuch gaudes a whit, not I:
Yet doth this trafh the mindes of many tempt
To loves delights, from whofe vile tyranny
Princes, no more then other, are exempt.
But onely him I lov'd, fo do I now,
And ever fhall; of whom both thought and dreamt
I have fo oft, that no man elfe may bow
My fettled heart: onely (were he alive)
He might, perhaps, prevaile againft my vow.

 And God, I begge it now, fo let me thrive,
If aught I fpeake the worlds good word to woo
Beyond my worth; but with his thunder drive
Mee quicke thofe ugly fhades of hell into,
Before, O fhamefaftnes! that I forfake
Thee, or yet any lawe of thine undoe.

 Might I with me my little *Henry* take
To fome remote and folitary denne;
Your noble prince, his fervant God him make,
(Whereto the people cried *Amen, Amen!*)
I could be well content no more to come
Among the preafe and multitudes of men.

Not that I doubt but vertuous there be fome,
I knowe there be, and many in this place.
This of my fpeech then is the very fumme;
That oft alone when I recount my cafe,
No life, me thinkes, is like to widdowhoode,
So God but guide it with his holy grace.
  Heereat the maide and wife aftoned ftoode.
Miftake me not, quoth then the lovely Queene,
For often hath it beene no leffe a good
To marry wel, then to live fingly feene.
Perhaps the more, if hearts as well as hands
Be rightly tied the married paire betweene:
Not altogether wedded unto lands,
Ne wealthy dowres. Ah! never may fhe thrive,
That on the purfe above the party ftands.
She that fo weds (as I know none that did)
Beguiles her husband; he hath but the hive,
Another eates the hony. God forbid
That ever any courtly dame fhould carry
A heart fo bafe within her bofome hid!
As for my felfe, had I not lov'd my *Harry*,
Perdy, I make a vow that, for my part,
No kingdome could have tempted me to marry
Againft the love and liking of my hart.
  But ah! not long had I enjoyed my joy,
When ugly Death comes ftealing with his dart,
(For hand of man could never him annoy)
And him of life, and me of love deprives.
Yet hath he left behinde a princely boy,
That in my breaft his heav'nly fhape revives.
So like the father doth he daily grow,

As any you have feene in all your lives,
Yea, like him he already learnes to goe:
So would he bend the bowe, fo would he looke,
His eies, his hands, he caft, he carried fo.

But whither have I, like a wandring brooke,
Thus err'd by love? Few liquid pearles then gufht
From out her eies, and then her breath fhe tooke.
But (Lord!) then how the lovely virgine blufht,
When all the people did the Queene purfue
With frefh applaufes; till, when all was hufh'd,
The Queene did her continued fpeech renew.

Ladies, it feemes (and therewithall fhe fate)
It feemes, I fay, to us, that each of you
So pleafed is with her peculiar ftate,
That all the world may not your wills reclaime.
Me lever alfo weare your love then hate,
Whereat no vertuous prince did ever aime.
Tyranny feare, and feare this hate begot.
What duety then can want a privy maime
That of the fubjectes love proceedeth not?
I then conclude, no kinde of life amis
That is fo fixt, and alters not a jot:
Unhappy moft the leaft refolved is,
When as the great commander in the warres
Affects the marchants life, the marchant his,
Who knowes each crooked motion of the ftarres:
The clerke againe envies the courtier,
And he the clowne. To leave particulars,
In us, and you, (for oft thus one may erre)
I muft (I hope to none of your difgrace)
Together when all courfes I conferre,

Of force define, that both refigne the place
To maidenhead ; as copper doth, or braffe,
When Indy gold their glory doth deface.
   A worthy wife, no doubt, *Sufanna* was,
Redeem'd from death, as fhe was thereto led ;
Yet did the widdow *Judith* her furpaffe ;
Who fmote off, as he breath'd his laft abed,
That horrid head, yet breathing warre and luft.
But unto *Mary*, well of maidenhead,
This, and that other yeeld of duty muft :
The Maide, where three times three months did repofe
The Sunne, in whom repofde is all my truft.
   A virgin is but ev'n a very rofe,
For once if hand of man thereon be laide,
Both fent and colour it will quickly lofe,
So tender is the bloome in ev'ry maide.
That innocent and ever happy ftate,
(Had our forefathers not fo fondly ftraide)
Wherein God humane nature did create,
In holy maidenhead refembled is,
Whence having falne too foone, we grieve too late :
When all the world doth point at our amis,
Then fee we naked fhame with open eies.
   Yea, maidenhead goes farre beyond all this ;
For in that earthly place of paradife,
As heere we doe, they did by Gods beheft :
But in that heav'n, where his owne owner lies,
As are his angells, fuch are all the reft ;
Maides and unmarried. Heere then I conclude
That maidenhead of all is only beft.
And as fhe faide, fo faide the multitude.

Then all three ladies (who did now relent,
And pardon aske that they had beene so rude)
Besought the night in sportes might now be spent;
Whom so to doe with many thankes she praide.
　　So they unto the foure and twenty sent
To certifie them what the Queene had saide,
And therewithall to bid them haste away.
The messenger so did, and they obaide.

　　Alacke for pitty! now what shall I say?
A wily traitor and a very thiefe,
That all the while in ambush closely lay
Among the maskers, is become the chiefe:
　　And to the castle is already come,
Good Queene, I feare me, to thy further griefe.

　　Herewith was heard the trumpet and the drum,
As if they had beene marching for the field:
By two and two they entred all and some,
Each after other offering up his shield,
　　While she, that in all curtisie did abound,
To every man particular thankes did yeeld.

The softer musicke then beganne to sound,
And eke the ladies were had out to dance:
It also pleasde the Queene to walke a round,
The courtly sportes the more to countenance,
　　With whom (bicause he did the measures leade)
To couple it was *Owens* happy chance.

　　Then all in order gan it softly treade
Up and downe, in and out: the planets seaven,
Rapt with harmonious spheres (as we may reade)
So daunce about the lofty pole of heaven.
　　The measures ended, it grewe very late,

Pancharis.

(For it was halfe an houre nigh paſt eleaven.)
Then bade the Queene, that one belowe the ſtate
A ſtoole for her ſhould ſet upon the ground :
This done, anone downe thereuppon ſhe ſate.
    Some in their cinqueapaſe did nimbly bound,
Some did the cros-point, ſome high capers cut,
And on the toe ſome other turned round ;
While ſtill the minſtrell on the trembling gut,
Strove with diviſion to outrunne the time
That haſted on the revells up to ſhut,
(For midnight now the clock began to chime.)
Then iſſued *Owen* out among the reſt,
Reſerved untill then, as onely prime
Of all the maſkers, and the very beſt.
    Love that did all the while no will forſloe,
That holp to ſett afire her ſnowy breſt,
Reſolv'd, at laſt, that it muſt needs be ſo.
    Wherefore, as *Owen* did his galliard daunce,
And grac'd it with a turne upon the toe ;
(Whether his eyes aſide he chaunc'd to glaunce,
And, like the lovely God, became ſo blinde,
Or elſe, perhaps, it were his happy chaunce,
I know not, and record none can I finde.)
This is the ſhorte : the Queene being very nigh,
He fell, and (as he forwarde downe declinde)
His knee did hit againſt her ſofter thigh.
I hope hee felt no great hurt by the fall,
That happy fall which mounted him ſo high ;
For up he quickly ſprang, and therewithall
He fetch'd me ſuch a friſk above the ground
That, O well doone ! cried out both great and ſmall.

The Queene arofe then, and dealt thanks around
To all of them, but unto *Owen* moſt :
The trumpets alfo they began to found,
For on ſhe paſſt, and after her an hoaſt
Of lovely ladies, while the people praied,
That God would guide her with his holy ghoſt.

Thus all the court was very well apaide,
And every dauncer in delight did ſwimme,
But *Owen* onely, who was ſo diſmaide,
That all the company came to comfort him.
Amongſt all, one wiſht it had beene his happe :
I can not blame him, though he loſt a lim,
That long'd to pitch in ſuch a princely lappe.

But out, alas ! what ſhall there more be ſaide ?
This was but ev'n an engine and a trappe,
That for the feely foule was lately laide :
The faireſt foule, I weene, that ever was,
This onely tricke ſo fowly hath betraide.

As into ſome one centre of the glaſſe
The funny beames we doe contract to light
Divine tobacco, that all blame doth paſſe,
Becauſe all union hath the greater might ;
So fierce *Cupido* cauſde his fiery brand
Upon that eagle-eye of his to light,
That in the very turning of a hand,
Reflected it might ſet afire her heart,
That obſtacles none might it once withſtand.

The wound did at the firſt not greatly ſmart,
For it was inward, and there foftly bled
Feeding the fire, till (having got apart)
Her yvory body laide in yvory bed,

Pancharis.

She there afresh of all beganne to thinke
(For idle fancies there be sooneft fed)
And unawares let love in softly sinke
Betweene the lillies of her lovely breft.
    What should she doe? she could not sleepe a wink,
Nor any respite take, nor any reft,
Nor once but dreame (for how can one awake?)
That it was got such an unruly gueft:
Which on the gods behalfe did greatly make.
    It was the very dead of drowfy night,
When every creature elfe his eafe did take
But onely yong Queene *Katherine* the bright;
Whofe eies (like two faire diamonds set in rings)
Awak'd her outward little world to light.
For ugly night with her broade raven-wings
Had overhild the golden goodly face
As well of heavenly as of earthly things,
And the dull humour powred downe apace
On weary miserable mortall men.
Loe! then beganne her eyes firft to embrace
An easie slumber: her devotions then
She softly sigh'd, and *Requiem* also saide
For her deere Lord: thus (having breath'd *Amen*,
And softer cheeke upon soft pillow laide)
Fell fast asleepe. Who then but *Cupid* sung?
Who laugh'd, who danc'd, or half such Herods plaid?
For here and there the fire about he flung,
As did in Ætna his suppofed fire:
That where before she was but only ftung
A little in the fancie with desire,
And quickely might have cur'd the same againe,

(Had fhe but ufde the meanes) his raging fire
Diffufde the venim now through ev'ry vaine.
  As elementar fire doth clofely creepe
Betweene fome plankes, the greater height to gaine,
Not daring out of his blinde cell to peepe,
Before, alas! (as oft it doth befall)
The goodman of the houfe be faft afleepe;
Then oppofition finding none at all,
About the noone of night invades the fparres,
And many hundred thoufand fparkles fmall,
About the welkin hurls to mocke the ftarres:
At laft in fmoaky flames it chokes the fkies,
And of the building all the beauty marres,
Or once the owner halfe can ope his eyes.
  O mercy God! O Love! O Charity!
What is this heate, or how doth it arife?
Is it begot but of a wanton eye,
And fo conceived in a gentle hart?
If it be fo, then afke I reafon why?
Thy felfe, O Love! of eyes deprived art.
But if by fatall revolution
Of any ftarre, O God! thou guide thy dart,
(Sith that we know the certaine motion
Of every ftarre in heav'n, both her degree,
Her oppofition, and conjunction,
With every other hidden qualitie,
Portending what is likelieft to befall)
Reveale, O God! reveale thou unto me
That am thy prieft (though worthy leaft of all)
So long have I rebel'd againft thy law,
Blafpheming it as ceremonial,

Pancharis. 49

Enacted onely fooles to keepe in awe:
Yet, fith I doe recant my folly now
That into danger youth might haply draw,
Reveale the reafon, and the caufe, why thou
In all thy deedes fo diverfe ever art;
And doe, I pray, inftruct thy Prophet, how
In every pageant thou doft play thy part,
Provoking here to love and there to luft.

   Why fhould a lady like with all her hart
(Her felfe borne under *Jove* and *Venus* juft)
A tawny face befur'd with fable haire,
Borne under old Saturnus ftarre combuft?

   What appetite the foule hath to the faire
Is evident; for every feely foule
Knowes with perfection how things long to paire:
But that the faire fhould ftoope unto the foule,
A wonder it doth feeme to me, no leffe
Then if an eagle fhould unto an owle.
Yet more may be then I can haply geffe:
I might be numbred eighth among the wife,
If all to know myfelfe I fhould profeffe.

   It is becaufe that in faire womans eyes
Blacke men feeme pearles (and women all, awis,
Would be, or elfe, which doth as well fuffice,
Reputed faire?) or is it haply this,
That any beauty layde againft the blacke,
Of much more beautie and more brightnes is?
Is it becaufe we like (though nought we lacke)
What others have? or elfe becaufe this hue
Lends livelier heate and moifture to the backe?

   Why fhould a queene, to whom fo many fue,

So many princes would be prowde to serve,
Bid all the glittering pompe of court adue,
And to a private love her sweets reserve?
Why should she spend with him her happy dayes,
That hardly doth to serve her but deserve?

   This is thy power, O Love! this is thy praise;
For unto Gods it only doth belong
The mighty downe to pull, the meeke to raise:
Thou findest likes, or else ere it be long,
Thou framest such of sundry qualities.
It is then open, and no petty wrong,
To charge thee so with incongrueties;
For onely thou alone in all thy deedes,
As at the first yet work'st by contraries.

   When as together all the sundry feedes
Of undigested *Chaos* did conspire
To mould the body that so many breedes,
The earth, the aire, the water and the fire,
(For each was unto either deadly foe)
To sundry rankes did all at once retire:
The leight got up, the heavy stay'd below,
The sea did start aside to show the land,
The windes did on the billowes stifly blow,
All which be now tied in so friendly band,
As they may not beyond their limits range,
And this was done by thy almighty hand.
Nor art thou, Lord (for all thou seeme so strange)
Yet halfe so mutable as any man,
But as resolved, and unapt to change,
As at the day when first the world began.

   Perhaps by some to scorne I shall be laught

For holding fo, fay all they what they can,
This is the truth, thus other fhall be taught:
Yea (though therefore I fhould be tortured)
I would not alter any word for aught,
For all is right, if it be rightly read.

FINIS.

RICHARDO MARTINO HUGO HOLLANDIUS
Optimo Oratori Peſſimus Poëta,
veteris et perfecti amoris ergò
novum ſed imperfectum poëma
mittit.

SONULUS HENDECASYLLABICUS.

Hoc, Martine, tibi vetus ſodalis
  Nuper mitto novum poema cœptum,
  Nec doctum ſatis id, nimiſve ineptum :
  Veſter Pegaſus eſt, nec ipſe talis
Qui tantis vehar incitatus alis.
  Verùm me videor ſat eſſe adeptum,
  Si carmen tibi tale ſit receptum ;
  Nec lectum tibi non fuiſſe malis.
Quod (ſi quid ſaperem) domo quietâ
  Annus debuerat videre nonus :
  O ſed famâ ego gloriaque ſpretâ
In peſſum cecidi poeta pronus ;
  " *Tanto peſſimus omnium poeta,*
  " *Quanto tu optimus omnium patronus.*"

TO SIR ROBERT COTTON, KNIGHT,
Lord of Cunnington.

My reaſons can no longer hold out nor yet my modeſty: nature indeed hath armed me againſt bluſhing, not againſt baſhfulnes. Have here then this double imperfect poëm. Firſt, though ill, not all done: Secondly, through all il done. The faults I confes in making (as they be many) are mine: the fault in ſetting forth (if it be any) is yours; and ſo much the more yours, by how much the more you would have mine publiſhed. It was (if you remember) the worke, or rather the paſtime of one vacation. Howbeit, that can no way iuſtly excuſe me. For (if the deſtiny of these leaves ſhould out-ſpin Nature in our lives) how ſhould poſterity be informed in how ſhort time the ſame were written? All the writings of old time were as the teſtaments of the writers: but moſt of the writers of our dayes are as executors to their writings; not unlike *Hecuba* in the tragedy, who in her own lifetime ſaw the death of all her children. And to ſay but truth (had not I beene the more indulgent father) theſe rimes of mine (which nigh upon two yeares have nowe layen by me) had long ſince made windeing-ſheetes for perfumed gloves in the EXCHANGE. The laſt ſummer I began to put this infant (then about ſome twelve-moneths old) out of his foule and ſwatheling clowts; and (like our *London* nurſes, who, when they bring their foſter-children to be ſhewed the friends, dreſſe them up in their beſt habiliments) wrote it out curiouſly with mine own hand, thinking to have gone into

Scotland and to have given it the king; towards whom my loyaltie, I was in thofe dayes as daring to powre into your bofome, as I found it ready to endure the fame. Your love to me, and our duty to him gave us both confidence thereunto: to fpeake nothing of particular intereft, his Maiefty and you defcended of two brothers, hee from *Rob. le Brufe*, and you from *Bernard*. But ill newes carried me into *Wales*, and upon my returne Maifter Secretary *Herbert* (with whom was in commiffion the noble and gentle Lord *Eure*, and the right worthy and vertuous Maifter Doctor *Dun*), being ready to goe into *Germany* (which was his thirteenth publike employment), I fignified to his Honour the defire I had, but once in my life, to fee the world (for untill then I had beene alwayes one of the Queenes deere), and he lovingly confented thereunto. Beleeve me, Sir *Rob.*, he eis the man I tooke him for, and told you of. I will not fpeake of honors and titles, things (like reprefentations in glaffes) actuated by other; but rather of his learning, his wifdome, honefty; the firft and laft whereof are goodly vertues in a man of his fortune, all three lying within the fpheare of our owne activitie. At *Amftelredam*, in my way homeward (for I returned before their Lordfhips) I met thofe good ill-newes of the Queens death, to whofe honour and memory (*neque me meminiffe pigebit* ELISAE), as by the Preface may appeare, I had once entended this firft booke of the Præparation or Præludium of the love betweene *Owen Tudyr* and the Queene; which Preface notwithftanding I will have printed with the reft, that I doe fo much right to that dead Lady, fometimes our foveraigne Queene and miftreffe. The very Gofpel it felfe (next which no gladder tidings could have pierced our eares, then that King JAMES his head fhould be invefted with the royall diadem) did allow the law, an honorable buriall. Neither fhould we fafhion our felves to fuch whofe affection to her waxed cold before her body, who thought they had done her a ftout piece of fervice, that they forfooke not her body before her foule did. I judge modeftly of them all, and hope it was but a longing they had to fee his Majefty, whom God of his mercy long preferve, left he, who hath freed us from one curfe of a kingdome, that is a woman, leave us unto another, that is, a childe. I have written an acrofticke fonet to his Maieftie, a canzonet to the Queene, and another acrofticke unto the Prince; whofe fervant I am by vow, and fubordinate fubject by birth. For I doubt not but his noble father will fhortly kiffe him, and deliver him the verge of gold, with his patent, whereby hee is entituled Prince of *Wales*: which (though now high in nothing but mountaines) I hope one day fhall be raifed by his Graces prefence; in whom we claime a double intereft, as well by *Walter Stewarte*, as *Owen Tudyr*, both of them lineally defcended from the moft haught and magnanimous Princes of *Wales*. My fecond booke (if God fpare life) of the entertainment of their love (which I principally vow to the honour of the better parte of his Graces principallity, my beloved country gentle Northwales, where by the way I am to fpeake fomewhat of the warres of *Owen Glindoure*, with the worthy deeds of the two thunder-bolts of warre, the noble Percies) I purpofe to confecrate unto his Highneffe: as alfo the third booke, of the perfection of their love, unto the Queens right excellent Majeftie. For unto whom fhould I dedicate the perfection of love but to the perfection of beautie? I fpeake this but by heare-fay: you have feene her, and know I flatter not, from which fault (if from any) I am moft free: for in flattery (faith *Tacitus*) is the foule fault of flavery, and freedom of fpeach will be thought malice. Howbeit, after the faire example of our good friend M. *Martin* (who, with like libertie as eloquence, was not afraide to tell the King the truth) I will fo comporte my felfe and wade warily betweene both, that I ever carry the heart of a monarchy, and the tongue of a common-wealth; the one loyall, the other liberall. In which refolution I end, commending this poëm to the conceipt of the reader, my felfe to you, and you to God.

Your very loving
HUGH HOLLAND.

INTRODUCTION.

THE ensuing drama is, in every respect, a most remarkable curiosity: it exists only in a single copy, and (with the exception, perhaps, of the "King Johan" of Bishop Bale) it is the earliest known specimen of that intermediate species of stage-representation which followed the old "Morality," consisting wholly of abstract impersonations, and the more modern "History" composed of real characters, such as we find them in the productions of Marlowe and Shakespeare. We apprehend (certainly upon no very distinct evidence) that the "Edward the Second" of Marlowe, though not printed until 1598, was written before 1590, and that it preceded the "Richard the Second" of Shakespeare, printed in 1597, but possibly not written until after the death of Marlowe in the summer of 1593. We only use the name of Marlowe as a representative of the immediate predecessors of Shakespeare, but to him might be added Peele, Kydd, Lodge, Greene, and others of less notoriety.

This, however, is not a point into which it is now necessary to enter, and the piece before us does not relate to English, but to Greek history: it is, in some sort, a companion to the old "Appius and Virginia" (Dodsley's *O. P.*, xii, p. 340, edit. 1825), dealing with events connected with the revenge of the son of Agamemnon in a similar manner to that in which the incidents of the Roman story were treated. As far as known dates are concerned, the author of "Orestes" had the precedence; for his drama was printed in 1567, while "Appius and Virginia" did not come from the press until 1575. The initials R. B. are given as those of the author of the latter; while John Pykering boldly places his names on the fore front of "Orestes." From the first page to the last the hero is called *Horestes;* and we may take it for granted that it was one of the many blunders of the early and ignorant typographer. Other errors of a glaring kind have been preserved in our reprint, and will be noticed as the reader proceeds; because our object has been to make an exact reproduction of the original, excepting, in a single instance, where we have added a word to a stage-direction, and where, in a few other places, for the sake of intelligibility merely, we have inserted a letter, always with the obvious distinction of brackets. The misprints begin on the very title-page, where "naturall" stands *naturtll*, "Menelaus" *Menalaus*, and "Hermione" *Helmione:* elsewhere *Meros* is put for "Mors," *gilt* for "gift," *despyare* for "desyare," *spare* for "fyare," &c. The spelling is arbitrary and corrupt even for the time when the production was printed. On p. 7, last line but one, the rhyme corrects the text; and on an earlier page, 2, the word "fight" is made part of the line, although clearly a stage-direction. These stage-directions are all singular, and indeed important, with reference to the manner in which the drama was got up and represented three hundred years ago.

In every dramatic piece of this intermediate description, the "Vice" is preserved from the old "Morality," for the purpose of giving vivacity and attractiveness to the performance; but in "Orestes" only (and the difference is of importance) he is made to sustain the parts of Courage and Revenge, for which he was furnished with proper apparel and disguises. The impersonation of Fame is used precisely in the same way and for the same purpose as Rumour in the second part of "Henry IV," or Chorus in "Henry V." The songs, with the ancient popular tunes to which they were sung, are also extremely interesting, and they are not only given to the Vice, as in some other early productions, but to Egisthus and Clytemnestra, who join in a duet in alternate stanzas. This last is to the old tune of "Lady, Lady;" also, as we here learn, called "King Solomon," which Elderton had used as early as 1559 in his ballad of "The Pangs of Love," and to which Shakespeare refers in two of his plays, " Twelfth Night," and "Romeo and Juliet." Other tunes appropriated to the Vice are "Over the water to Florida" (which was the same as "Sellinger's Round") and "The Painter," regarding which, we have no information. The most noticeable reference of this kind is near the conclusion of "Orestes," where a ballad is quoted which had been entered in the Stationers' Registers in 1557, "Who is merrier than the poorest sort."

The species of Epilogue, at the conclusion, is very peculiar, because it shews that the drama was publicly represented, if not in the presence, by permission of the Lord Mayor and Aldermen of London; who, however, soon after 1567, became so hostile to theatrical exhibitions, that they did their utmost to suppress them. They, happily, did not succeed; and between 1570 and 1580 three theatres were built and opened expressly for public performances.

We have evidence that a play with the title of "Orestes" was represented before Queen Elizabeth the year after the drama in the hands of the reader was printed; and we consider it more than probable that it was the identical production. On the whole, "Orestes" is, in our opinion, the most valuable performance of the kind in our language, in reference to the progress and improvement of our stage; and it is not long since it was discovered, among some other rare books (but no plays) in the closet of an old mansion of Wiltshire. We are happy to add that it is now deposited in the library of the British Museum: how long precisely it has been there we know not, but we lighted upon its title on accidentally turning over one of the many and confusing catalogues of that institution. We earnestly recommend that, instead of being kept in miserable half-binding, "Orestes" should be put into a cover somewhat consistent with its real worth, and as in every respect a unique specimen of our early dramatic poetry. When we venture to call it "poetry," the reader must be prepared to measure it, not by the standard of our perfect Shakespearian drama, but merely by that of the day when it was produced.

There is no greater desideratum in our language than a series of early dramas, properly arranged, shewing the gradual advance of our stage, from the earliest simple Scriptural Play, through the complex "Morality", and its periodical improvements by the introduction of real characters, until it culminated in the Historical Drama of the latter end of the reign of Elizabeth. Such a series, if only reasonably encouraged, we would gladly undertake, without the slightest view to pecuniary advantage. It might easily be comprised within three volumes of the size of our

A NEWE

Enterlude of Vice, Conteyninge the Historye of Horestes, with the cruell revengment of his fathers death upon his one naturll Mother.

BY

JOHN PIKERYNG.

THE PLAYERS NAMES.

The Vice.	*Clytemnestra.*	*Sodyer.*	*Truthe.*
Rusticus.	*Halterfycke.*	*Nobulle.*	*Fame.*
Hodge.	*Hempftryng.*	*Nature.*	*Hermione.*
Hroreftes.	*Neftor.*	*Provifyon.*	*Dewtey.*
Idumeus.	*Menalaus.*	*Harrauld.*	*Meffenger.*
Councell.	*A Woman.*	*Sodyer.*	*Egeftus.*

Commones.

THE NAMES DEVIDED FOR VI TO PLAYE.

The fyrft the Vice and Nature and Dewtey.   3.
2. Rufticus, Idumeus, 2 Sodyer, Menelaus, & Nobulles.   5.
3. Hodge, Counfell, Meffenger, Neftor, & Commones.   5.
4. Horeftes, a Woman, & Prologue.   3.
5. Haulterficke, Sodyer, Egiftus, Harrauld, Fame, Truth, and Idumeus.   7.
6. Hempftrynge, Clytemneftra, Provifyon, & Helmione.   4.

¶ Imprinted at London in Fleteftrete, at the figne of the Falcon by Wylliam Gryffith, and are to be folde at his fhope in S. Dunftons Churcheyearde.   Anno. 1567.

* ‡ *

HORESTES.
An Interlude.

The Vyce. A, fyrra! nay foft; what? Let me fee.
God morrowe to you, fyr, how do you fare?
Sante a men. I thincke it wyll be
The next day in the morning, before I com thear.
Well, forward I wyll, for to prepare
Some weapons and armour, the catives to quell:
Ille teache the hurchetes agayne to rebell.
Rebell? ye fyr, how faye you thereto?
What! you had not befte their partes to take:
Houlde the content, foole, and do as I do,
Or elles, me chaunce, your pate for to ake.
Ye, and thats more, for feare thou fhalt quake
Before Horeftes, when, in good fouth, he
Shall arryve in this lande, revenged to bee.
Well, forwarde I wyll, thynges to pourvaye,
In good fouth, for the wares, as I fhall thincke good.
Farre well, good man dotterell; and marke what I faye,
Or eles it may chaunce you to feke a new houd;
You would eate no more cakbread, I thinke, then, by the roud:
If that, that fame poulle from your fhoulderes were bent,
You would thincke you were yll, if fo you were fhent.
     [*Hear entryth* RUSTYCUS *and* HODGE.
 Ruft. Chyll never, nabore Hodge, have a glade harte,
Tyll Egiftous, the kynge, hath for his defarte

Received dew punnyſhment; for this well I knowe,
Horreſtes to Crete with Idumeus did go,
When his father was ſlayne by his mother moſt yll:
And therefore I thincke that com heather he wyll,
And revenge the injury of his mother moſt dyare,
Waſtinge our lande with zworde and with vyare.

 Hodge. Jeſu, nabor! with vyar and zworde? zaye ye zo?
By gys, nabor, chyll zave one, I tro;
For iche have ſmaull good, by giſe, for to loſe,
And therefore iche care not how ever it goſe:
But chyll not be zlayne, chyll love nothinge worſſe,
Chyll never be bowrnt for the mony in my pourſe.
Iche have ſmall rouddockes; and ſodyers, I kno,
Wy·ll robbe the riche chorles, and let the poore knaves go.

 Vyce. A ſyrre! nowe ſtaye, and pauſe their a whyle,
Be not to haſtye, but take all the daye:
Be God, I am weary with comming this myle,
And having no money my horſe heyare to paye,
Who how, I rode on my fete all the waye.
Jeſu! what ground, ſince yeſterday at none,
Have I gut thorow with this pare of ſhoune.

 Ruſt. Nabor Hodge, be goge, hatche none I veare,
That this lyttell hourchet the devayaunce doth beare.
Come, let us go, and of him, in good ſouth,
We woll conquear out the verey truth.

 Vyce. Hurchyt? goges oundes, gyppe with a wanyon!
Ar you ſo louſtey, in fayth, good man clound?
Oundes, hart and nayles, this is a franion!
Ille teache you to floute me, I hould you a pounde.
O that it weare not, in fayth, for my gound!
It wyll I be knoc um, yet for all that.   [*Fight.*

Hodge. Hould, good mafter! you mare my new hat.
 Vyce. Ha, ha, he! mar his hat, quoth he; thear was all
    his thought.
Tout, tout! for the blofe he fet not a pyn.
That garment is dyer that with blofe is bought.
Well, fieres, to in treat me fyth you begyn,
I am contentyd, my blade now fhaull in.
But tell me, fyeres, tell me no[w] whearefore of me
The caufe on this fort your taullkynge fhould be?
 Ruft. By gis, and iche chyll, mafter, for all my great payne,
Of this matter to you to tell the veary playne.
My naybor Hodge and I, in good fouth,
Mot hear in the veldes, I tell you the truth;
Now as we wear talkinge, marke what I zaye,
You came in ftraight, and of us croft the waye.
Which thinge for zartyn when I did efpye,
This fancey vlouncht in my head by and by;
And to Hodge I zayde that, by gys I dyd veare,
That your mafhyp, good mafter, the devyaunce doth beare:
And be caufe you weare lyttell, and of ftature but fmaull,
Your perfon a hourchet, in fayth, I dyd caull.
But, by gis, be contentyd, vor chyll neaver more
Ofvend you a gaine, but cham zorey thearvore.
 Vyce. Yf they weare not twayne, I cared not a poynt;
But two is to meyney, the proverbe douth tell:
Elles, be his oundes, I would jobard this joynt,
And teache them agaynfte me againe to rebell.
O! that I wear abull the knaves vor to quell,
Then would I tryomphe paffinge all meafure.
 Hodge. Zentyl man, zentyll man, at your owne pleafure
In fayth we be; and thearvore we praye,

What thy name is to us vor to zaye?
  Vyce. My name would ye kno? marrey, you fhaull.
Harke, frynde, fourft to the I wyll it declare:
Mafter Pacience, mafter Pacience, many on doth me caull.
But com heather, nabor Hodge; thou muft have a fhare.
By gys, unto the I wyll not fpare
The fame for to fhowe; whearfore, my frend,
My name is Pacience, if thou it perpend.
  Hodge. Paft fhame? Godes gee, naybor, paft fhame?
By godes be, naybor, thates a tryccom name.
  Vyce. Tell a mare a tall, and fhyell gerd out a fart.
Se how the as my wordes douth miftake
Would it not anger a faynt at the hart
To fe what a fcoffe of my name he douth make?
O, oundes of me! as ftill as a ftake
He ftandith, nought caring what of him may be tyde:
Be his woundes, I wod have a arme, or a fyde.
Sought! let me fe; it is beft to be ftyll,
Good flepinge in a hole fkynne, ould foulkes do faye;
Notwithftandinge, I wis, ill have myne owne wyll.
Naye, I wyll be revenged, by his oundes, and I maye.
Syrra, you good man Ruftycus, marke what I faye:
Harke in thine eare, man; this dyd I fee,
A hoge of thyne wearyed to be.
  Ruft. Godes gee, maifter Pacience, I praye you me tell,
What horfon chorles doge my hogge fo dyd quell?
Iche zware by gife, and holye zaynt blyve,
Chyll be zwinge him, and ich be a lyve.
By godes de, cham angry, and not well content:
Chould ha wear hear, chould make him repent.
Ich had rather gyven vore ftryke of corne,

Then to had my hogge on this wyfe forlorne:
But if I knewe whous dogge chould be,
Revenged well inough, iche warrent the.
    Vyce. Ha, ha, he! by God, Rufticus, I maye faye in no
        game,
I knowe the perfon whofe dogge fo did flaye
Thy hogge: fye, fye, man! it was vearey fhame
For thy naybor Hodge to let it, by this daye.
Well, I wyll go to him, and fe if I maye
By aney meanes procure him to make amendes:
Ille do the beft I can to make you both frendes.
    Ruft. Chyll be no frendes, chad rather be hanged,
Tyll iche have that oulde karle wel and thryfteley banged;
And tweare not your mafhyppe dyd me with hould,
To fwing the ourchet iche chould be boulde.
    Vyce. Ha, ha, he! nay, nay, fpare not for me;
Go to it ftrayght, if thear to ye gre.
    Ruft. Hodge, I harde fay, thou illy haft wrought,
For my hogge unto death with thi dog thou haft brought.
Iche byd the thy vaute to me to amend,
Or chyll zwaddell the, iche zweare, in my bat end.
    Hodge. Zwaddell me? godes get! chyll care not a poynte;
Iche have a good bat thy bones to a noynte:
Thou old carle, I zaye, thy hoge hurtyd me,
And therefore I wyll have a mendes now of the.
My rye and my otes, my beanes and my peafe,
They have eaten up quight, but fmall for my eafe;
And therefore iche zaye, all thy hogges kepe vafte,
Or iche wyll them wearey as longe as they lafte.
By godes get! I can never come in my ground,
But that zame zwyne in my peafe iche have founde.

Vyce. Tout, tout! Rufticus, thefe wordes be but wynd.
To him, man, to him, and fwaddell him well:
Ye, neaver leave him as longe as thou can fynd
Him whot, but teache him a gaine to rebell:
What nededeft thou care, though his wordes be fo fell.
Tout, tout! tharte unwyfe; and followe my mynde,
And I warraunt the in end fome eafe thou fhalt finde.

Ruft. Godes gee, hourfon Hoge, paye me for my zwine,
Or eles larne to kepe that cockefcome of thyne.

[*Up with thy ftaf and be readye to fmyte, but Hodg fmit
firft, and let the Vife thwacke them both and run out.*

Hodge. Godes de, do thy worft, I care not a poynte:
Chyll paye the none, chyll jobard a joynte.

Vyce. Nay, ftand I ftyll? fome what, I wyll lend:
Take this for a reward; now a waye I muft wend.

Ruft. O Godes get! cham zwinged zo zore,
Iche thincke, chaull neaver lyve one houre more.

Hodge. O godes! ge I thincke my bownes will in zonder;
Yf ich get home, by gis, ittes a wounder:
Farwell, Rufticus, for by gis ich chaull,
When I mete the againe, bezwinge the vor all.

Rus. Naye, letes be frendes, and chyll, in good part,
Of browne ale at my houfe give the a whole whart:
What, Hodge, fhake handes, mon; be merey and lauffe,
By godes ge, iche had not the beft end of the ftaffe.

Hodge. Cham content, naybor Rufticus, fhaull be ene fo.
Come, to they houfe I praye the, let us go.   [*Go out.*
                                    [HORESTES *entrith.*

Horeftes. To caull to minde the crabyd rage of mothers
     yll attempt
Provokes me now all pyttie quight from me to be exempt.

Yet lo! dame nature teles me, that I muſt with willing mind
Forgeve the faute, and to pytie ſome what be inclynd.
But lo! be hould that ulltres dame, on hourdome morder vill
Hath heaped up, not contented, her ſpouſaule bed to fyll
With forrayne love, but ſought alſo my fatal thred to ſhare,
As erſt before my fathers fyll, in ſonder ſhe dyd pare.
O paterne love! why douſte thou ſo, of pytey me requeſt,
Syth thou to me waſt quight denyed, my mother being preſt:
When tender yeres this corps of mine did hould, alas for wo,
When frend my mother ſhuld have bin, then was ſhe chefe
    my fo.
Oh godes! therfore ſith you be juſt, unto whoſe poure & wyll,
All thing in heaven, and earth alſo, obaye and ſarve untyll,
Declare to me your gracious mind: ſhall I revenged be,
Of good Kynge Agamemnones death, ye godes, declare
    to me?
Or ſhall I let the adultres dame ſtyll wallow in her ſin?
Oh godes of war! gide me aright, when I ſhall war begyn.
    Vyce. Warre, quoth he, I, war in dede? and trye it by the
        ſworde.
God ſave you, ſyr; the godes to ye have ſent this kind of
    word:
That in the haſt you armour take your fathers foſe to ſlaye,
And I as gyde with you ſhall go, to gyde you on the way.
By me thy mind ther wrathful dome ſhalbe performd in
    dede.
Therfore, Horeſtes, marke me well, & forward do procede,
For to reveng thy fathers death; for this they all have ment
Which thing for to demonſtrat, lo! to the they have ſent me.
    Hor. Ar you, good ſyr, the meſſenger of godes as you do
        ſaye?

Wil they, in revenging this wrong I make not long delay
   Vyce. What nede you dout? I was in heaven when al
      the gods did gre
That you of Agamemnons death, for fouth, revengid fhould
    be.
Tout tout! put of that childifh love: couldft thou with a
    good wil
Contentyd be, that one fhould fo thy father feme to kyll?
Why wayght thou man? leave of I fay; plucke corrage
    unto the:
This lamentation fone fhall fade, if thou embrafydeft me.
   Hor. What is thy name, may I inquear? O facred wight!
      I pray
Declare to me, & with this feare do not my hart difmaye.
   Vyce. Amonge the godes celeftiall I Courrage called am.
You to affyfte, in veary truth, from out the heavens I cam,
And not without god Marfis his leave I durft hear fhow my
    face,
Which thou fhalt fele, if that thir gift thou doft forthwith
    imbrace.
   Hor. And fith it is thear gratious will, welcom thou art
      to me,
O holy wight! for this thear gyft, I thanke them hartelley.
My thinkes I fele all feare to fley, all forrow griefe & payne:
My thinkes I fele corrage provokes my wil for ward againe,
For to revenge my fathers death and infamey fo great.
Oh! how my hart doth boyle in dede with firey perching
    heate.
Corrage, now welcom by the godes: I find thou art in dede
A meffenger of heavenly goftes. Come, let us now procede,
And take in hand to bringe to pas revengyd for to be

Of thofe which have my father flaine : but foft ! now let me fe.
Idumeus, that worthy kinge, doth com into this place ;
What fay you, Corrage, fhal I now declare to him my cafe ?
 Vyce. Faull to it, then, and flacke no time, for tyme once paft away
Doth caufe repentence but to late to com old foulks do fay.
When ftede is ftolen, to late it is to fhyt the ftable dore.
Take time, I fay, while time doth give a leafure good therfore.
 Idum. What ever he be that fceptar beares, or rules in ftate full hie,
I[s] foneft down through fortunes eyar, and brought to myferey ;
As of late yeares the worthy kinge, Agamemnon by name,
Whos prais throughout the world is bloun by golden trump of fame :
His wel won fame in marfhall ftoure doth reache unto the fky,
Yet, lo ! through fortunes blind attempt, he lo in earth doth lie :
He that had paft the fate of war, where chance was equall fet,
Through fortunes fpight is caught, alacke, with in olde Meros net ;
And he which fomtime did delight in clothed coat of maylle,
Is now conftraynd in Carones bote over the brouke to faylle,
That flofe upon the fatall bankes of Plutofe kingdome great,
And that in fhade of filent wodes and valeys greene do beate ;
Where foules of kinges and other wights a poynted are to be
In quiet ftate, there alfo is this worthey reall tree.

Of south, I joye for to behold Horeſtes actyve cheare,
The which in father ſomtime was, in ſon doth now apear.
But where is he that all this day I neaver ſawe his face?
    Hor. At hand, O king, thy ſarvant is, which wiſsheth
        to thy grace   [*Knell downe.*
All hayl, with happey fate certayne, with pleaſures many
    fould!
But yet, my liege, a ſute I have, if I might be ſo bold
To crave the ſame, my ſoferayn lord, wherby I might aſpyer
Unto the thing which very much, O king, I do requier.
    Idum. What thing is that? if we ſuppoſe it laufull for
        to be,
On prynces faith, without delaye, it ſhall be given the.
    Vyce. Tout! let him alone now, we ſay in good ſouth;
I was not ſo luſtey my pourpoſe to get.
But now, of my honeſtey, I tell you of truth,
In revenging the wronge his mynd he hath ſet.
It is not Idumeus that hath power to let
Horeſtes fro ſekinge his mother to kyll.
Tout! let hym alone, hele have his own wyll.
    Hor. Sith that your grace hath willed me this my deſiar
        to ſhow,
Oh, gratious king, this thing it is I let your grace to know;
That long I have requeſt to vew my fathers kingley place,
And eke for to revenge the wrong done to my fathers grace
Is myne intent: wherefore, o king, graunt that without
    delaye,
My earytage and honor eke atchyve agayne I maye.
    Idum. Stey their a whyle, Horeſtes mine, tyll Councell
        do decree
The thing that ſhall unto your ſtate moſt honorabell bee.

My counciler, how do you thinke? let us your councell have:
How think you by this thing the which Horeftes now doth
    crave?
  Counc. As I do thinke, my foferayne lord, it fhould be
    nothing ill
A prynce for to revenged be on thofe which fo dyd kyll
His fathers grace; but rather fhall it be a feare to thofe
That to the lyke at anye time their cruell mindes difpofe:
And alfo, as I thinke, it fhall an honer be to ye
To adjuvate, and helpe him with fome men revenged to be.
This do I thinke moft fytteft for your ftate, and his alfo:
Do as you lyft, fieth that your grace my mind herin
    doth know.
  Idum. Sith Councell thinkes it fyt, in ded, revenged for
    to be,
That you, Horeftes, in good fouth, for to revenge I gree:
And alfo to mayntaine your war, I graunt you with good
    will
A thoufand men, of ftomake bolde, your enimife to kyll.
Take them forth with, and forward go, let flyp no time
    ne tyd,
For chaunce to leafure to be bound, I tell you, can not byd.
Go therfore ftraight, provide your men, and like a manly
    knight,
In place of ftouer put forth thy felfe, affay with all thy
    might
To win the fame, for glorey none in chambering doth reft.
Marke what I faye: to get thy men I take it for the beft.
  Vyce. Come on, Horeftes, fith thou haft obtayned thy
    defier.
Tout, tout, man! feke to dyftroye as doth the flaming fier,

Whofe properte, thou knoeft, doth gro as long as any thing
Is left wher by the fame may feme fom fuckor for to bring.
    Hor. I thanke your grace: I fhal fequeft your gratius mind herin.   [*Go out.*
    Vyce. Se, fe, I praye you, how he joyfe that he muft war begin.   [*Go out.*
    Idum. My Councell, now declare to me, how think you by this wight,
Doth not he feme, in fouth, to be in tyme a manley knight?
By all the godes, I thinke in fouth, a man may eafeley kno
Whofe fon he was, fo right he doth his fathers fteppes follow.
    Counc. Undoubtedly, my foferaynd lorde, he femeth unto me
Not to fequeft his fathers fteppes in feates of chevallrey;
But rather for to imitate the floure of Greation land,
I meane Achilles, that fame knight by whofe one only hand
The Greacians have obtaind, at laingth, the conqueft of old Troy,
For which thei did holl x. yeres fpace their labor great imploy.
    Idum. Syth he is gon for to purvaye fuch thinges as fhall, in dede,
Suffife to farve his tourn in wares wherof he fhal have nede,
Let us depart, and when he fhall retourne heather a gayne,
To fee the mufter of his men we wyll fure take the payne.   [*Go out.*
    [*Entrithe and fyngeth this fong to the tune of have over the water to floride or felengers round.*
THE SONGE.
    Halterfycke. Farre well, adew that courtlyke lyfe,
        To warre we tend to gowe;

It is good fport to fe the ftryfe
Of fodyers on a rowe.
   How merely they forward march
   Thefe enemys to flaye:
   With hey trym and tryxey to,
   Their banners they difplaye.
Now fhaull we have the golden cheates,
When others want the fame:
And fodyares have foull maney feates
Their enemyes to tame.
   With couckinge heare, and bomynge their,
   They breake thear fofe araye;
   And louftey lades amid the feldes
   Thear enfines do difplaye.
The droum and flute playe loufteley,
The troumpet blofe a mayne;
And ventrous knightes corragioufley
Do march before thear trayne.
   With fpeare in refte fo lyvely dreft
   In armour bryghte and gaye,
   With hey trym and tryxey to,
   Thear banners they difplaye.

        [HEMPSTRINGE *commeth in and fpeaketh.*

Hempftring. Goges oundes! Haulterfycke, what makes
   thou heare?
Hault. What! Jacke Hempftringe, welcom; draw near.
Hemp. By his oundes, I have foughte the, fome newfe
   the to tell.
Hault. Godes bloud! what newfe? ist the devell in hell?
Hemp. In faythe, thou art mearey; but this is the matter:
Douft thou hear, Halterficke? each man doth clatter

Of warres, ye, of warres; for Horeftes will go
His erytage to wyn, boye: the truth is fo.

Hault. Nay, but Jacke Hempftringe, leafe of this prate;
Yf thou caull me boye, then beware thy pate.

Hemp. What! hould thy peace: as far as I fe,
We be boyfe both; thearfore let us gree.

Hault. Boye! naye, be god, though I be but fmaull,
Yet, Jacke Hempftringe, a hart is worth all:
And have not I an hart that to warres dare go?
Yes, Hempftringe, I warrant the; and that thou fhouldeft know,
If Dycke Halterfyckes mynde thou move unto eyar:
Colles neaver bourne tyll they be fet one fyare.

Hemp. Ye, but if they bourne fo that they flame,
Yet water, Dycke Halterfycke, the bourning cane tame.
But, harke thee, my mafter will venter a joynt,
And me to wayte on him he all readye doth poynt.
But, hearfte thou, thou knoweft my mafter loves well,
Now and then, to be fnappinge at fome dayntye moffell.
But by goges bloud, Hallterfycke, if thou love me,
Take fome prytey wenche our laundrar to be;
And be goges bloud, I am contentyd to beare
Halfe of her chargis, when that fhe comes thear.

Hault. As fyt for the warre, Jacke Hempftringe, thou art,
In fayth, as a be is to drawe in a carte:
He is lyke to be manned, that hath fuch a knight
Under his banner, I fweare, for to fight.
When Horeftes in fight mofte bufieft fhalbe,
Then with thy gynney we muft feke the.

Hemp. Goges oundes, hart, and nayles! you are a franion:
Come of with a myfchiefe, my gentell companion.

By your lieve, fire Haulterficke, I thinke that a be
As good a fodyer as ever was ye.
   Hault. He hath learned his leffon; but, of fouth, I feare
He hath quight forgotten the waye for to fweare.
Oundes, hart, and nayles! marcy, hes no lad,
And he be not hanged, he wyll be ftarke mad.
   Hemp. Hange me no hanginge; yf ye be fo quicke,
Roube not to hard, left Hempftringe do kycke.
   Hault. Had better be ftyll, and a fleepe in his bead:
Yf a kycke me, me chaunce to breake his head.
                                                      [Flort him.
   Hemp. Goges bloud! good man Halterfycke, begyne you
      to flout me?
   Hault. No, not at all; he douth but lout ye.
What, Hempftringe, I faye, are you angred at jefte?
In fayth, goodman lobcocke, your handfomley drefte.
                                       [Flort hym on the lipes.
   Hemp. Goges bloud! fo to flout me, thou art much to
      blame.
   Hault. Why, all that I do, man, is but in game.
   Hemp. Take thou that for thy jefte, and flout me no more.
                               [Give him a box on the eare.
   Hault. For that fame on blowe thou fhault have a fcore.
Drawe thy fword, vylyne, yf thou be a man,
And then do the worft that ever thou can.
   Hemp. Naye, fet fword a fyde, and at boffetes well trey
Wheather of us both fhall have the mafterey.
   Hault. Goges oundes! thou art bygger, yet I care not a
      poynt,
Yf to be revenged I jobard a joynt.
                             [Fyght at bofites with fyftes.

Hemp. I have coylyd the well, but I holde the a grote
Yf thou meddell with me, I wyll fwinge thye cote.
 Hault. In dede, I muft faye, I have cought the worft ;
But I wyll be revengyd, or eles I fhall bourfte.
Yf tyme did not call me from hence to depart,
I fhould anger the, Hempftring, even at the hart.
Therefore farwell, tyll an other daye.
But, hearfte thou, take this, to fpend by the waye.
     [*Give him a box on the eare, and go out.*
 Hemp. Goges oundes! is he gon? naye, after I wyll,
And of the flave, by his oundes, I wyll have my fyll.
              [*Go out.*
    [*Let the drum playe, and* HORESTES *enter with
     his men, & lette him knele downe and fpeake.*
 Hor. O godes! be profperous, I praye, and eke preferve
  my band ;
Show now that ye be gods in ded, ftretch out your mighty
  hand,
And give us hartes and willes alfo, where by we may
  prevayll ;
And fuffer not, you godes, I praye, our courragis to fayll :
But let our hartes addytyd be, for aye as we pretend,
And of that vile adultres dame, oh gods! now make an end.
My hands do thryft her blod to have: nought can my mind
  content,
Tyll that on her I have perfourmed, oh gods! your juft
  judgment.   [*Stand up.*
 Nature. Nay, ftey, my child; from mothers bloud with-
  draw thy bloudy hand.
 Hor. No, nought at all, oh Nature! can my purpofe now
  withftand.

Shall I for geve my fathers death? my hart can not agre,
My father flayne in fuch a forte, and unrevengyd be.
    Nat. Confider firft, Horeftes myne, what payne for the
        fhe toke.
    Hor. And of my fathers death, againe, O Nature! do thou
        louke.
    Nat. I do confeffe a wycked facte it was, this is moft
        playne;
Not withftanding, from mothers bloud thou muft thy hands
    refrain.
Canft thou, alacke, unhappey wight! confent revenged to be
On her whofe pappes before this time hath geven foud to the?
In whom I, Nature, formyd the, as beft I thought it good?
Oh! now requight her for her pain; withdraw thy hand from
    bloud.
    Hor. Who offendith the love of God, and eke mans love,
        with willing hart,
Muft by that love have punifhment, as dutey due for his
    defart.
For me therfor to punifh hear, as law of gods and man
    doth wil,
Is not a crime, though that I do, as thou doft faie, my
    mother kil.
    Nat. The cruel beafts that raung in feldes, whofe jaufe
        to blod are whet,
Do not confent their mothers paunch in cruell wife to eate.
The tyger fierce doth not defiare the ruine of his kinde;
And fhall dame Nature now in the fuch tyraney once finde,
As not the cruell beftes voutfafe to us in aney cafe?
Leve now, I fay, Horeftes myne, and to my wordes give
    place,

Leſt that of men this facte of thine may judged for to be
Ne lawe in ſouth, ne juſtys eke, but cruell tyraney.
  Hor. Pythagoras doth thinke it, lo, no tyraney to be,
When that juſtyſe is myneſtryd as lawe and godes decree.
If that the law doth her condemne as worthy death to have,
Oh Nature! wouldſt thou wil that I her life ſhould ſeme
    to ſave?
To ſave her lyfe whom law doth ſlay is not juſtiſe to do,
Therefore I ſaye, I wyll not yeld they heſtes to com unto.
  Nat. Yf nature cannot brydell the, remember the decaye
Of thoſe which heretofore, in ſouth, their parents fought
    to ſlay.
Œdippus fate caull thou to minde, that ſlew his father ſo;
And eke remember now what fame of him a brode doth go.
  Hor. What fame doth blowe I forſe not I, ne yet what
    fame I have;
For this is true, that bloud for blood my fathers deth doth
    crave,
And lawe of godes and lawe of man doth eke requeſt the
    the ſame:
Therefore, oh Nature! feaſe to praye, I forſe not of my name.
  Nat. For to lament this heavey fate I cannot other do.
Alacke, alacke! that once my chyld ſhould now conſent
    unto
His mothers death: wherefore farewell, I can no longer
    ſtey.   [*Go out.*
  Hor. Farwel, dame Nature. To my men I ſtraight wil
    take my way.   [*Go out.*
              IDUMEUS.   [*Enter.*
  Idum. To ſe this mouſter let us go, for I ſuppoſe it tyme.
Where is Horeſtes? why ſteaſe he? the truth to me define.

Counc. Oh, foferayne lord! me thinkes I here him for to be at hand.

Yft pleafe your grace, he is in fight even now withal his band.
> [*Let the drum play, and enter* HORESTES *with his band: marche about the ftage.*

Idum. Come on, Horeftes, we have ftayd your mofter for to fe.

Hor. And now at hand my men and I all redy armed be.
Lo, mighty king, thes champions here agre with me to wende:
Oh, gratious king! that they fhall fo wylt pleafe you condiffend.

Idum. I do agree; and now a whyle give eare your king unto.
It doth behoufe corragious knightes on this wyfe for to do:
That is, to ftryve for to obtayne the victorey, and prayfe
That lafts for aye, when death fhall end the find of thefe our dais.
Wherefore be bold and feare no fate, the gods for you fhall fight,
For they be juft, and will not fe that you, in cafe of right,
Shall be defstreft: wherefore attend, and do your bufey payne,
The crabyd rage of enymyfe by forfe for to refftrayne.
And as to me, your trufteynes hath here to fore be knowne,
So now in this Horeftes here let eke the fame be fhowne.
Be to his heaftes obaydient; be ftoute to take in hand
Such enterpryfe which he fhall thinke moft for his ftate to ftand:
Which if you do the fame is youres; the glorey and renoune
That fhal arife of thes your facts throughout the world fhal found:

The which you may, I pray the godes your gydes here
　　in to be.
And now farewell, but not[e] that well that I have fayde to ye.
　　Sodyeares. The godes preferve your grace for aye, and
　　　you defend from wo.
That we have don as you comaund ful wel your grace
　　fhal kno.
　　Idum. Now, harke, Horeftes: fince thou muft of men the
　　　gyder be,
And that the wyll of godes it is thou muft now part from me,
Take yet my laft commaundement, and beare it in thy
　　minde.
Let now thy men courragiousnes in the their captayne
　　finde ;
And as thou art courragious, fo lyke wyfe let their be
For fafe gard of thy men a brayne, well fraught with
　　pollicye.
For over rafhe in doinge ought doth often damage bringe,
Therfore, take councell firft before thou doft anye thinge.
For councell, as Plaato doth tell, is fure a heavenly thinge;
And Socrates a certaynte doth fay, councell doth brynge
Of thinges in dout ; for Lyvy fayes, no man fhall him repent,
That hath before he worked ought his tyme in councell
　　fpent.
And be thou lybraull to thy men, and gentell be alfo,
For that way at thy wil thou mayft have them through fire
　　to go ;
And he that fhall at any tyme deferve ought well of thee,
Soffer him not for to depart, tyll well reward he be.
Thus have you hard, Horeftes mine ; remember well the
　　fame :

An Interlude.

In doing thus you fhall pourchas to the immortaull fame :
The which I hope you wyll affaye for to atchife in dede.
The gods the blis, when in the war thou forward fhalt pro-
    cede.
    Hor. I thanke your grace ; and now of you my leave I
    here do take.
    Idum. Farwell, my fonne Horeftes ; I thy partinge yll
    fhall take.   [*Imbrace him.*
Yet eare thou go, let me imbrace the once, I the do praye:
Alacke, alacke, that now from me thou muft nedes part
    away !
Yet whyell thou art in preafent place receave of me this
    kys :   [*Kys him.*
Farwell, good knight, for now I fhal thy fwete imbrafings
    mys.
    Hor. The facred godes prefarve and fave thy ftate, oh
    king, I pray,
And fend the helth, and after death to rayne with him for aye!
Come on, my men ; let us depart.
    Sodyers. As pleafe your grace, with all our hart.
                                    [*March about and go out.*
    Idum. Ah, ah ! how grevous is his parting now, my
    Councell, unto me !
The godes him bles and fend him helth, I pray them hartele.
Wo worth the time, the day and our, now may Horeftes
    wayle :
And Clytemneftra may lament that fo fhe dyd affayle
His father deare ; for now on bloud Horeftes mind is fet,
And to revenge his fathers death, fure, nought their is can let.
In voyding of a mifchefe fmal, they have wrought their
    decay :

For now nought elles in Horeſtes but ſore reveng bears
  ſway.
 Councell. For t[w]o cauſes, my ſoferayne lord, revengment
  ought to be :
The on, leaſt others be in fecte with that that they ſhall ſe
Their princes do : the other is, that thoſe that now be yll,
May be revoked and may be taught for to ſubdew their wyll.
Plato, a wiſe phyloſopher, dyd thinke it for to be
A pryncely facte, when as a king ſhall puniſhe ſeriouſley
Such perſons as dyd trayne their lyfe to follow that was
  naught,
The which their prince at ani time ſhal by miſchaunce have
  wrought :
Protegeus an evell kinge a carrayne likenes to,
Which all the place about the ſame to ſtinke cauſeth to do.
Therefore, O king! if that her faute ſhould unrevenged be,
A thouſand evylles would inſu their of your grace ſhould ſe.
Her faute is great, and punnyſhment it is worthy for to have;
For by that meane the good, in ſouth, from daungers may
  be ſauſe.
For, lo, the unyverſaull ſcoll of all the world, we knowe,
Is once the pallace of a kinge, where vyces chefe do flow.
And as to waters from on head and fountayne oft do ſpring,
So vyce and vertue oft do flo from pallace of a kinge.
Whereby the people ſeeing that the kinge adycte to be,
To proſecute the lyke they all do labor, as we ſe.
Therfore the gods have wylled thus, Horeſtes for to take
His jorney, and a recompence for fatheres death to make.
 Idum. Sith gods have wild the ſame to be, good lucke the
  gods him ſend.
Com on, my Councell; now from hence we purpoſe for to
  wend.   [*Go out.*

[*Enter* EGISTUS *and* CLYTEMNESTRA, *singinge
this songe, to the tune of king Salomon.*

Egis. And was it not a worthy fight,
Of Venus childe, kinge Priames sonne,
To steale from Grece a ladye bryght,
For whom the wares of Troye begon.
Naught fearinge daunger that might faull,
   Lady ladie!
 From Grece to Troye he went with all,
   My deare lady.
Clytem. When Paris firste arived there,
Where as dame Venus worshyp is,
And bloustringe fame abroade dyd beare
His lyveley fame, she dyd not mys
To Helena for to repayre,
   Her for to tell
 Of prayse and shape so trym and fayre,
   That dyd excell.
Egis. Her beautie caused Paris payne,
And bare chiefe sweye with in his mynde:
No thinge was abell to restraine,
His wyl some waye fourth for to finde,
Where by he might have his despyare,
   Lady ladye!
 So great in him was Cupids fyare,
   My deare ladye.
Clytem. And eke as Paris dyd desyear
Fayre Helena for to possesse;
Her hart inflamid with lyke fyear,
Of Paris love despiard no lesse;
And found occasion him to mete,

In Cytheron :
When each of them the other dyd grete,
The feaſt uppon.
Egis. If that in Paris Cupides ſhafte,
O Clytemneſtra! toke ſuch place,
That tyme ne waye he never left,
Tyll he had gotte her comley grace,
I thinke my chaunce not ill to be,
Ladye ladye!
That ventryd lyfe to purchaſe ye,
My dere ladye.
Clytem. Kynge Priames ſonne loved not ſo ſore
The Gretian dame, they brothers wyfe :
But ſhe his perſon eſtemed more,
Not for his ſake ſavinge her lyfe ;
Which cauſed her people to be ſlayne,
With him to flye ;
And he requight her love a gayne,
Moſt faythfullye.
Egys. And as he recompence agayne
The fayre quene Hellyn for the ſame,
So whyle I lyve I wyll take payne
My wyll alwayes to yours to frame.
Syth that you have voutſafe to be,
Ladye ladye!
A Queene and ladye unto me,
My deare ladye.
Clytem. And as ſhe lovyd him beſt, whyle lyfe
Dyd laſt, ſo tend I you to do,
Yf that devoyd of warr and ſtryfe,
The Godes ſhall pleaſe to graunt us to.

Syeth you voutfafeſt me for to take,
O my good knyght!
And me thy ladye for to make,
My hartes delyghte.

Egis. As joyfull as the warlyke god is Venus to behoulde,
So is my hart repleate with joye, much more a thouſand fould,
Oh Lady deare, in that I do poſſes my hartes delyghte.—
What menes this found? for very much it doth my hart aflight. [*Let the trumpet blowe with in.*
 Clytem. Feare nought at all, Egiſtus myne; no hourt it doth pretend:
But lo! me thinkes a meſſenger to us heather doth wend.
[*Enter.*
 Meſſenger. The Gods preſarve your eaquall ſtate, and ſend you of their blys!
 Clytem. Welcom, good meſſenger: what newefe, I pray the, with the is?
 Mes. Yft pleaſe your grace, even now there is aryved in this land
The mightey knight Horeſtes, with a mightey pewſaunt band,
Who purpoſith for to invade this Mycœne Citie ſtronge;
And as he goeſe he leyſe both tower and caſtell all alonge:
It boutes no man defence to make, for yf he wyll not yeld,
By ſodyeres rage he ſtraight is ſlayne in mydeſt of the felde.
[*Go out.*
 Clytem. Ah, fyr! is he come in dede? he is wellcom, by this daye.
Egiſtus, now, in ſouth, with ſpede from hence take you your way

In to our realme, and take up men our tyghtull to defend.
Tyll your retourne, this citie I to kepe do sure intend:
For all his strength, he shall not get to entter once hear in.
The walles be strong; and for his forse I sure set not a pyn.

Egis. Syth you be abell to defend this citie, as you saye,
Farwell! in south, to get me men, I now wyll take my waye.
And sone againe I wyll returne his pamprid pryd to tame.

Clytem. Farwell, Egistus! and, in south, I strayght will do the same. *Go out.*

[*Enter a woman, lyke a beger, ronning before they sodier; but let the sodier speke first, but let the woman crye first pitifulley.*

Sodyer. Yeld the, I saye; and that by and by,
Or with this sword, in fayth, thou shalt dye.

Woman. Oh! with a good wyll, I yeld me to the.
Good master sodier, have mercye on me!
My husband thou hast slayne in most cruell wyse,
Yet this my prayer do now not despyse.

Sodier. Come on, then, in haft; my pryfoner thou art:
Come, followe me, I saye; we must nedes depart.

[*Go a fore her, and let her fal downe upon the [sodier], and al to be beate him.*

Woman. A horson slave! I wyll teach the, in faye,
To handle a woman on an other waye.
To put me in feare with out my dezarte?
I wyll teache the, in faye, to playe such a parte.

Sodyer. Be contentyd, good woman, and thou shalt be
Neaver heare after molysted for me.

Woman. Naye, vyllyn slave! a mendes thou shalt make.
In that thou be fore me as pryfiner dydest take,
Nowe I have cought the, and my pryfoner thou art.
By his oundes, horson slave! this gose to they harte.

Sodyer. Naye, fave my lyfe, for I wyll be
Thy pryfoner : and, lo, I yelde me to the.
    Woman. Come, wend thou with me, and they wepon
        thou fhalt have,
[*Take his weapons, & let him ryfe up, & then go out both.*
Syth that thou voutfafyfte my lyfe for to fave.
[*Enter the* VYCE, *fynginge this fong, to the tune of the Paynter.*
    Vyce. Stand backe, ye flepinge jackes at home,
        And let me go.
    You lye, fyr knave! am I a mome?
        Why faye you fo?
Tout, tout ! you dare not come in felde,
For feare you fhoulde the gofte up yelde.
    With blofe, he gofe, the gunne fhot flye,
    It feares, it feares, and thear doth lye.
A houndreth in a moment be,
        Difftroyed quight :
Syr faufe, in fayth, yf you fhould fe,
        The gonne fhot lyght,
To quake for feare you would not ftynte,
When as by forfe of gounfhotes dynte,
The rankes in raye are tooke awaye,
As pleafeth fortune oft to playe.
    But in this ftower who beares the fame?
        But onley I :
    Revenge, Revenge, wyll have the name,
        Or he wyll dye.
I fpare no wight, I feare none yll,
But with this blade I wyll them kyll :
For when myne eayre is fet on fpare,
I rap them, I fnap them; that is my defyare.

Farwell! a dew, to wares I mufte
 In all the haft.
My cofen cutpurffe wyll, I trufte,
 Your purffe well taft.
But to it, man, and feare for nought :
Me faye to the it is well fraught
Wyth ruddockes red : be at a becke ;
Beware the arfe, breake not thy necke.   [*Go out.*
 [HORESTES *entrith with his bande, & marcheth
 about the ftage.*
Horeftes. Come on, my fodyers, for at home aryved their
 we be,
Where as we muft have our defyare, or els dye manfulley.
The walles be hye, yet I intend uppon them firft to go ;
And, as I hope, you fodierrs will your captayne eke follow.
Yf I for fake to go before, then fley you eke be hynde,
And as I am, fo eke I truft my fodyers for to finde.
Com hether, Harauld: go proclame this mine intent ftraight-
 way :
To yonder cittie fay that I am come to their decaye.
Unleffe they yeld I will deftroye both man, woman & childe;
And eke their towers, that for the war fo ftrongly they do
 bylde.
Byd them in haft to yeld to me, for nough[t] I do a byde,
But for their aunfwear, or elles fourthwith for them and
 theres provid.
 [*Let the trumpet go towarde the Citie and blowe.*
Harraulde. Your gratious minde ftraight fhalbe don.
 Cum, trompet, let us go.
That I have don your meffage wel, your grace ful wel fhal
 kno.

Hor. Flye the apafe, and let me have agayne an aunfweare
   fone ;
And then a non thou fhalt well fe what quickely fhalbe
   done.
   Harr. How! whow is their that kepes the gate? geve eare
      my words unto!
   [*Let the trumpet leave foundyng, & let* HARRAULD
      fpeake, & CLITEMNESTRA *fpeake over the wal.*
   Clytem. What wouldft thou have, Harald? declare what
      haft thou her to do ?
   Har. My mafter bydes the yeld to him this citie out of
      hande,
Or elles he will not leave on ftone on other for to ftand :
And all things elles within this towne he wil have at his wil,
As pleafeth him by any meanes to fave or elles to fpyll.
What you will now, therfore declare, & aunfwere to him fend.
   Clytem. This citie here againft him and his I wyll defende.
   Harr. Then, in his name, I do defye both the and all
      with in.
   Clytem. By him and his, tell him in fouth, we do not
      fet a pyn.
   Harr. Yf it pleafe your grace, this word fhe fends: fhe
      wil not yeld to ye,
But yf you com, unto your harme fhe fayes that it fhalbe.
               [*Let the Haraulde go out here.*
   Hor. Sith that my grace, and eke good will, they on
      fuch fort difpife,
For to deftroye both man and chyld I furely do devyfe.
Come on, my men! bend now your forfe this citie for to wyn :
Save no mans lyfe that on[c]e fhould make ryfiftaunce there
      within ;

And when you fhall poffes the towne, and have all things
  at wil,
Loke out my mother, but to her do ye no kynde of yll:
Let her not die, though that fhe would defiar the death
  to have,
For other wyfe my fathers death revengment doth crave.
  Sodyer. We fhall your heftes obaye with fpede. Oh cap-
  tayne! we defiar
That we were there, for to revenge, our hartes are fet
  on fyar.
  Vyce. Lyke men, by God I fweare, wellfayd! Horeftes,
  let us gow:
Nowe to thy men lyke manly hart I praye the for to
  fhowe:
And, as thou feifte, be firfte the man that fhall the citie wyn.
How, how! now for to flye all ready they begynne.
  Hor. With lyvely hartes, my troumpeters, exault your
  tubal found;
And now, my fodyers, in your harts let courrage eke be
  found.
Com, let us go: the godes for us fhall make an eafey wayᵉ:
Spare none a lyve, for I am bent to feke their great decaye.
  [*Go and make your lively battel, and let it be longe eare
  you can win the citie; and when you have won it, let
  HORESTES bringe out his mother by the armes, and
  let the droum feafe playing, and the trumpet alfo:
  when fhe is taken, let her knele downe and fpeake.*
  Clytem. A lack, what heaps of myfchefes great me, felly
  wight, torment!
Now is the tyme falune me upon, which I thought to
  prevent.

Yet beſt I ſeke my lyfe to ſave, perhappes he will me here.
A lacke! revengment he dothe crave for ſlaying his father dere.
Yf aney ſparke of mothers bloud remaynd within thy breſte,
Oh, gratious child! let now thine eares unto my words be preſt.
Pardon I crave, Horeſtes myne; ſave now my corpes from death;
Let no man ſaye that thou waſt cauſe I yeldyd up my breath:
I have offendyd, I do confeſſe, yet ſave my lyfe, I praye,
And to they mother this requeſt, o knight! do not denaye,
  Hor. For to repent this facte of thine, now that it is to late,
Can not be thought a recompence for kylling of thy mate.
Go; have her hence therfore with ſpede, and ſe her ſureley kepte,
And for the fact a fore thou dydeſt, thou ſurley ſhouldſt have wept.   [*Go out with on of the ſodiares.*
  Vyce. Nay, far you well; in fayth, you have an aunſwer; get you hence.
Oundes of me, I would not be in her cote for forty pence.
Nay, nay, a way, far well, a dew; now, now it is to late,
When ſtede is ſtollen for you, in ſouth, to ſhut the ſtable gate.
She ſhould have wept when firſt ſhe went the king about to ſlay:
It makes no matter; ſhe foull well dyd brede her owne decaye.   [*Let* HORESTES *ſyth hard.*
Ounds of me, what meane you, man? begyn you now to faynt?
Jeſu god! how ſtyll he ſittes; I thinke he be a faynt.

O oo w! you care not me; nay, fone I have don, I war-
   rant ye.
             [*Wepe, but let* HORESTES *ryfe and bid him peafe.*
   Hor. By all the godes, my hart dyd fayle my mother
      for to fe
From hye eftate for to be brought to fo great myferey,
That all moft I had graunted lyfe to her had not this be
My fathers death, whofe death in fouth, chefe caufer of
      was fhe.
   Vyce. Even as you faye. But harke! at hand Egiftus
      draweth nye,
Who purpofeth the chaunce of war, Horeftes, for to trye.
         [*Let* EGISTUS *enter, & fet hys men in a raye; & let
            the drom playe tyll* HORESTES *fpeaketh.*
   Hor. And by the godes, I purpofe eke my honour to
      defend.
Com on, my men! kepe your araye, for now we do pretend
Eather to be the conquerer, or elles to dye in felde:
Lyft up your hartes, and let us fe how ye your blofe can yeld.
   Egiftus. Lyke manley men adreffe your felves to get
      immortall fame:
Yf ye do flye, lo, what doth reft behynde but foull defame?
Strike up your drums, let trumpets found, your baners eke
      difplay!
And I my felfe, as captayne, to you wyll lead the waye.
   Hor. Thou traytor to my father dere, what makeft the
      here in feld?
Repent the of thy wyckednes, and to me ftrayght do yeld.
   Egis. Thou pryncoks boy, and baftard flave! thinks thou
      me to fubdew?
It lyeth not with in thy powre, thou boye, I tell the trew.

But yf I take thy corpes, it fhalbe a fode the byrdes to fede.
Stryke up your droums and forward now! To wars let us
    profede.
> [*Stryke up your drum, & fyght a good whil, & then
> let fum of* EGISTUS *men flye, & then take hym,
> & let* HORESTES *drau him violentlye, and let
> the drums feafe.*

Hor. O vyllayne trayghtor! now the gods ne mortall
    man fhall fave
Thy corps from death, for blud for blud my fathers deth
    doth crave.
O tyraunt fyrfe! couldeft thou voutfafe my father fo
    to flaye?
But now no forfe, for thou haft wrought at laft thine one
    decaye.
> *Egis.* Alacke, a lacke! yet fpare my lyfe, Horeftes, I
> the praye.
> *Hor.* Thy lyfe? naye, trayghtor vyle, that chefe I do
> denaye.

For as thou haft defervyd fo I fhall thy facte requit,
That once couldft feme to me and mine for to work fuch
    difpight.
Therfore com forth, and for thy facte receave dew pun-
    nifhment:
Repent, I fay, thy former lyfe, for this is my judgment:
That for my fathers death, the which we finde the chefe to be
The caufer of, thou fhalt be hanged, where we thy death
    may fe;
And as thou for my fathers death dew punnifhment receive,
So fhall my mother in lykewife, for that fhe gave the leave
Him for to flaye, and eke to it with good will condyfende.

Therfore com of, and fone dyfpatch, that we had made
    an end.
  Egis. Ah, heavy fate and chaunce moft yll, wo worth this
    hap of mine!
For give my faute, you facryd godes, and to my wordes
    incline
Your gracious eare; for caufer furft I was, this is moft plaine,
Of Agamemnons death, wherefore I muft receave this paine.
Pardon, I crave; voutfafe, ye godes, the fame to graunt it me!
Now, fodier, worke thy will in haft, I praye the harteley.
    [*Fling him of the lader, and then let on bringe in
    his mother* CLYTEMNESTRA, *but let her loke
    wher* EGISTUS *hangeth.*
  Clytem. Ah, heavey fate! would God I had in tormoyle
    great byn flayne,
Syth nothing can Horeftes hands from fheding bloud
    reftraine.
  Vyce. How chaunce you dyd not then lament his father
    whom you flew?
But now, when death doth you prevent, to late ites for
    to rew.
  Clytem. Yet hope I that he will me graunt my lyfe that
    I fhould have.
  Vyce. Even as much as thou voutfafeft his fathers lyfe
    to fave.
Therfore come of: we muft not ftay all daye to wayght
    on the.
Lo! myghtye prince, for whom ye fent, lo, preafent here
    is fhe.
  Clytem. Have mercy, fonne, and quight remitte this faute
    of mine, I pray:
Be mercyfull, Horeftes myne, and do not me denaye.

Confider that in me thou hadeft thy hewmayne fhape
    compofid :
That thou fhouldft flay thy mother, fon, let it not be
    difclofyd.
Spare to perfe her harte with fword; call eke unto thy mynd
Edyppus fate, and as Nero fhowe not thy felfe unkynde.
              [*Take downe* EGISTUS, *and bear him out.*
  Hor. Lyke as a braunche once fet a fyare doth caufe the
    tree to bourne,
As Socrates fuppofeth, fo a wicked wight doth tourne
Thofe that be good, and caufe them eke his evell to fequeft.
Wherefore the poete Juvenal doth thinke it for the befte,
That thofe that lyve lycentioufley fhould brydlyd be with
    payne ;
And fo others, that elles would fyn, therby they might
    reftrain :
For thus he fayeth, that cities are well governed in dede
Where punnifhment for wycked ones by lawe is fo decrede;
And not decrede, but exerfyefd, in punnyfhinge of thofe
Which law ne pain from waloing ftill in vice their mind
    difpofe.
And as thou haft byn chiefes[t] caufe of yelding up they
    breath,
So call to minde thou waft the caufe of Agamemnons death:
For which, as death is recompence, of death fo eke with the,
For kyllinge of my father, thou now kylled eke fhault be.
This thinge to fe accomplyfhyd, Revenge with the fhall go.
Now have her hence, fieth that you all my judgment here
    do kno.
  Clytem. A lacke, a lack ! with drawe thy hand, my fon,
    from fheding bloud.

Vyce. Thou art a foule thus for to prate; this doth
    Horeftes good :
Com on a way! thou douft no more but him with words
    moleft.
A foulyfhe foull! that thou wart ded he takes it for the beft.
    Clytem. Yf ever aney pytie was of mother plante in the,
            [*Knele downe.*
Let it apeare, Horeftes myne, and fhowe it unto me.
    Hor. What pyttie thou on father myne dydeft curfedley
        beftowe,
The fame to the at this prefent I purpofe for to fhowe.
Therfore, Revenge, have her a way, and as I judgment gave,
To fe that fhe in order lyke her punifhment dew have.
    Vyce. Let me alone. Com on away, that thou weart out
        of fight !
A peftelaunce on the crabyd queane! I thinke thou do
    delyght
Him to moleft: com of in haft, and troubell me no more.
Come on, com on! ites all in vaine; and get you on a fore.
        [*Let* CLYTEMNESTRA *wepe and go out,* REVENGE *alfo.*
    Hor. Now, fyeth we have the conqueft got of all our
        mortall fofe,
Let us provide that occafion we do not chaunce to lofe.
Stryke up your droumes! for enter now we wyll the citie
    gate ;
For nowe refeftaunce none there is to let us in there at.
[*Enter in* FAME; *and let all the fodyers folow him in araye.*
    Fame. As eache man bendes him felfe, fo I report his
        fame in dede.
Yf yll, then yll, through iarne trump his fame doth ftraigh[t]
    profede ;

Yf good, then good, through golden trump I blo his lyvely
    fame :
Through heavens, throgh earth, & furging feafe I bere abrod
    the fame.
Perhaps what wind me heather drives with in your minds
    you mufe ?
From Crete I com : to you, my frends, I bring this kind of
    newfe ;
That Agamemnons brother is arivyd in this land,
And eke with him his ladey fayre, Quene Helen, underftand ;
Whom for to fe a great frequent of people their aryve :
This newfe to fhew at this prefent me heather now dyd drive.
        [*Enter the* VYCE, *finging this fonge.*
            Vyce. A newe mafter, a newe !
                No lenger I maye
                A byde : by this daye,
                    Horeftes now doth rew.
                A new mafter, a new !
                    And was it not yll
                    His mother to kyll ?
                I pray you, how faye you ?
                A new mafter, a new !
                    Nowe ites to late
                    To fhut the gate,
                Horeftes gines to rew !
    Fame. Denique non parvas animo dati gloria vires :
Et fœcunda facit pectora laudis amor.
As Ovid fayeth, I am, in dede, the fpure to each eftate ;
For by my troumpe I often caufe the wicked man to hate
Is fylthey lyfe : and eke I ftoure the good more good to be.
So much the hart and will of man ys lynked unto me.

Vyce. A new mafter, a new! naye, I wyll go.
Tout, tout! Horeftes has be com a newe man.
Now he forroweth : to bad that it is fo.
Yet I wyll dreffe him, by his oundes, and I can.
Who, *faintie amen!* God morrowe, myftres Nan!
By his oundes, I am glad to fe the fo trycke :
Nay, may I be fo bould at your lyppes to have a lycke?
Jefus! how coye do you make the fame.
You neaver knew me afore, I dare faye.
In fayth, in fayth, I was to blame
That I made no courchey to you by the waye.
Who, berladye, Nan! thou art trym and gaye.
Woundes of me! fhe hath winges alfo.
Who, whether, with a myfchefe, douft thou thinke for
 to go?
To heaven, or to hell? to purgatorye, or Spayne?
To Venys? to Pourtugall? or to the eylles Canarey?
Nay, ftay a whyle, for a myte or twayne
I wyll go with the, I fweare by Saynt Marey.
Wylt thou have a bote, Nan, over feay the to carey?
Now, yf it chaunce to rayne, as the weathers not harde,
It may chaunce this trym geare of thine to be marde.

Fame. Omnia fi perdis, famam fervare memento,
Quæ femel amiffa, poftia nullus eris.
Above eache thinge kepe well thy fame, what ever that
 thou lofe;
For fame once gone, they memory with fame a way it gofe:
And it once loft thou fhalt, in fouth, accomptyd lyke to be
A drope of rayne that faulyth in the bofom of the fee.
Me, Fame, therfore, as Ovid thinkes, no man hath powre to
 hold :

To thofe with whom I pleafe to dwell I am more rich then
    gold.
What caufid fome for countris foyle them felves to perell
    caft,
But that the[y] knew that after death the fame of thers
    fhall laft.
Not on, but all, do me defiare, both good and bad lykewyfe;
As may apeare, yf we perpend, of Nerofe enterpryfe,
Which firft did caufe his mafters death, and eke wheras
    he laye
In mothers wound to fe, in fouth, his mother dyd ftraight
    flay.
With this Horeftes eke takes place, whofe father being
    flayn
Throgh mothers gile, from mothers blod his hands could
    not refraine.
But lyke as he revengyd the death of father in his eyare,
So fathers brother, in lyke fort, Revenge hath fet on fyare.
For he is gon for to requeft the ayde of prynces great;
So fore his hart is fet on fyare, throught raging rigrous heat.
What to detarmyne all the kynges of Grece aryved be
At Neftores towne, that Athens highte, their judgment to
    decre.

    Vyce. Oundes, hart, and nayles! naye, now I am dreft.
Is the kinge Menalaus at Athenes aryved,
And I am be hind? to be packinges the beft,
Leaft the matter, in fouth, to fone be contryved.
Auxilia humilia firma, confenfus facit: this alwayes provided
That confent maketh fuckers moft fure for to be.
Well, I wyll be their ftrayght wayfe you fhall fe.

    Fame. As Publius doth well declare, we ought chefeft to fe

Unto our felves, that nought be don after extremite.
Ab alio expectes, alteri quod feceris. [*Go out.*
For loke, what mefure thou doft meate, the fame againe fhalbe
At other tyme, at others hand, repayde againe to the.
Therefore, I wyfhe eache wight to do to others as he would
That they, in lyke occafion, unto him offer fhould.
Wel, forth I muft, fom newfe to here, for Fame no where can ftay;
But what she hears throughout the world abrod she doth difplay.
 Provicion. Make roume and gyve place! ftand backe there a fore!
For all my fpeakinge, you preffe ftyll the more.
Gyve rome, I faye, quickeley, and make no dalyaunce:
It is not now tyme to make aney taryaunce.
The kinges here do com: therefore, give way,
Or elles, by the godes! I wyll make you, I faye.
Lo, where my Lord Kynge Neftor doth com!
And Horeftes with him, Agamemnons fonne.
Menelaus, a kyng lykewyfe of great fame.
Make rome, I faye! before their with shame!
 Nest. Now fyeth we be here, Kynge Menelaij,
Unto us, we praye you, your matter to faye:
For thefe prynces here, after they have perpendyd,
If ought be amys it fhall be amendyd.
But, fyrra Provifion, go in hafte and fet
Good Kynge Idumeus: tell him we are fet.
 Prov. As your gracis have wylled, fo tend I to do;
I wyll fetche him ftrayght, and bringe him you to. [*Go out.*
 [*Paufe awhile till he be gon out, and then fpeak tretably.*

An Interlude.

Hor. If ought be amys, the fame fone fhall be,
If I have commytted, amendyd of me :
But lo, Idumeus, the good kyng of Crete,
Is come to this place us for to mete.
    [*Enter* IDUMIUS, *and* PROVISION *comming with his cap in his hand afore him, and makinge waye.*
Idumeus. The Gods prefarve your gracis all, and fend you health for aye.
Nest. Well com, fier kinge, the fame to ye contynewalley we pray.
Menal. Two things there is, o kings! that moves me thus your ayds to pray :
And thefe be it, the which to you I purpofe for to faye.
The one is this, where with I fynde my felfe agrevid to be,
That on fuch fort my fyfters flayne, as all your gracis fe.
The other is, that fo her fonne, without all kind of right,
Should to his mother in fuch cafe (I fay) worke fuch difpight.
Thefe two be they, wherfore I crave your ayds to joyn with me,
To the infent of fuch great ylles revengyd I may be.
That thus he dyd, be hould the ftate of all my brothers land,
And fe, I pray you, in what place the fame doth prefent ftand.
His crueltie is fuch, in fouth, as nether tower ne towne,
That letted once his paffage, but is brought unto the ground.
The fatherles he pyttied not where as he ever went,
The agyd wight whofe yeres before their youthly poure had fpent,
The mayd whofe parentes at the fege, defending of their right,

Was flaine, the fame this tyrant hath opreffyd throuh his
  might;
The wido that through forrayne wars was left now com-
  fortles
He fpared not, but them and theres he cruelly dyd dyftres.
Wherfore fith that he thus hath wrought, as far as I can fee,
From Mycœne land we fhould provid him exylyd to be.
   Hor. Syth that you have accufyd me, I muft my aun-
  fwere make;
And here before thefe kings of Greece this for my aun-
  fwer take.
O ounckel, that I never went revengment for to do
On fathers fofe, tyll by the godes I was comaund there to:
Whofe heaftes no man dare once refufe, but wyllingly obaye.
That I have flayne her wylfully untruely you do faye;
I dyd but that I could not chufe: ites hard for me to kycke,
Syth gods commaund, as on would fay, in fayth, againft
  the prick.
In that you fay I fparyd none, your grace full well may fe,
That lyttell mercy they fupppofyd, in fouth, to fhow to me.
When as they bad me do my worft, requefting them to yeld,
It is no jeft when fodyares joyne to fight within a felde.
Thus I fuppofe fufficiently I aunfwered have to end
Your great complaynt, the which you fo mightely did defend.
   Idum. In dede, as Hermes doth declare, no man can
  once eftew
The judgment of God moft juft, that for his fautes is dew:
And as God is moft mercyfull, fo is he juft lyke wyfe,
And wyll correcte moft fuerley thofe that his heaftes
  difpyfe.
   Neft. As you, good Kyng Idumeus, have fayd, fo lyke-
  wife I

Do thinke it trew; therefore as nowe I do him here defye
That one dare fay that he hath wrought the thing that is
    not right,
Lo, here my glove to him I give in pledge with him to fyght.
I promys here to prove there by Horeftes nought dyd do
But that was juft, and that the gods commaundyd him
    there to:
That he is kinge of Mycœne land who ever do deney,
I offer here my glove with him therfore to lyve and dye.
Yf none there be wyll under take his tyghtull to with faye,
Let us be frendes unto him nowe, my lordes, I do ye praye.
It was the parte of fuch a knyght revengyd for to be:
Should Horeftes content him felfe his father flayne to fe?
No, no; a ryghteous facte I thinke the fame to be in dede,
Syeth that it was accomplyfsht fo as godes before decrede.
    Menel. In dede, I muft confeffe that I revengyd fhould
    have be,
If that my father had byn flayne with fuch great cruelte.
But yet I would, for natures fake, have fpard my mothers
    lyfe.
O wretched man! o cruell beaft! o mortall blade and
    knyfe!
    Idum. Seafe of, fyr kyng; leave morning: lo, nought can
    it you avayle;
Not with ftanding, be rulyd now, we pray, by our counfaylle.
Confider firft your one eftate, confider what may be
A joyefull mene to end at leyngth this your calamytie.
Horeftes he is younge of yeares, and you are fomwhat olde,
And forrowe may your grace to fone within her net infolde.
Therefore ites beft you do forget; fo fhall you be at eafe,
And, I am fure, Horeftes wyll indevor you to pleafe,

So far as it for him may be with honor lefe to do.
He will not fhry[n]ke but wyll confent your gracis bydding
    to:
For affuraunce of your good wyll, Horeftes here doth crave
Your daughter, fayre Hermione, in maryage to have.
Thereby for to contynew ftyll true love and amytie,
That ought, in fought, betwixte t[w]o fuch indefferent for
    to be.
  Menel. As for my frendfhyp, he fhall have, the godes his
    helper be;
But for my daughters maryage, I can not graunt to be.
She is but yong, and much unfet fuch holy ryghtes to take:
Therefore, fyr kyngs, at this prefent no aunfwere I can make.
  Neft. She is a dame of comeley grace; therefore, kyng
    Menelaye,
Graunt this to us this ftryfe to end, o kyng, we do the praye.
For eache of them a grede be the other for to have:
Good fyr, graunt this that at thy handes fo juftley we do crave.
  Menal. O, nobell king, what that it were I could not
    you denaye.
I muft nedes graunt, when nought I have againft you to
    repley.
Horeftes, here before thefe kinges my fonne I the do make.
  Hor. And the, o kynge, whyle lyfe doth laft, for father I
    do take.
  Neft. Ryght joyfull is this thinge to us, and happey for
    your ftate.
Therfore with fpede let us go hence the maryage to feley-
    brate;
And all the godes, I praye, prefarve and kepe you both
    from wo.
Come on, fyr king, fhall we from hence unto our pallace go?

Menal. As it fhall pleafe your grace, in dede, fo we con-
fent to do.
Idum. And we lykewyfe, oh gratious Prynce, do condi-
fend there to. [*Go out all.*
　　　　[VYCE *entrith with a ftaffe and a bottell*
　　　　　　　　　　　　　　　　or dyfhe, and wallet.
Revenge. I woulde I were ded, and layde in my grave!
Oundes of me, I am trymley promouted:
Ah, ah, oh! well now for my labor thefe trynketes I
have.
Why, fe you not, I praye you, how I am flouted?
A bagge and a bottell; thus am I louted!
Eache knave, nowe a dayes, would make me his man.
But chyll mafter them, I, be his oundes, and I can.
A begginge, a begginge, nay now muft I go.
Horeftes is maryed; god fend him much care:
And I, Revenge, am dryven him fro.
And thun ites no marvayll, though I be thus bare.
But peace! who better then beggars doth fare?
For all they be beggares, and have no great port,
Who is meryer then the pooryfte fort?
What shall I begge! nay, thates to bad.
Is their neare a man that a farvaunt doth lacke?
Of myne honeftye, gentle woman, I would be glad
You to farve but for clothes to put on my backe.
A waye with thefe rages! from me the[y] shall packe.
　　　　　　[*Put of the beggares cote and all thy thinges.*
What! thinke you fcorne me your fervaunt to make?
A nother wyll have me, yf you me forfake.
Parhappes you all mervayll of this fodayne mutation,
How fone I was downe from fo hye degre:
To fatisfye your myndes I wyl yufe a perfwation.

This one thinge you knowe, that on caulyd Amyte
Is unto me, Revenge, moſt contrarey;
And we twayne to geather could not abyde.
Whych cauſyd me ſone from hye ſtate to ſlyde,
Horeſtes and his ounckell, Kynge Menalaus,
Is made ſuch ſure frendes, without peradventure,
Through the pollycye of olde Idumeus,
That, as far as I can ſe, it is hard to enter;
Ye, and thates worſſe, when I ſought to venture,
I was dryven, out comfort, awaye from their gate:
I was glad to be packinge, for feare of my pate.
Yet befor I went, my fancey to pleaſe,
The maryage ſelebratyd, at the church I dyd ſe.
Wyllinge I was them all to dyſeaſe,
But I durſt not be ſo bold; for maſter Amyte
Sot by Menalaus, and bore him companye.
On the other ſyde Dewtey with Horeſtes boure ſwayc;
So that I could not enter by no kynde of waye.
Well, ſyeth from them both I am bannyſhyd ſo,
I wyll ſeke a new maſter, yf I can him finde:
Yet am I in good comfort, for this well I knowe,
That the moſt parte of wemen to me be full kynde;
Yf they ſaye near a worde, yet I knowe their mynde.
Yf they have not all thinges when they do deſiare,
They wyll be revengyd, or elles lye in the myare.
Nay, I knowe their quallytes, the leſſe is my care,
As well as they do knowe Revengys operation.
Ye, faull to it, good wyves, and do them not ſpare:
Nay, Ille helpe you forward, yf you lacke but perſwacion.
What man a moſte is free from invaſion?
For, as playnely Socrates declareth unto us,
Wemen for the moſt part are borne malitious.

Perhappes you wyll faye, maney on, that I lye;
And other fume, I am fure, alfo wyll take my parte:
Not withftandinge what I have fayde, they wyll veryfye,
Ye, and do it, I wys, in fpyght of thy hart.
Yf, therefore, thou wylt lyve quyetlye, after their defart,
Reward then, fo fhault thou brydell their affection,
And unto they wyll fhall have them in fubjection.
In Athenes dwellyd Socrates, the phyllofopher dyvine,
Who had a wyfe named Exantyp, both develyfhe and yll;
Which twayne, beenge faulne out uppon a tyme,
Perhappe caufe Exantyp could not have her wyll,
He went out of dores, fyttinge there ftyll:
She cround him with a pyfpot, and their he
Was wet to the fkynne, mofte pytifull to fe.
I praye God that fuch dames be not in this place,
For then I might chaunce neare a miftres to get.
Nay, yf ye anger them, they wyll laye you on the face,
Or elles their nayles in your chekes they wyll fet;
Nay, lyke a rafor fome of their nayles are whet,
That not for to pare, but to cut to the bone:
I count him moft happeft that medelles with none.
Well, far you well! for I muft be packinge:
Remember my wordes, and beare it in mynde.
What! fuffer the myll a whyle to be clackinge,
Yf that you intend aney eafe for to fynde:
Then wyll they be to you both lovinge and kinde.
Farwell, cofen cutpurffe! and be ruled by me,
Or elles you may chaunce to end on a tre.   [*Go out.*
    [*Enter* HORESTES *and* HERMIONE, NOBILYTYE
        and COMINYALTE, TRUTH *&* DEWTY.
  Horeftes. Syth the gods have geven us grace this realme
    for to poffes,

Which floryfheth aboundauntlye with gold & great riches,
Let us now fe how much the wilds and minde of all this land,
Is unto us, and of their ftate lykewyfe to underftand.
   Herm. I deme of them, Horeftes myne, that they contentyd be
With humbell hart for to fubmyte, o kyng! them felves to ye :
Wherefore, my love, inquiare their ftate this preafente tyme,
And of their hartes good wyll to us, o king! let them devyne.
   Hor. As I do love,the ladye bright, fo eke I thynke, in dede,
That love for love as equallye fhalbe rewarde of mede.
   Herm. The godes never prolonge my lyfe that day I fhall a peare
To breake my fayth to the now plyght, my loving lord fo dere!
[*Let* DEWTY *&* TRUTH *take the crowne in their right hands.*
   Hor. Come on, my lordes and commons eke, let me now underftand
Of all your mindes, for I defiare to know what cafe this land
Doth now confyft; voutfafe the fame therfore to fhew to me,
And yf that ought be now amyfe, amendyd it fhalbe.
   Nobelles. Moft regall prynce, we now are voyd of mortall wars vexation,
And through your grace we are joyned in love with every nation ;
So that your nobelles may now lyve in pleafaunt ftate fartaine,

Devoyd of wars and civill ſtryfes while that your grace
    doth raine.
The which you may, I pray the God, with happy days
    and blys,
And after death to ſend you there where joyſe ſhall
    never mys.
As fyne of our obedyence, lo, Dewty doth the crownd,
And Truth alſo, which doth me bynd they ſubjecte to be
    found.
              [*Let* TRUTH *and* DEWTY *crowne* HORESTES.
  Hor. My Nobells all, I gyve you thankes for this now
    ſhowed to me,
And as you have, ſo eke will I the lyke ſhow unto ye.
My Commons, how goſe it with you? your ſtate now let
    me know.
  Commons. Where as ſuch on as you do raine there nedes
    muſt riches gro.
We are, o king! eaſyd of the yoke which we have ſo deſiard:
The ſtate of this our common welth nede not to be
    inquiard.
Peace, welth, joye and felycitie, o kinge! it is we have,
And what thing is their the which ſubjects ought more to
    crave.
  Hor. Syeth all thinges is in ſo good ſtate, my Commons,
    as you ſaye,
That it may ſo continew ſtyll the ſacred godes I praye.
And as to me your truſteynes ſhall anye wayes be found,
So ſtyll to mayntayne your eſtate I ſureley ſhalbe bound.
And for your faythfull harts, the which you graunted have
    to me,

Both you, my lords and commons eke, I thanke you hartele.
Therfore fith time wil have an end, and now my mind you know,
Let us give place to tyme, and to our pallafe go.
　Nobelles. We both wil waight upon your grace, yft pleafe you to depart.
　Commons. Eeven when you pleafe to waigh[t] you on I fhall with all my hart.
　Truth. A kyngdome kept in amyte, and voyde of diffention,
Ne devydyd in him felfe by aney kynde of waye,
Neather provoked by wordes of reprehention,
Muft nedes long continew, as Truth doth faye,
For defention and ftryfe is the path to decaye;
And continuinge therein muft of nefecitie
Be quight ruinate, and brought unto myferye.
　Dewtey. Where I, Dewtey, am neglected of aney eftate,
Their ftryfe and dyffention my place do fupplye:
Cankred mallyfe, pryde, and debate,
Therefore to reft all meanes do trye.
Then ruin comes after of their ftate, whereby
They are utterly extynguyfhed, levinge nought behynde
Whereof fo much as their name we maye fynde.
　Truth. He that leadeth his lyfe as his phanfey doth lyke,
Though for a whyle the fame he maye hyde,
Yet Truth, the daughter of Tyme, wyll it feke,
And fo in a tyme it wyll be difcryde;
Yet in fuch tyme as it can not be denyed,
But receave dew punnifhment, as God fhall fe,
For the faute commytted, moft convenient to be.

As this ftorye here hath made open unto ye,
Which yf it have byn marked much prophet may aryfe.
For, as Truth fayth, nothinges wryten be
But for our learninge, in anye kynde of wyfe.
By which we may learne the yll to difpyfe,
And the truth to imitate ; thus Truth doth faye :
The which for to do I befech God we maye.
   Dewtey. For your gentle pacience we geve you thankes
       hartely.
And therefore, our dewtey wayed, let us all praye
For Elyzabeth our Quene, whofe gratious majeftie
May rayne over us in helth for aye :
Lykwyfe for her Councell, that each of them maye
Have the fpyryte of grace their doinges to dyrecte,
In fettinge up vertue, and vyce to correcte.
   Truth. For all the nobylytie and fpiritualtie let us praye ;
For judges and head officers, what ever they be :
According to our boundaunt dewties, efpetially I faye
For my Lord Mayre, lyfetennaunt of this noble Cytie ;
And for all his brytherne, with the comminualtie,
That eache of them, doinge their dewties a ryght,
May after death poffes heaven to their hartes delyght.

             FINIS.   qd J. P.

¶ Imprinted at London in Fleteftrete, at the figne of the
   Faucon, by Wylliam Gryffith, and are to be fold at
      his fhoppe in Saynte Dunftones Church
         yarde. Anno Domini. 1567.

INTRODUCTION.

THE work here reprinted is in every respect unique : only a single copy of it has been preserved, and it is in a form of versification of which we have never seen any other specimen.

The subject of it is anglo-historical; but it has few claims to be considered an important addition to our national poetry, excepting as regards the versification ; for the unnamed and unknown author can have no pretension to rank himself with such contemporaries as Daniel or Drayton, both of whom (to mention no others) have left behind them highly finished proofs of genius in the same department of literature. The author of " The Preservation of Henry VII" was sufficiently well read, and his biblical and classical allusions are numerous, and apposite; but the frame of his mind was remarkably unoriginal, and his own reflections are always common-place.

He promised in the outset to extend his labours to five books ; but he seems to have paused near the commencement of his second division, as if waiting to learn what degree of favour his production obtained from the Queen, to whom it is especially addressed; and from the public, whose taste he hoped to wean from " the gingle of rhyming mother-wits."

Yet he is throughout guilty of singular inconsistency ; for while condemning rhyme, he professes, however loosely and lawlessly, to adopt it ; and, as it were, strives to reconcile and combine the classical measures of antiquity with the poetical ornament handed down to us by our gothic ancestors. Thus we have a series of so called rhyming hexameters, occupying more than sixty pages; and, although the writer is not deficient in self-confidence, not to call it self-conceit, he seems, as he proceeded, to have lost faith in his own experiment, and to have become weary of the double shackles to which he had voluntarily submitted. He tells us in one place that Abraham Fraunce had preceded him in this species of mingled composition; but if he did so, the attempt has never fallen in our way.

He gives us a hint of his family when he says, "I come myself of a Trentham," but we have no other clue to his connexions; and although in the outset we fancied that Sir Edward Dyer, who liked such experiments, and did not die until 1607, might possibly be the writer of this work, we were convinced, as we advanced, that it was far inferior to his pen. In one place our author almost follows the very wording of a stanza in Sir Walter Raleigh's famous poem called "The Lie"; and, in another, he literally translates a line which Chapman placed on the engraved title-page of his translation of Homer.

The original volume is an oblong quarto, for the sake of avoiding the turning of the lengthened lines, and of inserting marginal references: the last, for greater convenience, we have transferred to the foot of our page. We willingly and thankfully acknowledge our obligations to Mr. H. Pyne, not only for directing our attention to this highly curious and, as far as we know, unexampled production, but for the use of a most beautiful and accurate transcript of it.

J. P. C.

THE FIRST BOOKE OF THE PRESERVATION OF

King Henry the vij. when he was but Earle

of Richmond, Grandfather to the

Queenes maiefty :

Compiled in englifh rythmicall Hexameters.

Vivit in eternum poft funera vivida virtus.
Vertue remaineth alive after death lively for ever.

Quo magis difficilior, eo pulchrior,
Hoc opus, hic labor eft.

⁋ Imprinted at London, by R. B. and are to be folde in Paules Church-yard, at the figne of the Bible.
1599.

TO THE PRINTER.

Print with a good letter this booke, and carefuly, Printer:
Print each word legibill, not a word nor a fillabil alter:
Keepe points, and commas, periodes, the parenthefis obferve;
My credit and thy reporte to defend, bothe fafely to conferve.

*To the Right honorabel, worſhipfull, gentel, and learned
Readers, whoſoever ; that are both trew favorits of
poetry, and of right ancient Heroicke
Hexameters.*

IGHT honored, worſhipfull, and gentell Reader, theſe Hexameters and Pentameters in Engliſhe are miſliked of many, becauſe they are not yet come to their full perfection; and ſpecially of ſome, that are accounted and knowne to be Doctors, and ſingularly well learned and great Linguiſtes : but eſpecially of the plaine Rythmer, that ſcarce knowes the footed quantitie or metricall ſcanning thereof; much leſſe to reade them with a grace according to the ſame. But for him, I ſay thus; *Scientia nullum habet inimicum, præter ignorantem :* whoſe bookes are ſtuft with lines of proſe, with a rythme in the end ; which every fiddler, or piper, can make upon a theame given. Nevertheleſſe, I confeſſe and acknowledge that we have many excellent and ſingular good Poets in this our age, as Maiſter Spencer, that was, Maiſter Gowlding, Doctor Phayer, Maiſter Harrington, Daniell, and divers others whom I reverence in that kinde of proſe-rythme ; wherein Spencer (without offence ſpoken) hath ſurpaſſed them all. I would to God they had done ſo well in trew Hexameters, for they had then beautified our language. For the Greekes and Latines did in a manner aboliſh quite that kinde of rythme-proſe ; and why ſhould not we doe the like in Englifhe? But the ignorant and adverfe part will fay, our fpeach is not copious enough. But I fay that it is; and, befides, it would be the more inriched, adorned, and more eloquent, if they would make triall thereof, or could compofe them artificially and eloquently to delight the Readers, to refound with a grace in their ears: *Nam nihil difficile volenti.* But this is the trew caufe why they do not fo; *Hoc opus, hic labor eft,* which the chiefe Doctors and beft learned of them all, cannot deny. And perhappes fome of the beft of them, that are curious carpers and reprehenders of this trew metrified verfe, though fkilful in other arts, cannot formally compofe the like as Fraunce did; who obferved a better Profodia then Stanihurft. For Tully was not fo good a poetician as he was an orator. God beftoweth his gifts feverally, and more bountifully on fome than on others. For Homer in Greeke, and Virgill in Latine, furpaffed all that ever were before or fince in trew footed hexameters; but not in profe. Neither were Homer and Virgill the firft that verfifyed in their naturall language; but others did attempt to poetize afore them, in the like verfe; or elfe, in truth, I fuppofe they could not have done fo well. Every thing hath a beginning, which at firft cannot be made fo perfect. Thofe verfes which Ennius made, before Virgill made any, were not fo well liked; as, for example: *Unus homo nobis cunctando reftituit rem:* yet Virgill moft commonly had his booke about him. Therefore, I reverence Stanihurft; who being but an Irifh man, did firft attempt to tranflate thofe foure bookes of Eneados, which (if he be living) I defire him to refile them over againe; and thus have written in verfe:

The Epiſtle dedicatorie. 5

If the poet Stanihurſt yet live and feedeth on ay-er,
I do requeſt him (as one that wiſheth a grace to the meter)
With wordes ſignificant to refile, and finely to poliſhe
Thoſe fower Æneïs, that he late tranſlated in Engliſh.
I doe the man reverence, as a fine, as an exquiſit author,
For that he firſt did attempt to tranſlate verſe as a Doctor.

For, at the firſt, Maiſter Aſkam had much adoe to make two or three verſes in Engliſh; but now every ſcholler can make ſome. What language ſo hard, harſh, or barbarous, that time and art will not amend? As I have written in another place, thus:

Naught can at once be begonne, or preſent made, to be perfect.
By travel all hard things are brought to ſingular effect.
Yet that Apelles could Cytheræas bewty depoliſh;
Had not he time to delyne, hir picture finely to fynnyſh?

This trew kinde of hexametred and pentametred verſe will bring unto us four commodities. Firſt, it will enrich our ſpeach with good and ſignificant wordes; ſecondly, it will bring a delight and pleaſure to the ſkilful reader, when he ſeeth them formally compyled; and, thirdly, it will incourage and learne the good and godly ſtudents, that affect poetry, and are naturally enclyned therunto, to make the like; fourthly, it will direct a trew Idioma, and will teach trew orthography, for as gould ſurpaſſeth leade, ſo the hexameters ſurpaſſe rythme proſe. And as concerning the ſame, this have I written:

As yelo gould purified doth ſurmount every mettell,
So fine verſe metrifyed this rythme-proſe greatly doth excell,
With wordes ſignificant ſuch rurall rythmery confound,
And metricall verſes with a new rythme lawraly compound:

For fily mufe feare not ; fince every paltery rythmor
With wordes unmetrifyed would feeme to be counted a
    Doctor,
Whofe workes feeme to be good, reprefenting Tantalus
    appels,
Which did apeare to be gold, but toucht were turned
    in afhes.

And in another place.

Clowde not your orient fine fkyll with dregges of a drowfy
Conterfaited profe : this Romane verfe hath a glory,
As redolent gilyflowers perfumes a delight to the fenfes,
Mens memories to refrefh : fo fcanning rythmery verfes
Bringes a delight to the mindes, &c.

For thefe ribaud and baudy Poets be but the divels agents, and are to be detefted ; but the vertuous and godly Poets are to be both reverenced and regarded, as I have here written :

As domiport flug-y fnayle, his paffage plainly to difclofe,
Leaveth a print as he goes, but a fhining flyme to no
    purpofe ;
So doth a bawdy Poet (his braineficke folly to publifh)
Write amorous madrigals; fome lewd love-toy to re-
    cognize.
Aime at a trew period, Chrift Jefus: flee from al evil ;
Roave not afide to detract his praife ; learne rightly to
    leavell.
Wits mifabus'd will apeare as a goulden ring in a fwine's
    fnowte.
Gods worde fuch reprobate lewde wits doth worthily
    confute.
Shew me the tree by the fruite : fo faith Saint Luke that
    Evangel,[*]
Do men gather grapes of thornes, or fygges of a thyftel ?

[*] Saint Luke, ca. 6, verfe 45.

Chrift fhewes by parables who be tares and who be the
  good feede;
Th' one by the divell fowen, and th' other fowne by the
  goddhead :*
Bothe to be reapt at a time, and both to be parted afonder:
Bothe to be bound in fheaves, and bothe to be laid from
  another:
Th' one to be laid in a barne, th' other to be throwne by
  Jehova
Into that burning lake, that burning fyry Gehenna.

And wee, that profeffe Chriftianity, fhould not ufe any paganifme to detract Gods glorie, as the paganis'd poets did, in the time of ignorance. For this I have written of them; I meane, of Homer, Virgill, and others:

Only the fault was this, they liv'd in a time then of error,
And to the Pagan goddes moft of them yeelded an
  honnor.
Thofe fecular fages, which gods new worde did abandon,
Wilfully loft them-felves, and others left at a randon.
But fhould we Chriftians (confeffing one God imortal,
Trinity, unity, one, deifyed with glory coequal)
Call to the Pagan gods, to detract praife from the
  Redeemer,
Our foules fole-faviour? Should we fuch blafphemy
  fuffer?

In truthe, all they that profeffe trew poetry fhould feek to further the advancement of Gods glory what they (which I pray God they may doe, to bannifh all thefe fond fantafticall and venereall Poets) and alfo to doe their beft endeavour, in trew hexameters, to abolifh this plaine rythmeprofe; that wee may imitate and follow the beft learned

* Saint Mathew, ca. 13, verfe 36, 37, 38.

and aunticent poets, as Homer, Virgill, and Lucan in Chronicles. For that an heroicall verſe compoſed in hexameters, is moſt correſpondent to a right honorable nature; as appeared by Alexander the great, as I have compoſed in hexameters following.

> When that Alexander did come to the tombe of Achilles,
> That monument to behold, he pronounced theſe very ſpeaches,
> And with a ſigh thus ſaid: Thrice Lariſſœus is happy,
> For that he greek Homer had to record his glory ſo worthy.
> And when he had conquerd great ſpoyles from king Darius,
> There was a cheſt of gould that, he ſaid, was fit for Homerus
> Bookes to be ſafely repos'd. For he kept them ſafe as a jewel,
> Under his owne beads-head: whoſe worke divinely doth excell.
> And Maro, laurigerent, in verſe moſt glorious enrold
> Venturous Æneas exployts, and worthines extold;
> Which brought Rome in a muſe, with a grace ſo loftily flowing,
> Whoſe praiſe ſtill wil abide, while ſeas or earthe ar abiding.

And that we may imitate them, as neere as we may, in poetizing of verified Chronicles, I have elſewhere written thus:

> Learne of Mœonides, who writeth of Hector, Achilles,
> Of Troilus, Diomede, of craft-contriver Uliſſes.
> If ſo be that Chronicles had not bin ſkilfuly written,
> Kinges valiant exployts, lordes fame, and knightes valor had bin
> Drowned in oblivion. For time (fames greedy devowrer)

Leaves fame unmemoriz'd ; as a tree confum'd with a canker.
You fine metricians, that verfes fkilfully compile,
(As fine artificers hard iron do refile on an anvile)
This verfe irregular, this ruftick rythmery bannifh,
Which doth abafe poetry ; fuch verfe, fuch meter abolifh,
For lily milke-white fwannes flote on ftreames cleare as a cryftall,
And in a fowle mud-y lake donguehill duckes ftrive for an offall.
Both Greekes and Latinifts fuch verfeleffe verfe did abandon,
Whofe verfe is purifi'd, as gould is try'd by the touchftone.
As vineger doth aford no pleafant tafte to the palate,
So wordes unmetrifi'd, which rythmers rudely promulgate,
Bringe no delight to the wits, nor found with a grace in a man's eare.
Every worthie poet will fuch rude rythmery forbeare.

Surely this kinde of fcanning verfe is not to be difcommended ; and who fo doth, hath no warrant fo to doe. And who fo doth difcommend Stanihurft, or Fraunce, let them make fo many verfes ; for many will difpraife their bookes, that cannot whiles they live make the like. For it is more eafie for every man to finde a fault, then to make fo many, as I have written, thus ;

For curious cavilift but a fmall mote eafily will fee
Sooner in each ftrangers eyfight, then a beame in his owne eye.
Hardly he will fuch bookes in a trew verfe notably perfect.
For many men ready be to finde faults, hafty to correct.
Such fycophant humorifts, like quayles, feede chiefly by poyfon :
Whofe ftoicall cenfures and felfe-mindes ftand for a reafon.

And whofoever fhall difcommend mine, I would requeft

him to make so many as I meane to make, in five bookes, in rythming hexameters. For, as I thinke, the rythme doth give them a grace, in our english tongue especially, above other tongues; so it be good rythme, though they be the harder to make. The best verse that Fraunce made was in rythming hexameters, of the nativitie of Christ. And if he make so many better, I will reverence him: if so many, and not better (so that he raile not) I will commend him. I discommend no mans workes, for that I know none have more defects then myne owne. For it is the enriching and beautifying of our language, and the credit and glory of the verse, that I regarde. For I am no mercinary man, nor write with an hyred penne, nor expect vaine glorie. But whoso doth slander these verses, and cannot amend them, nor make so many, let him keepe his winde to coole his potage; for my answere shall be silence. As Diogenes answered one that asked him a foolish question; saying that silence was an answere fit for such a fond demaund: and in respect of them I will say, as the bird said to Cæsar, *Operam et laborem perdidi*. But as for you, that are trew favorits both of poetry, and of this trew metricall and scanning verse, I wholly submit and referre myselfe to your favorable censures and assistance; to see if we can yet once againe set on foote this footed verse, that it may runne smoothely, with a grace and credit. I would I were but as Ennius to a fine Maronist, or to a skilful Mœonides. And also I request you to take in good part these simpel verses of mine, wherin at idel times, I have both taken pleasure and paines. For al those that professe learning (and especially such as are descended of honor or of trew gentilitie) should chiefely like of this kinde of heroicke hexameters : as Alexander did of Homers, or Auguftus of Virgils. And if thefe fhall like you, I fhall be glad ; and do purpofe (God willing) yer that a yeare come about, to fet forth another booke.

I doe not utterly difcommend or condemne this profe-rythme; but do only prefer this Romane verfe farre above it. And I know, moft of them that be learned wil fo thinke; and efpecially when it is brought to perfection : unleffe they be fome carping cavilifts, paradoxically captius or prejudicius. For I know plainefong is good, but pricke fong is knowne to be better ; and there is great difference betwixt an orient pearle, and a blacke fimpel bugel. If you finde any faults in my booke, I would requeft you to amend them, and to fend them in a privie note to the Sta-tioner. But now, leaft I fhould be too tedious, wifhing to you all as to my felfe, in our Lord and Saviour Chrift Jefus, I moft humbly take my leave ; refting yours in all love and duetie to command.

A Briefe rule or prosodie, for the un-
derſtanding of the quantitie of ſome peculiar
wordes in this booke; untill I have ſet
forth a Verball, or littel Dictionarie,
with a Proſodia requiſite for
Poetry.

THIS monaſillabel, on, being an adjective, is indifferent, either long or ſhorte; but being an adverbe, alwaies ſhort.

Alſo, mee, thee, yee, hee, and ſhee, are long or ſhort.

All words ending in O are indifferent.

Pre and pro, in diffylabels, are indifferent; in trifyllabels, likewiſe indifferent; except it be an anapœſt, as preminence, preſident, prevalent, and the like. In ſome quadriſyllabels, long: as premeditate, predominant, precogitate, and the like. And in ſome quadriſyllabels, long or ſhort; as for exampel, prepoſterous, preſumptuus, and the like. The Latin and the Engliſh quantitie in ſome wordes are not alike, but are meerely diſſonant. And we are to follow our naturall prenuntiation and accent in words, yet following the Latin as neare as we may, obſerving the right euphonia; as, for exampel, we ſay in Latin, orâtor, long in ra; but in Engliſh we make ra, in orator, ſhort.

De, in dyffyllabels and triſſyllabels, is alwaies ſhort. In

A briefe Rule or Prosodie.

some quadrissyllabels it is long; as demerited, depopulate, demonicall, and such like. And againe, in other some it is either long or short; as, denunciate, determinate, denominate. And in words of five syllabels it is short, as dedication, deprehension. And in words of six syllabels it is long; as determination, delapidation, and such like.

My, why, thy, and by, are indifferent.

Besides, there are some wordes, which sometimes by pronunciation we make but monasyllabel, as ayre, fire, flowre, powre, showre; which as dissyllabels are written thus, ay-er, fy-er, flow-er, pow-er, show-er.

And likewise sometime we make dissyllabels, trissylabels; as desire, de-si-er; require, re-qui-er; and such like.

And wordes having doubel consonants in the middel of dissyllabels (as account, attend, applause, afford, and the like) by figure are made short, by the detraction of a letter; as acount, atend, aplause, aford; and so in polysyllabels likewise. Lastly, some words are indifferent, as cre, in credit; co, in comet; pee, in peepel; and ci, in civil; and such like. Which I will, God willing, in my Verball and Prosodia set forth more at large. In the meane while, gentel Reader, have patience. For I meane not to compose these hexametered verses irregularly.

THE AUTHOR TO HIS BOOKE.

Stay, bifie booke, for a while. What rage conftraines thee to wander,
Like fugitive vacabond, into the world to be feene?
Pofte not in hafte, fo deform'd : let faultes be reform'd by thy mafter.
Art not afham'd to repaire unto the court of a Queene?
Unpolifhed to repaire to the regall throne of an empreffe,
Our Queene Elizabeth? onely the worldes diamonde,
Crown'd with an eternall diademe ; whofe glorious highneffe
Treafures of poetry, chiefe in all arts doth abounde.
Thou art fcarce purifi'd, to be feene of her exquifit Highneffe.
Better I thinke it, at home fafe in a cheft to remaine,
Then to depart fo deform'd, poore cloath'd, and plaine as an hermit.
Selfe love, felfe arogance, makes many fooles to be faine.
If that I leave thee fo rude, hir Grace may worthily blame mee.
What, wil a prince, think'ft thou, of fo renowned a lande,
When thou com'ft to the court fo defafte, vouchfafe to perufe thee?
Thy reverent Soveraigne greater afaires hath in hand.
Go not away gadding from mee that lov'd thee fo dearely,
But com againe, that I may once yet againe thee perufe ;
Quickly returne to thy freend, with me to remaine in a fafety :

The Author to his booke.

Com to thy maifter againe, com to me, com to thy Mufe.
Manes, that Diogens fervant, ran away in a fury:
   Some wifhed Diogen for to go fetch him againe;
Not fo, faid Diogen, but laught, and thought it a folly;
   But, prety booke, I do feeke how that I might thee retaine.
What fhal I do? For alas! my booke runs haftily gadding
   In metrifi'd poetry, not poetiz'd as I meant.
Some faultes, you learned, tolerate; fooles love to be fcoffing:
   Since that I thee manupend, now I to late do repent.
If that he chaunce to repaire to the court, I the courtier
     exhort,
   Not caviling to deface this prety booke that I pend,
Though that he comes not adorn'd with robes, yet friendly
     to fupport,
   And to reforme his faultes, if that he can them amend,
No body fhal thy report with a glofing diftiction extoll,
   Like popular parafite, or Thrafo grandiloquent.
Let thy defert be thy praife; feeke not to be prais'd as an
     idole.
   Better I had thee refil'd, if that I were eloquent,
Since that I plainely do fee, thou wilt goe from mee fo
     fimpel;
   Therefore I leave thee my booke, friendles alone to depart:
Like Peregrine pilgrime traveling but meane in aparel,
   And with a name unknowen, which is a griefe to my
     heart;
For that I fee many faultes, and have no time to reforme
     them.
   Runne not away from me fo; thy fily ftate I do rew;
For many will difalow, and will thee fhamefuly condemne.
   Zoilus is but a doult. My prety libel, adieu!

A FAREWELL TO HIS BOOKE.

My prety book, farewell: God fend thee profperus acceffe
Unto the court; to the Queene vouchfafe my name to be
    namelesse:
Thy foveraigne patroneffe (if pleafe her grace to defend thee)
Can patronize thy defectes. Whom God preferve, as a
    bay tree,
Long to be predominant, with lords of her privie Counfail.
Namely, the Lord Keeper, with learned lawes who doth
    excell:
That Metropolitan eake, whom I think my felf to be
    bound to;
Th' Archbifhop at Lambeth: that wife Lord Treafurer alfo;
And fenator Cecill, that apeares to the realme a defender,
Sonne to the Lord Burleigh, late deade, his wife wilie father,
That fapient Neftor, which did by pollicy compaffe
Much quiet unto the realme. For like as Cœlifer Atlas,
On large broad fhoulders fore preffed, propped up heaven;
So with his experience, this noble realme was upholden.
For why? The ftate of a Prince confifteth chiefly by councel
Of wilie grave fenators, whofe witte with vertue doth excel.
And I befeech God bleffe that noble pillar of highneffe,
Glorius Earle Talbut, ftout Earle of Shrewsbury; doubtlefle
Vertues trew prefident, of al humane curtefy mirror:
Mirror of omnipotence. Whofe nobel name was a terror
Unto the Frenche regiment: to the Crowne ftill knowne to
    be a conftant;
Worthy to be credited with a prince, as a faithful atendant;
And to be chiefly prefered, that he may with bounty the
    better

Stand a defenfe to the Prince, to the publick weale as a pillar.
And God graunt to that Earle of Oxford, mirror of highnes,
Happines in this world: God bleffe his ladie the Counteffe,
Elizabeth Trentam, that right trew maiden of honnor,
Immaculat virgin; whofe houfe and name I doe favor
With reverence, as I fhould. For I came my felfe of a Trentam,
Aunt to thee, lady renoun'd: yet I am not known to thee,
    Madame.
Loth I am yet to be knowne; for I fhould be knowne to
    the beft fort:
Knowne to that Earle Devereux, whom I pray God daily
    to comfort.
Vere, Devereux, Talbot, three nobel principal howfes,
Are to be greatly renoun'd for their nobilitie peerleffe.
And I do charge thee, my book, with things not rafhly to
    meddel
Which ar above our reach, that concerne us but a littel;*
Nor to detract my fame from peeres or ftates that are higheft.
For littel meddling of moft is thought to be wifeft:
As the poet poetiz'd, that Nafo poetical author,
Frugaly live to thyfelfe;† flee far from great men of honnor.
For many men that atend fome lords, or daily do follow,
Do but as Æfops dogge, that a fubftance loft for a fhaddow.
Yet many men be preferd by the meanes of great men of
    honnor;
Such fpeciall perfons which they moft dearely do favor.
Farewel againe, prety book; be dutiful unto thy betters:
Humbly, with al reverence, fubmit thy felfe to thy rulers.

        * Quæ fupra nos nihil ad nos.
        † Ovid. Vive tibi, et longè nomina magna fuge.

The Dedication of the booke to the Queenes Majestie.

Unto the magnipotent, the renowned princes of Europ,
Emperes Elizabeth, this petie libel I give ;
Which I prefent to thy Grace as a prime primirofe or a
  couflip.
  Onely the flow-er of all our chronicles, I beleeve :
Skilfuly pend by the knight Sir Thomas Moore, then a
  courtiè'r,
  Learned in arts ; who delin'd that that he knew to be trew,
Grounded on experience, requifite to be read of a ruler.
This donative, Soveraigne, deigne to receive to thy view.
Give but a grace to my verfe, it mounts, O Queene, in a
  moment,
  Up to the fpang'd element, up to that ayry Lion :
Give but a check to the fame, it falles downe (throwne
  with a contempt)
  Downe to the Tartarian river of hell, Phlegeton.

A Prayer.

O my God ! O God of hoftes, God of Abraham, and God of
And the God of Jacob (thou that didft regaly ranfack [Ifack,
  Tartarus infernal, who gave him felfe as a ranfome,
And here was crucifi'd, to redeeme our foules from a
  thraldom),
Sanctifie thy creature : infpire thy grace to my fpirit :
Stand my defence : guide me with thy celeftial eyefight.
O my God ! O Saviour ! vouchfafe me grace to my fpeeches :
Then wil I magnifie thee ; my mouth fhal fing to thee praifes :
Unto thee only, my God, my voice fhall ftil be refounding
Perpetuall praifes, while breath and life are abiding.

The Epistle to the Queenes most Excellent Majesty, my renowned Soveraigne and Princesse, Elizabeth, Queene of England, Fraunce, and Irland, &c.

So, I the man that am he, that afourds small praise to the Muses;
And yet in hexameters I meane to metrifie verses
Unto the worldes Diamond, to the Phœnix rare; that doth excel
In pre'minence as a prince: whose praise my wits ar unabel
Here to record as I should: as a worke to large, or a matter
Fit for a Mœonian fine skilfull penne to decypher;
Whose stout progenitours great fame her glory doth advance:
Which, if I could poetize, is a worke yet worthie remembrance.
Graunt to me no learning, Muses, thou Pagan Apollo,
Cynthia, with Charites, thou blandiloquent mery Pytho,
Mercury, with Sappho, Pallas nam'd also Minerva,*
Graunt to me no favour: but thou, thou mightie Jehova,
Thou, Lord Emmanuel, Lord of celestial heaven,
Only God imperiall, to mee wretch terrestrial harken.
Since litel helpe they graunt, and cannot aford any favor,
To those idolatrous pagan goddes yeald not an honnor;
Yeald reverence to the Lord, who is the creator of all us,
And do not here atribute any praise, but wholy to Jesu.

* A contradictory to the paganiz'd invocation.

20 *The Epiſtle to the*

Shall we Gods anger by wilful blaſphemie kindel?
When John kneeled afore that bleſſed glorius angell,
Do not ſo, ſaid he, for I am but thy felo ſervant:*
Give thou praiſe to the Lord, to the Lord, that is only
    triumphant;
Unto whom only belongs all praiſe, and glory for ever.
Shall we, his creatures, then adore and invocat other?
That ſonne of Shelomith, which Gods name wilfuly blaſ-
    pheam'd,†
Was not he ſton'd to death, by the Lord God rightfuly
    condemn'd?
Sorcerer hight Elimas was juſtly depriv'd of his eyeſight,
For that he by ſpeaches did deputy Sergius excite‡
For to renounce our God; whom Paul and Barnabas alſo
Taught him afore to beleeve. We ſhould ſuch blaſphemie
    forgoe.
Barnabas (in ſynagogues) and Paul (that faithfull Apoſtel)
Preached at Iconium; by faith Paul healed a crippel.§
When the peepel ſaw it, they would have done to them
    honnor,
And brought them ſacrifice, not praiſing God the creator.
Barnabas of the peepel was called Jupiter; and Paule,
Mercury; but they gave praiſe to the Lord God imortal.
And in amongſt them went, and rent their clothes in an
    anger:||
Wee are but creatures as you, Gods glory to further.
Shall we detract any praiſe from Chriſt, our Lord God of
    heaven;

---

* Revel. 22, verſe 8, 9.   † 24 of Levit. v. 14 and 23.
‡ Act. 13, ver. 8, &c.   § Act 4. v. 12, 3 14.
|| Act. 14, ver. 12 and 13.

Like bify-fnowted fwine, which uproot hearbes from a
 garden?*
Let paganiz'd parafites, that purpofe fmoothly to flatter,
Call to the pagan gods, their goddes, to reforge up a matter.
Right reverent foveraigne, the renowned Princes of England,
Glorious Elizabeth, Queene of Fraunce, Queene of al Irland,
I (he that am too too bould) this fimpel gift, but a trifel,
Unto thy Grace dedicate; my fimpel fkill to difabel.
If that I could poetize thy deferts, to thy glory coherent,
Might not I greatly rejoyce? But I want arte, and fkil is
 abfent.
Your luculent eyefight to my rude mufe regaly diftill,
For radiant funnebeames difplai'd will fhine on a dounghill.†
If that I were Chorilus, yet a faithfull minde of a fubject,‡
Deigne to receive, Soveraigne, with a princelike bountiful
 afpect:
Like Artaxerxes, ftout king; whofe gracius hignes§
Thankfully dranke water from palmes of filly Zinetes;
And in a cuppe of gold he fent to the poore man a thoufand
Goulden maffy darecks; yet he was but a poore fily peafant.
Like that princely Philippe, king of Macedonian empire,
Who great curtefie fhew'd, when a poore man gave him a
 dinner:
And Chrift our Saviour vouchfafe to receive of a woman,
Which was a Samaritan, water drawne forth of a fountaine,‖
Named Jacobs well: and Chrift faid, If fhe the perfitte
Gift of God did know, and him that did fo demaund it,
She would have afked Chrift Jefus freely the water
Of life eternall, who could that water aford her.

* Similie. † Similiè. ‡ Exampel. § Plutarke in Regum Apo
‖ 4 cha. of John, vers. 6, 7, 8.

Deigne then an eare to my mufe, thou Queene, whom
    mighty Jehova
Regaly doth beatize, as a fortunate Elizabetha.
Whofe very magnificence to the type of glory doth afcend ;
Which to the world al abroad thy regall vertue doth extend.
As Phœbe with radiant bright beames this world doth
    iluftrate,*
So to thy realme (O Prince) thou do'ft thy mercy pro-
    mulgate.
All pretious diamondes and pearles do not equaly glifter,†
Some ftarres more glitering ; one prince furmounteth another.
So my benigne Soveraigne, thou Queene (our gratious
    Empreffe)
Art as a trew period, of trew perfection endleffe :
Like to the ftarres in fky, to the fand incountabel in fea,‡
So be the Lords benefits to thy felfe, O Queene, to thy
    country.
For why ? The Lord God of Hoftes preferves thy pro-
    perus eftate
Gainft forraine enemies, whofe driftes he decrees to be
    fruftrate.
For men on earth purpofe, but God that ruleth in heaven§
Ruleth on earth as a God. Juft God difpofeth of all men.
Gods providenee hidden is : what man can poffibly forefhow
What future age wil afourd ? God alone mans deftiny doth
    know.
That God above, God alone, preferve thy Grace as a patterne
Long to be fceptriferent, this ftout realme wifely to governe.
And for al his benefits, let us all to the Lord God of Hofts
    graunt

  * Similie.   † Similie.   ‡ Similie.   § Sentence.

Perpetuall praifes, who to thee ftill ftands as a gardaunt.
Rightfully crowned a Queene, as a rightfull Queene, as a right heire
Unto the regal crowne, and lawfuly knowne to be daughter
Of King Henry that eight, late king, w[h]o rul'd as a puifant
Conquerer of kingdomes, with fame and glory triumphant.
His father Henry the feav'nth,* thy wife ftout grandfather, obtain'd
Th' imperiall diademe ; who vice and tyrany difdain'd,
As Chronicles do report. This king, by the ftates privie confent,
Elizabeth maried, promifed by former agreement,
Which was a Plantagenet, firft and eld'ft daughter of Edward,
Namely the fourth, who flew at Bofworth field bludy Richard,
That tyranus cruel hogge, moft worthily plagu'd for ofences.
He, by the faid mariage, did unite thofe notabel houfes,
Yorke and Lancafter; whofe long contentius envy
Caus'd civil inteftine warfare. This conquerus Henry,
Venturus and valiant, was afygn'd by the Lord to be ruler.
Every king hath a time : thus this worlds glory doth alter.†
I he that once could not, nor meant, in heroical Englifh
Rythmecal hexameters, any book fo timely to publifh,
Yet when I knew that I could compofe new rythmery verfes,
Lately become metricall, which are right verfes of antike ;
Then did I wifh that I could dedicate fuch bookes to thy perfon,
Worthy fo great a Regent, thy deferved glory to blazon,
Which fro the eaft to the weft doth fpread. Whofe fame to decypher

* Grafton.   † Virg.   Sic tranfit gloria mundi.

More praife demeriteth than I can now poffibil utter.
Like as a cryftall fpring tranfparent unto the bottome,*
Flowes with a filver ftreame ; fo (puifant prince) to thy kingdome,
And to thy common weale, thou shew'ft thyfelf as a princeffe
Mercifull, and liberall ; thy good life vertue doth expreffe.
God to thee gave many gifts, more then my minde can imagine,
Which do atract to thy felfe moft hearts with a force adamantine.
I he the fame man afore, as a man fcarce knowne to the Mufes,
Boldly prefume to prefent foote-fcanning rythmery verfes
Unto thee, world's Soveraigne : vouchfafe, O Queene, to perufe them ;
Stand as a princely patrone, nor (ofenfive) juftly me condemn.
If tonitr'ant bifie Jove fhould alwaies ftrike in his anger†
Every man that ofends, with lightning flame of a thunder,
Should not he then be bereft or defpoild quite of his armor ?
So, if I have many faults, yet, good Queene, ftand my protector.
And I, with all reverence, do befeech your gratious Highnes,
Though many things ar amiffe, yet pardon graunt to my rudeneffe.
Though that I Mœonides (who writeth of Hector, Achilles,
Of Troilus, Diomede, of craft-contriver Uliffes)
Nor Maro Laureat am (who the laurel crowne to the Romans
Wanne, as a princely poet, who recorded fame to the Trojans)
Yet, for a zeale that I have, thefe primer fruites of a fubject

* Similie. † Poeticè. Si quoties peccant, &c.

(Lately befeem'd a poet) with a regall friendlines accept :
For why ? My pipe is of ote, not Apollos, fkilfuly compact,*
Nor Ciceroes eloquence I retaine : for a worke that is exact,
Truly thy princely benigne acceptance of my beginnings
Shall my minde animate, to record fome greater atemptinge.
For my delight (O Queene) my drift and only my purpofe,
Is to record Chronicles; metricall verfe fitly to compofe,
And to refyne our fpeach, to procure our natural Englifh
Far to be more elegant ; that verfe may fkilfuly florifh.
Which when it is re'difi'd, eloquent, and knowne to be perfit,
Unto thee, and to thy realme, (O puifant Prince) what a
    credit !
Hexameters will amend our fpeach (thou facred Eliza)
Publifh an orthography, and teach us a trew idioma.
Stories are requifite to be read of ftates that are higheft,
As kings imperial, thron'd in regalitie chiefeft.
If fo be that Chronicles had not bin fkilfuly written,
  Kinges valiant exployts, lordes fame, and knightes valor
    had bin
Drowned in oblivion. For time (fames greedy devowrer)
Leaves fame unmemoriz'd, as a tree confum'd with a canker.†
Hiftoricall Chronicles, well penn'd by the learn'd (as
    aforefaid)
Doth manifeft reprefent (as a comedy fhewes, on a ftage
    plaid)
Mens vice and vertues ; as a trew glaffe vifibly doth fhew‡
Mens face and favor, their faults in vifnomy to viewe.§
For by the great diligence of men, mans memorie (chiefeft
Treafurer of knowledge, with learning fkilfuly furnifht)
Enroules in Chronicles the renowned deeds of heroick

   * Poeticè.   † Similie.   ‡ Similie.   § Similie.

And valiant Worthies, their fame and victorie warlike.
For Chronicles do recite faultes and falles of many princes,
Horribly that tyraniz'd, fore plagu'd for their fory vices.
Was not lofty Babel firft built by proude fory Nimrod,*
Whofe arogance had a fall? and was not merciles Herod
By greedy vermin fpoild, that murderd fo many children?†
And Nero that tyrant, the detefted monfter of all men,
Stab'd himfelfe with a knife.‡ The wicked king Jeroboam
Plagu'd by the Lord, that he di'd.§ And lewd ungodly
    Jehoram
Was by godly Jehu through fhoulders fhot with an arrow,||
Which through pearced his heart, that he languifht for
    very forrow.
When that a prince hath a will, whofe will doth ftand for a
    reafon,
Lulled in errors lappe, that will infectes as a poyfon
Both to the king and realme. For wherein proud fory
    princes
Fondly delyre, pitiles fubjects ar plagu'd with a witneffe.¶
Thankes be to God, our Queene doth rule with finguler
    advice,
And with mercy benigne as a prince doth quallifie juftice:
Our Soveraigne doth apeare, as goulden Cynthia fhining,
Glides by the firme element, her bright beames cheere-
    fuly fhewing
Unto this earthly chaos: fo her grace (glorius extant)
Shines to the common wealth, with love and mercy
    regardant:

---

* Genefis, ch. 10 and 11. † Act. 12, v. 21, 13.
‡ Suetonius, fol. 162, cha. 49. § 2 Chro. ch. 13, vers. 20.
|| 2 of Kings. ch. 9, ver. 24.
¶ Horace. Quicquid delirant reges plectuntur Achivi.

Whofe fpeciall rare gifts and vertues daintily lufture,
Like orient diamonds, or fplendent pearles on a vefture.*
All you princely regents, you kings (well knowne to be rulers)
Learne to refraine from finne. Our Lord God terribly finners
Impenitent doth plague: not a king, not an emperor, he fpares;
All eftates are alike. Who with Gods dignitie compares?
Caft downe your diademes, your crownes and dignity defpife;
Meere vanities count them, but feeke to do good, to do juftice.
Yeald reverence to the Lord, to the Lord your duty to performe:
You are Chriftes fubjects, your fubjects peaceably governe.
Your pre'minence but a charge, your life but a blob, but a bloffom:
When death ftrikes with a dart, what availeth a king or a kingdom?
That Platonift, Socrates, did afirme, that a mans bodie living
Was but a grave to the foule;† which to felicitie lafting,
Should by deferts demigrade: moft divine fpeach of an heathen!
For by the faith in Chrift we come to the kingdome of heaven.
As radiant rud-y Phœbe exhales his vapory moyfture‡
Unto the firme element, with his ardent hot fun-y lufture,
So the God omnipotent, our foules with finnes hevie loden,
Freely by mercy benigne, extolles to the kingdom of heaven.
Death bringes every thing to decay; for like as a frefh flower§

* Similie.   † Erafmus in decla. de morte.   ‡ Similie.   § Similie.

Springs for a time redolent, but can not poſſibil endure,
So doth a king for a while reigne with great dignitie preſent,
Whoſe great glorie decaies, whoſe prowde pompe dures but
    a moment.
Like as a man doth in yeares wax ould, ſo ſhould he be
    wiſer ;
And as he groweth in age, ſo ſhould his life be the beter.
Thinke this world to be vaine, and thinke this life to be
    mortal,
And to the King of kings let us yeald our ſelves to be loyal ;
Who to redeeme our ſoules, ordained his only begotten,
Only beloved ſonne, to be ſent downe freely from heaven,
And to be here crucifi'd (as a ſinleſſe man for a ſinner)
To mitigate Gods wrath, t' appeaſe his infinit anger :
Who by the death that he di'd hath cleans'd us freely from
    evill,
For that he conquered hath ſinne, death, and alſo the divell.
Whiles we do live, let us al live well. Time ſtailes away
    leapes,*
Like as a cloud vaniſheth. For, as every ſteppe that a man
    ſteppes,
Is but a ſteppe to the grave, ſo plodding age, *pedetentim*,
Stouping, creepes on a paſe. Age is to death as a pilgrim,
Which for a time doth abroad wander, but in end he re-
    turnes home ;†
So for a time we do live, but in end death will be the
    bridegroome.
No body can ſtay time. Time ſtaies for no body.‡ Time
    ſwift
Flyeth away on apaſe, as a bird that flyes from a mans
    ſight.§

* Similies.   † Similie.   ‡ Sentence.   § Similie.

Therefore, princely regentes, both vice and tyrranny forgoe;
For what availeth a king, what availeth an emperor alfo,
If that he lofe his foule, to live here fortunat alway?*
As patient Job faid, each mortall king to thy felfe fay,
Naked I came to the world, fro the world hence naked I
    fhall go :†
Formed of earth was I firft, to the earth yet againe fhall I
    turne to.
That fapient Salomon naught here but vanitie could finde,‡
With manyfould miferies, with great vexation of minde.
What man alive can afourd (as Gods word plainely doth
    expreffe)
One cubit unto his height by carking cares that ar endleffe?§
Let not a man be to bolde, though God be mercifull,
    and ftaies,‖
For when he ftrikes, his ftroke is a ftroke importabil alwaies :
And then he plagues when he ftrikes. For where th' al-
    mighty Jehova
Rightfuly plagues for ofenfe, what availeth a mans cata-
    plafma ?
For with a flouthfull pafe Gods anger goes to revengement;
But when he comes, he rewards eternall paines for a torment.
Here I wil end, O Queen. O Lord! our only creator,
(Our Lord Emmanuel, our Chrift and fole mediator)
Adde to thy life many yeares, as he did to the king
    Ezechias ;¶
Safely defend thee from harme, as he fafely preferved
    Elias :
And that he graunt to thy Grace, after this life (as a chofen

---

* Mark, ch. 8, vers. 36.   † Job, ch. 1, ver. 21.   ‡ Ecclefiaftes 1.
§ Mat. 6. 27.   ‖ A proverbe.   ¶ 2 of Kings, ch. 20, ver. 6.

Veffel of his, purify'd) joyes in celeftiall heaven ;
Joyfully there to remaine with Jefus Chrift the Redeemer,
Imparadiz'd as a faint, with faints in glory for ever.
As two Greeke letters in Grecian alphabet, Alpha
Firft letter plafte is, but placed laft is Omega :
So wil I continuall, firft and laft, praife thee for ever,
If that I could poetize, as I would, thy glory to further.

   Your Graces fubject, in faith, love, duty to

      commaund :

THE FIRST BOOKE OF
The preservation of King Henry the vij. when he was but Earle of Richmond.

FATHER Omnipotent, our Lord and only Redeemer,
    (Which on a throne, deifi'd, there fits, and fhines as a
       jafper,
And as a fardine ftone, incompaft round with a raine-bow,*
Like to the bright emeraud) with thy grace my fpirit endow:
From which throne lightnings, voices, with lowde flafhy
       thunders
Duly proceed: where fowre and twenty colaudibil elders
Seated in as many feats, all cloth'd with a white lily garment,
Crown'd with crownes of gould, on their heads ftately
       refulgent:
Seaven lampes of fire ar there eternaly burning,
Gods very godly fpirits, on God there faithful atending.
Neare to the throne is a fea of glaffe, which fhin'd as a cryftall:
There fowre beafts ful of eyes ar about that ftately tribunal.
Firft was like a lyon, next feemed a calfe to refembel,
Third had a face of a man, fourth beaft was form'd as an
       eagel.
Every beaft of them fix wings had them to belonging,
And ful of eyes ar within, day and night joyfully finging

    * The firft part of the Revelation of Saint John in effect verbatim.

Three times holy be God th' almightie, that ever is holy :
Holy before which was, which is, which fhall be God only.
And when thofe fowre beafts gave praife to the Lord God
    Iefus,
Which on that throne fate (who for ever liv'd, who re-
    deem'd us)
Thofe reverent elders their crownes commendably threw
    downe,
And fell flatly before that Lord that fate on a tribune,
Worfhiped him that liv'd, and lives with glory for ever.
For thou glory deferv'ft that made all things by thy power :
Unto whom Archangels and Angels greatly rejoycing,
With Cherubins, Seraphins, are there eternaly finging.
Thou father only my God, which art, waft, fhalt be for ever :
Who the tereftriall orbe (which ftaies itfelfe by the center)*
Quadruply partiting, fire, ayre, earth, watery fubftance,
Out of an ugly chaos did'ft frame, and ftore with abundance
Of feverall creatures, and made man laft (as an image
Like to thyfelfe) upright, to behold this globe with a vifage :†
Placed him in Paradice, in a facred garden, in Eden ;
Where, by the fondnes of Eve, they loft thofe joyes then of
    heaven :
Thou Lord only for aye, whofe power and glory fupernall
This ftar-y fpang'd element, and this whole world univerfal
Made‡ (as a mightie monarche) in fix daies; only the
    feaventh
Day he referv'd, to be kept as a facred day, as a Saboth,
Which God by Moyfes did apoint and confecrat holy :
And that day to be kept (by the cov'nant) from labor, only.

---

   * Gen. ch. 1, ver. 1, 2, &c.   † Gen. ch. 1. v, and 27.
        ‡ Genefis, ca. 2, vers. 2.

Thou, he the same very God, three persons, one God in essence,
Raise up aloft to thy selfe, my weake spirit hale to thy presence.*
Leavy the lines that I write, let thy law still be my load-starre,
Still to direct mee my course, here trewly to write; that I differ,
No not a word, fro thy word; that I may in minde as a Christi'an
Glorify Christ crucifi'd, to detest that sect of a pagan.
Sanctify me, my Jehove, in Christ I repose al afiance:
Therefore I humbly beseech of thee, my Lord, an asistance.
Grant that I may poetize that credibil history, written
By Sir Thomas Moore, of an English story the maiden,
For why? The learned knight wrote that, that he knew to be certaine;
Trouth with his art to deline, credit of both safely to maintaine.
For that he was then alive in court, in prime of his young yeares,
And by that experience, that he knew and learned of others
By good inteligence, he reserv'd for his historie faultlesse,
Thereby the truthe to deline; quite voide of flattery doubtlesse.
Which when he had manupend, in briefe prose skilfuly finnisht,
Streight he the same (to be knowne) in print did apoint to be publisht.
In which book I do meane, by the grace of God, to deliver

---

* Exod. ca. 20, ver. 8, 9, 10.

Nothing els but a trouthe; Gods name and glory to further.
Nor with a penne that is hyr'd I write, verfe fmoothly to compile,*
Like glavering parafite, with a veile, lewde ftates to depenfile:
If fo that envy repine, and flaundring tongues do calumnize,
Trouth wil in end be my praife, and fhame the reward to the divelifh.
Feare not at all, fil-y Mufe, to report fo thankles an errant;
Boldly declare to the beft their faults, trouth fhal be thy warrant.
This knight, Sir Thomas, was made Lord Chauncelor after,
Who was knowne to be learn'd, of a chiefe affembly the fpeaker:
He both loft his life, of his office made a refufall,†
For that he would not agree to the king's fupremacy regal.
My Mufe incouraged (firft praifing God as a giver
Of all good benefits) thefe words fhe began to deliver.
North Soveraigne Phœnix, thou ftout Queene, famus Eliza,
Of grace and fapience (peereleffe prince) facred idea,
Deigne with a gratius eye to perufe (O Chriftian Empreffe)
This pretty booke manupen'd, manumiz'd to thy gratius Highneffe.
Al you earthly kings, you kings adventurus, hearken;
You ftates pontificall, with atentive eares to me liften:
You lords imperiall, of her Highneffe wife privie counfel,
(Whofe fapient wifdomes to record my wits are unabel)
You lords in generall, that atend in court on a princeffe
(Only the world's foveraigne) lend liftning eares to my verfes.

* Similie.   † Grafton.

You catholike divines, graduat divinity doctors,
Which be the favory falt, of Gods word lively profeffors;
You fapient fenators of Innes of Court, that are ordain'd
To minifter juftice, by the Queenes authoritie conftrain'd;
Arts reverent amatifts, of both* univerfity famus
(Whofe orient fine wits of Romane verfe be defirus)
Deigne to beholde this verfe, although it feem but a trifel.
For many times you fee that a pearle is found in a mufkel.†
Here I do meane to recite how our Queenes grandfather, Henry,
That king magnanimus, with a ftout and conquerus armie,
With valerus chivifance did a tyrant manfuly conquer,
Richard, lately the king, that vile and fhameful ufurper:
Henries fame to report, in fcanning verfe, as I purpofe,
Prince Edward ftratagiz'd, and Richards tyranny difclofe.
When ftout King Edward, at a field neere Teuxbury gotten,‡
Where Queene Marg'ret was, with her eld'ft fonne, forcibly taken,
Nam'd to be Prince Edward: which was there bluddily murdred
By tyranus Richard,
And fhe fent prifoner to London: where fhe remained
Till that her owne father had (that French duke nam'd to be Reiner,
Of Sicyl alfo the king) with a raunfome kindely redeem'd her.
When Jafper (ftout Earle of Pembrooke), natural uncle
Unto this Earle Richmond, when he knew how ftoutly the battel

* Figure.   † Similie.   ‡ Grafton.

Was fought and manupriz'd, and faw all things to go
    backward,
How ftout Earle Warwick was flaine by conquerus Edward,
And how Henry the fixt in Towre fafe kept was abiding;
How London citizens difdain'd him now to be their king;
How his confederates and frieends grew weaker on each
    fide,
And how King Edward, himfelfe and his cofen envi'd,
Wittily confidering (as a wife Earle) fought to prevent it,
Both their lives to preferve, where they might fafer inhabit.
In peril ambiguus that courfe is beft to be taken,*
Which fhal availe to do good. In time privy danger is
    holpen,
As by the fequel apeares.
Mindfuly, Mufe, memorize, firft how this vertuus Henry
(Saved alive many times by the Lords protection only)
Came to the crowne as a king, here fent by the Lord his
    apointment;
Sent to the realme as a prince, that fhould here make an
    atonement:
For Gods facred elect are ftraungely preferv'd by the Lord
    God.†
Our Lord and Saviour was fav'd from murtherus Herod;
From the lyons, Daniell; from ftrength of mighty Golias,
Holy David; Jofeph, from brethren; faithful Elias,
From wicked Jezabel; that younger godly Tobias
Sav'd by the Lords Angell: and was not truftily Jonas
Kept in a whales bely fafe, three nights? God fav'd Ma-
    chabeus;
Noe with his owne families was fav'd from deftiny grievus;

* Sentence.   † Exampels in divers places of the Bibel.

Mofes, throwne in a flagge to be drown'd, was fav'd by the
    daughter
Of tyranus Pharaoh,* manumiz'd to be nurft by the mother :
Ifrael and Shadrach, Mefhach with Abednego likewife,
Gods divine providence his bleffed will wil acomplifh.
Firft, when he was, but an earle, he being then but of young
    yeares,†
Was by the Lords providence preferved from many dangers
And peril of lofing his life ; and life of his uncle,
Martial Earle Pembrocke, who behav'd himfelfe as a nobel
And valiant chival'ir, when they were like to be taken
By Roger hight Vaghan, who thought them furely to
    murder,‡
Rightly received a death that he purpos'd falfely for other.
Thofe fraudulent judges, that accufed falfely Sufanna,
Rightfully were condemn'd by the Prophet fent by Jehova ;
Worthily fton'd to death, as they had wrongfuly judged
Godly Sufanna to die : thus God th' ungodly rewarded.§
And on a gallow tree that proud prefumptuus Hamon
Rightly was hang'd, that aledg'd to guiltleffe Mardoche
    treafon.||
This forefaid Vaughan was charg'd, by the king his apoint-
    ment,
For to aprehend thofe Earles ; but he therein mift of his
    intent.
Each felf-will of a king, or commaund, is not a godly
Thing to be done ; for a prince enraged fiercely with envy
Seekes to do wrong caufeleffe, which God will avenge in
    his anger :

* Exod. cha. v, 6, 7, 8, 9. † Grafton, fol. 712, Edw. 4.
‡ Grafton, fol. eodem. § Hiftory of Sufanna. || Efter.

(For God on high, God above, knowes all) for he plagues
    an ofender.
Marke what a chance foloed. Thefe Earles fled thence to
    the caftel
Of Pembrooke ;* who were eftfoones purfu'd by the fubtil
Fierce Morgan Thomas, who the caftel ftrongly befieged,
Environed with a trench, yet they were fafely preferved
By David ap Thomas, who the fiege rais'd ; yet very brother
Unto the faid Morgan. Can men Gods purpofes alter ?
Was not godly David, by the meanes and faithful atonement
Of Jonathan, preferv'd from King Saules murderus intent ?†
Henry the fixt propheci'd (who this Earles ftate and very
    favor
View'd for a while, noting his princelike witty behavi'or.)
Lo, this is he, for a truth, that in end fhall furely by
    wifdome,‡
By valor of knighthood, and ftoutnes, ataine to the
    kingdome.
This good king (as a prince infpir'd) did prophecy trewly,
For what he told proov'd trew, by Gods revelation only :
For God alowes his elect feverall gifts. Every perfit
Good gift comes fro the Lord, by the gift of Gods very
    fpirit.§
For the Prophets propheci'd of Chrift : God gave his
    Apoftels
Marvelus and ftrange gifts, as he gave his glorius Angels.‖
Now to my matter againe.
Thefe Earles, fafely preferv'd, durft not ftay there any longer,
But got away in all haft from thence for feare of a danger.

---

    * Grafton.   † 1 Sam. ch. 20, ver. 35, &c.
    ‡ Grafton, fol. 692, Edw. 4.   § Sam. 1, 17.   ‖ 1 Pet. 1, v. 10, 11.

Like as a light foote roe, from quick-fent houndes to the greene-wood*
Luftily bounceth away, to fave life, fkips on a maine fcud ;
So thefe Earles got away from thence to Timby, that haven
Towne in Wales ; to the which by conftraint luckily driven,
They made provifion for fhippes. And like as a fwallow
Quickly the fkyes doth fheare ;† or rather, like as an arrow
Flies from a ftrong mans bow, fo they from thence with a navie
Sail'd to the Duke Francis,‡ who received them both very friendly ;
Faithfully them promifing that they fhould have his afiftance
For to do them pleafure, and what they wanted, alowance.
Where thefe fortunate Earles, in great fecurity living,
Safely remained a while, King Edward's anger avoiding,
Joyfully there paffing their time ; where he with his uncle,
Highly regarded at armes, at tylt and turnee did excell.
Every time hath a chaunge : we in times mutabil alter :§
Gods will prefcient prefcribes a determinate order,
His great glory to raife.
Can mindes affociat to kingdomes amity fofter ?
Or perfit lovers, can they rivality fuffer ?
Cæfar could not abide to be fubmiffe, or to be loyall
To valiant Pompey,‖ that acounted no man his equall.
Every king hath his heyre, or next to the crowne, in a fufpect ;
For that he thinks that he will not prove fo trew as a fubject.

* Similie. † Similies. ‡ Grafton, fol. 713, Edw, 4.
§ Tempora mutantur, &c. ‖ In Lucan.

Love to be kings, and kings breed brothers mutual hatred,*
No faith obferving, like tyrants fet by no kindred.
Can faith and falfhoode in felfe fame feat be refiaunt?
Such contrarieties are placed flatly repugnant.†
Marke what a chaunce hapned, that counter-chekt, in a moment,
All their courtly delights to their cleane contrary judgement;
For when as Edward, namely the fourth, did know for a certaine
That thefe venturus Earles were failed fafely to Brittaine,
Unto the forefaid Duke, and there liv'd friendly together,
Highly regarded of him, nor at all did feare any danger,
Thefe fory new tidings did aflict his minde not a littel,‡
For that he thought thofe Earles might bring him quickly to trubbel.
Embaffadors, therefore, to the Duke he fent of a purpofe,
With grave difcretion his meffage wifely to difclofe;
Who did acomplifh his heafts, like wife ftates, made many proffers
Unto the Duke, promifing large gifts and bountiful offers,
So that he would vouchfafe thofe Englifh lords to deliver.
Unto whom immediate this Duke thus framed an anfwere:
So to do, it were not requifite, nor ftood with his honnor.
But leaft that thofe lords fhould feeke elfwhere any fuccor,
To prejudice their king, he devis'd to feclude them afunder
With vigilant perfons, to be fafe kept one from another,
And from them to remove each page and every fervant
Which was an Englifh man, that there were on them atendant.

* Sentence.   † Sentence.   ‡ Grafton, fol. 715, Edw. 4.

Anfwered in this fort, they toke their leave with obeifance,
And fo return'd to the king, to fhew their faithful atendance.
Who, when he heard thefe newes, he beleev'd that he
    ftoode in a fafety;
His minde was quieted, quite freed from factius envy.
Therewithal, he to the duke forth with them wrote in a
    letter,
How that he would him yearely reward, with thankes for
    his anfwer;
Friendly requefting him that he would thofe words but
    acomplifh,
Which of his owne free will he did fo faithfuly promife.
See what a fufpitius minde works: how greedines of gould
Princelike mindes doth ataint, by force of flattery contrould!
Like as a fulphurus heate (encompaft round) lyeth hollow,*
Clos'd in a vapory clowd, there ftruggling ftrives for an iffue;
Which, with a ftraunge rattling, with a rumbelo lowd flafhy
    thunder,
Filles th' element with a noyfe, and center of earth with a
    wonder:
So privy fufpition, conceived in heart with a fury,
Breedes great difpleafure, and raging cankerus envie.
For when King Edward had bettere pondered all things,
He (that had experience) fought firft to prevent the
    beginnings,†
Leaft that he might be depos'd. When a wound with
    mallady feftreth,
And growes inveterate, that fore what furgery cureth?
When nature vanifheth, which cannot worke any longer,

* Similie.   † Ovid. Principiis obfta. Serò medicina paratur, &c.

What medicine can availe mans former health to recover?
Flexibil at firſt is young tender tree to be bowed;
Growne by continuance very bigge, diſdeignes to be moved.
For when he confidered that rightly this Earle fro the lynage
Sprouted of Henry the fixt, then he fought for a further avantage,
For that he knew wel inough, if that there were any living*
Righteus heire to the crowne, that lin'aly came from his ofspring,
Might bring his diademe and regal fcepter in hazard.
Therefore againe to the duke he charg'd grave men to go forward,
Doctor Stillinton with two more, fent with a treafure
Once yet againe to prefent his grace more largely to pleaſure,
If that he would but alow and permit curteus Henry
(Nam'd Earle of Richmond) with them to returne in a fafety,
For fpeciall caufes; that their king, bountiful Edward,
Would joyne in mariage (wherein then he feem'd to be forward)
Elizabeth to this Earle; which was wel knowne to be daughter
To their liege Soveraigne: which luckily fortuned after.
Thereby this Earle might have thofe landes that he claim'd in afurance,
If that he were maried fo nere to the king in alyance.
And fo the king ſtood ſure that none might make any tytel
Unto the crowne, but he might all forraine faction expel.
They in al haft get away their meffage wifely to tranfpofe,
Who to the duke at large each particularity difclofe.

* Grafton, fol. 732, Edw. 4.

When that he their meſſage did know, he pauſ'd for a good while
What was beſt to be done, ſince th' earle liv'd there but in exile;
But when he conſidered that he ſhould be match'd with a virgin,
Their owne kings daughter, to be linkt in league with his owne kinne,
Where that he might be prefer'd to ſome great dignity preſent,
There as an earle, or a duke, to rule by the king his apointment,
Firſt he began to deny, but pleaſ'd with treaſure given,
What with ſoliciting, and gould ſo gainfully gotten,
Kindly this anſwer he gave: that he was content to deliver
Henry that Earle, not a ſheepe to the wolfe, but a ſonne to the father;*
And in a letter he wrote how th' Earle was much had in honor
Both for his own wiſdome, valiaunce, and witty behavi'our.
They then ſeiz'd of a prey, which they had greatly deſired,
Thankfully tooke their leave, and from thence quickly departed
Unto the towne of Saint Malo, bord'ring neare to the ſea ſhore,
Minding thence to depart when ſhips were made ready. Wherefore
Th' Earle, when he knew that he ſhould be return'd home, for very ſorrow
Since that he was ſo betrai'd, he fell ſore ſicke of an ague;

* Similie.

Imagining that he fhould, as foone as he landed in
   England,
Be ftratagiz'd. But fee! who can Gods dignity withftand?
Gods divine providence and facred dignity fupreame
Ruleth al humane caufe, though humane caufes ar ex-
   treame.*
Marke Gods omnipotence, whofe workes ar wonderus,
   extant,
Still to be feene; who preferv'd this venturus Earle at an
   inftant,
Sav'd (as a ftrange miracle) by the faithfull love of a
   ftranger.
For many times men ar helpt, and fav'd by the meanes of
   another;
Like as a phyfition doth feeke mans health to recover,
So wil a friend for a friend in trubbels ftand a defender.
Vulcan againft Troy was, but Trojans friend was Apollo,
And Venus indiferent, Pallas not: mortally Juno
Malliced Æneas, as alyed wholly to Turnus;
Yet was he by Venus helpe preferv'd from her enmitie
   grievus.
Undubitate Pylades was a friend to woful Oreftes;
To Damon, Pythias; Patrocles friended Achilles;
Alcyde ayded Hylas, Æneas friend was Achates,†
Eurialus, Nifus; Diomedes friended Uliffes;‡
And to be chiefe memoriz'd, that firme and trufty Zopirus
Who cut his owne eares off Babilon to procure Darius.
Darius, ftout king, in his hand faire pomegranat having,§
One of his efpecial friends afkt him (merrily jefting)
What things efpeciall (if he might have that he wifhed)

* Sentence.   † Divers examples.   ‡ Virg.   § Plutarch in Apo.

Would he requeft for his owne ? As there were graines to
  be counted,
So many friendly, Zopyres (as a wife king) wifely did
  anfwer :
For what more pretius then a friend that friendeth another ?*
As fire and heate both cannot be parted afonder,
So love and friendfhip cannot be without one another.
For when on John Chewlet (that was for a courtier only
Counted a ftout man at armes) who lov'd this gratius Henry,
Heard that he was very fick, and from thence like to be
  conveigh'd,†
Shortly to King Edward, he (therewith wofuly difmaid)
Pofted amaine to the court, and prefent ftept to the Kings
  Grace,
Heavily perplexed ; who, looking fad with a pale face,
Stood as amafed afore this duke, with a ftearne hevy
  count'nance,
And not a word did fpeake, as a man that wanted his
  uttrance.
Therewithal aftonied to behold fo feareful an object
(Like as a prince vigilant) he did fome treachery fufpect ;
Yet, when he confidered this knights ftate, chearefuly thus
  fpake :
Shew me the caufe (good John) that thou fo monefuly doft
  looke.
Therewithal he, to the duke reverent, with an humbel
  obeyfance,
Boldly declar'd what he meant, and fpake with a treatibel
  uttrance.
Pardon I crave, Soveraigne, if I fpeake : Truth verely never‡

* Pluta. in Apo.   † Grafton, fol. 738, Edw. 4.   ‡ Sentence.

Shameth his own mafter. What availes than fondly to flatter?
Heare then a truth, O Duke! for like as Cynthia fhining,
Inveloped with a clowde, obfcures her-felfe from iluftring,
Semblably truth for a time obfcur'd, many times lieth hidden;*
Truth yet in end wil apeare: truth never permaneth unknowne.
O my renowned Duke! wilt thou now falfify promife,
Firmely betroth'd to this Earle? What a fault is this, what a blemmifh?
O that I were buried! Shal I live to know thy difhonor?
Truly my minde (O Duke) is vext with an infinit horror,
For that I greatly to grieve, that this ftout Earle to the flaughter
Should (as a lambe) be betrai'd, and there to be flaine of a butcher.†
This wil bring thy renowne, O Prince (which every mans mouth
Extols up to the clowdes) to decay. For (plainely to tell trouth)
If fo be (my Soveraigne) thou wilt fo fhamefuly fuffer
Henry this Earle to depart, thou ftain'ft thy glory for ever:
Thy former valiance and fame, that fhine to the world's end,
Shall as a fmoke pas away. Shal a Prince fuch craftines intend?
Peace, good John (quoth the Duke) peace, peace! I pray thee, beleeve me;
For thefe embafadors do proteft and fay that he fhal be

* Similie. † Similie.

Spows'd to the kings daughter (which their king faithfuly
    promift*)
And to be next to the king plafte in authority chiefeft.
Well, faid John to the duke, in whom fhall fhame be reputed,
If that he dye by the way, or in Englifh realme be beheaded?
For that I dare venture my life, that it is but a practice
This fily foule to deceive, this ficke Earles life to relinquifh.
If that he fhal be beguil'd in fuch fort, let me no longer
Live to repaire to thy court : if he fhould dye, dye had I
    rather.
When Dionife the tyrant would needes have Plato be-
    headed,†
Zenocrates anfwer'd : not afore that mine be deprived.
But many fay that a king that knowes not how to difembel
Knowes not at all to rule : fuch fleights be devis'd by the
    divell.
If that I may be fo bould to fpeake but a word in his
    abfence,
O my benigne Soveraigne! lend eare and give to me
    credence,
For why? This Earle of a truth lyes fick, and likely to
    perifh.
If fro thy realme he depart, what prince will truft to thy
    promife?
Nothing more perilus then a compound poyfonus honny ;‡
No body more treacherus then a foe that feemes to be
    friendly.
With tunes harmonicall fweete finging merrily mermaides
Falfly betray mariners : fo thefe men, fent as aforefaid,§

* Grafton, fol. 738, Edw. 4. † Laertius, lib. 4, chap. 2.
    ‡ Similie. § Simile.

Smoothly deceive your grace with faire fpeach and mony
    given :
Under a cloake of love his conceal'd craftines hidden.
O fond difcretion, on faire words wholly relying !*
Experiment beft is where wordes and deedes are agreeing.
Craft hath a godly pretence, but a murderus end. For a
    fowler
Merrily playes on a pipe when he craftily taketh a plover.†
Ifcariot Judas, that falfe and wicked apoftel,
Falfely betrai'd with a kiffe, and fould our Lord for a trifel.
Laomedons falfhood (Priamus father, and fon of Ilus)
Caufed his owne bludy death, and loffe of Troy, city famus.
Was not Alexander, by craft of King Ptolemæus,‡
His falfe fath'r in law, depriv'd of his empery famus ?
Bluddy Polymneftor (which of gould was fo defirus)
Beaftly did obtruncate Priamus fonne, young Polidorus.
More to recite, what availes ?§
Therefor I humbly befeech your Grace (O Duke) to re-
    member
This difconfolate Earle, that lyes neare dead of a fever.‖
Send that he may be retain'd. Let not thy glory be
    blemmifht :
Keepe faith inviolate, let a prince performe what he promift.
Thus this knight to the duke his whole minde (wofuly
    diftreft)
Plainely without any guile or diffimulation expreft.
Laftly by perfwafions this wife Duke (ruled by the counfell
Of good John Chewlet, who this earles ftate knew to be
    feebel)

* Sentences.   † Similie.   ‡ 1 Macha. ch 11.   § Virg.
‖ Grafton, fol. 739, Edw. 4.

when he was but Earle of Richmond. 49

Sent Peter Landoyfe, chiefe Treafurer, only the forefaid
Embaffadors to delay, that th' Earle might fafely be convai'd
Unto the Sanct'ary there; which was with fpeede then efected,
Which fo delighted his heart that his health there quickly revived.
Like as an hart in a chace, that is hurt or pincht with a greyhound,
Bounceth away on a maine, and runnes moft fwiftly, to get ground,*
Yer that he fhould b' imboft, fro the greyhound fpeedily doth get,
And privy lewnes in a brake, imbaies himfelfe in a thicket,
There to recover his hurt: fo this Earle (efcapt from a daunger)
Liv'd in a place priviledg'd, his former health to recover.
Would to God every prince, that ruleth in every kingdome,
Would be fo rul'd by the good wife counfell, and by the wifdome
Of plaine trouth-fpeakers, and alfo that every courti'er
Would not aledge any lyes to the Prince to defame on another.
Now to my matter againe.
When thefe embafadors perceiv'd they were fo deluded,
Both of an Earle, their prey, and of gould freely deliver'd,
Tould Peter Landoyfe, their king would take it in ill part,†
They to retorne, fo deceiv'd of their Earle and mony, homeward:
But Peter Landoyfe affured them that he fhould be
Safe in a fanct'ary kept (which they would warily forefee)

* Similie.   † Grafton, fol. 739, Edw. 4.

Or to be ftreightly detein'd in a fafer cuftody forthwith;
So they neede not at all to doubt or feare any mifchiefe.
They, pacifi'd by the meanes of Landoyfe curteus anfwere,
Thought it a folly to ftay in Brittain realme any longer,
But willed Landoyfe (to the Duke their duty remembring)
Thofe promifes to be kept, their leave there thankfuly
    taking:
Who promifed that he would.
So thefe embafadors fail'd thence, and landed in England,*
And there tould to the king each chiefeft point of his arrand.
Who, when he heard their fpeach, perfwaded partly by reafon,
How that he fhould be detein'd there fafe, or fafe in a prifon,
(He not at all fearing th' intendment of fory perfons)
Shew'd himfelf as a prince more bountiful unto the
    commons,
And liberal to the poore.
But time his courfe hath; time ftayleffe daiely doth happen,†
With fwift breach cureleffe, with gould not againe to be
    gotten.
O wavering fortune! when thou feem'ft moft to be fmiling,‡
Mutabil intendment meaneft, and mifchievus ending.
Every time hath an end. O worldly varietie, never
Knowne to remaine conftant! What is here that per-
    maneth ever?
For ftout King Edward, when he found himfelfe to be
    fore fick,
And when he thought that he was (in a manner) paft any
    phyfick,
Streight to the Queenes kindred did fend on away in a
    pofte-hafte

---

   * Grafton, fol. 755, Edw. 4.   † Sentences.   ‡ Poeticè.

Unto the Lord Rivers* (whom he knewe to be firme, to be
    ftedfaft)
And to the Lord Haftings (Lord Chamberlaine then of
    England)
And to the Lord Marqueffe (whom fhe firft had by her
    husband
Named Sir John Gray, which was made knight in a battel
Fought at Saint Albons, & there was flaine : who did excell
In valor of knighthood)
Willing them to repaire to the court with fpeedines eftfoones,
And to refort to the king for divers and many reafons.
Who to the court in all haft did come, who courtly faluting
Were refaluted againe, on another femblably greeting.
Every lord that came to the courte, by the king his apoint-
    ment,
Went to the kings prefence. When he faw them there to
    be prefent,
He took them by the handes (though inward pangs with a
    forrow
Greatly molefted his heart) and, underfet with a pillow,
Spake to them as foloweth.
My lordes and kynfmen, your prefence hartily welcom,†
Whofe frendfhippes I found more fure to me than a
    kingdom.
My life is but a blaft, I feele death woful aproching,
And I rejoyce that I have my freendes here at my departing :
My body wafteth away, I fynd myfelf to be feebel,
Alfo my blud to decay; I feele myfelf but unabel

* Grafton, fol. 760 & fol. 761, Edw. 5.
† King Edward's laft will, or admonition to the Queene, his children, and nobility.

For to pronounce many wordes. Therefore, my lordes, to
    me liften.
Concord in friendfhip, be faythful unto my children;
And to my fonne, your Prince, I charge you for to be loyall,
Safe to preferve his grace, to defend this realme univerfall.
For the Cicil tyrants could find no greater a torment
Then cruel envy, that hagge, which fofters deadly re-
    vengement.
Marcus Agrippa declar'd that fmall thinges, daily, by
    concord,*
Eftfoones grow to be great; and great thinges, fondly by
    difcord,
Quickly declyne to ruine.
That grave ould fapient Scyllurus, named Chironefis,†
(Fowre fcore fonnes who begate) when he lay fick, thus did
    he publifh.
Every one, deare fonnes, in his hand here take but an arrow,
And break them forthwith. Which they did fpeedily.
    But now
Each on a fheafe of fhaftes, my fonnes, take, forcibly break
    them:
Which to do each did afay, but could not. Then with a
    folemne
Speach thus he fpake: As you could not them break, fo,
    my children,‡
Trew fyrme and conftant conjunction of many brethren
No body can diffolve. Therefore, live frendly together.
If fo be you feperate your felves each one from another,
Then fhall your enemies (as a prey fnatcht up of a tyger)

    * Seneca in Epift. lib. 14.   † Plutark in reg. Apotheg, & Stob. fer. 82.
                        ‡ Similie.

You (difagreeing fo) with a fmall force eafily conquer.
So, my beloved lordes, if you, by malicius envy,
Shall fall at variaunce, which of you ftands in a fafety?
Profperus are kingdomes, publick weales ftatefuly florifh,
Where ftates concording do perfect amity ftablifh ;*
But when a realme difagrees, that realme is feene very feldom
Long to remaine a monarche. For certaine, every kingdome
Hatefully diffevered (fayth and tranquillity wanting)
Turned is up fide downe, ruinus difconfolat ending:
Hate doth a realme ruinate. Therefore, my lordes, I be-
    feech you,
Every one to be frendes, my precepts duly to follow.
Every lord by the hand there prefent tooke on another
(Who did apeare to be frendes) though their heartes were
    far afunder.
And then he fpake to the Queene fore greev'd, who mourne-
    fuly looking,
Teares from her eyes gufht forth, as bubbling blobbes from
    a welfpring.
Farewell, dearly belov'd; your children charily cherifh;
See them well to be bred with good and fingular advife.
And you, my children, be dutiful unto the mother:
Ufe thefe your kinfmens counfayle, in ftead of a father;
For litel yong children fhould wifely be rul'd by the
    counfayle
Of wity grave fenators, whofe fame and vertue doth excell.
And, with a forroful hart his children fadly beholding,
Stretched his hand to them all, thefe fame wordes faintily
    fpeaking.

          * Sentence.

God bleffe you children, farewell lordes dearly beloved ;
Who with trickling teares (fad fighing) wofully mourned.
And then he held up his hands to the Lord, his mercy befeeching,
And to receive his foule to the joyes that ar ever abiding.
Therewithal he faynting in a fwoune grewe ftraight to be fpeachleffe :
Gafping breath who did yeald, with a pale face and body fenfeleffe.
Whofe foule imparadiz'd, I believe is with the Creator,
Our Lord Emmanuell, our Chrift, and fole mediator.
Who, when he had regaliz'd 3. yeares and credibly twenty,
Tomb'd in a faire monument, at Windfore lies, in an abbey.
How that he dy'd many men did doubt, for he dy'd on a fuddayn.
Sundry by furfet afirm'd, which no body knew to be certayn ;
But many thought that he was put away by the vile privy treafon
Of tyranus Richard, by the meanes of fome fory poyfon ;
As Sir Thomas More, in his owne book fkilfuly penned,
Thought (by the fpeach that he learn'd) that he was fure privily poyfned.
And not a thing unlyke; for he fpared no body, whofe life
Might dominire for a king, whofe life might work him a mifchiefe.
He was a vile Machavile, and ftill tooke time at avauntage :
To worke fuch ftratagemes his lew'd mind gave him a courage.
As wax is molify'd, and clay made hard, by the fun-fhine,[*]

[*] Similie.

So to the word of God good mens hearts daily wil enclyne ;
But lewd are hardned by the word. Such obftinat error
Permaneth in reprobates, whofe end is damnable horror.
This valiaunt Edward was a prince of a beautiful afpect,*
Whofe face fhyn'd with a faire fanguine complexion indeckt;
Whofe yelo burnifhed haire did fhyne like glorius amber,
Whofe gray eyes twinkling, like ftarres, did cheerefuly
    glifter :†
Comelines of perfon, very tall of bodily ftature ;
Exquifit every part was featured ; and of a nature
Merciful and liberal ; whofe ftout hart (bouldly by wifedom
And politick valiaunce) of right did atayn to the kingdom.
He was a prince patient, in great profperity pleafant,
And not at all arogant ; in great adverfity conftant,
Not timorous, wavering ; to fteadfaft friend very faithfull ;
To fra'dulent enemyes fevere, implacabel, hatefull ;
Fortunat in warfare ; but fomewhat gi-ven (in exceffe)
To womanifh daliaunce, as his hiftorye plainly doth
    expreffe.
This ftout king Edward many times would fay, that he
    lov'd well
Three fpeciall paragons, in fev'ral gifts who did excell :
Firft was wily by kind ; but another feem'd to be godly ;
Shores wife was merieft, as a woman void of al envy.

   * Defcription of Edward the fowerth.   † Similies.

The just and lawful title that Richard
Duke of Yorke, father to King Edward, made to the Crowne of England.

Richard Plantagenet, Duke of Yorke, rightly the garland
Sought by law to regaine, his right to the Crowne then of
 England;
And he preferred a byll to the nobil common afembly*
Held at Weftminfter. Where, after merciful Henry
(Namely the fixth) his death, they all (there jointly to-
 gether)
Gave this realme to the Duke, his right heires in the
 remainder.†
But this ftout Richards ftout luckleffe mynd was unabel
For to prolong fo long; but in end was flaine in a battel,
Neare to the towne Wakefield (and left here thefe many
 children:
Edward, George, Richard; all three well knowne to be
 brethren)
And yet he fware many times by folemne othes, that he
 never‡
Would any treafon atempt, or againft him raife any power.
His three fonnes, whom I nam'd, were like three martial
 Hectors,
All of a ftoutnes alike, on anothers glory detractors.
This forefaid Richard to the forefaid fortunat Edward
Was father undubitate; fonne and heire namely to Richard,

* Grafton, fo. 757 et 758.   † Graunted by parliament.
‡ Stow, fol. 944 & fol. 972.

Stout Earle of Cambridge.
Who maried Dame Anne, fole heire and daughter of
    Edmund
Mortimer, Earle of March, Richards niece, namely the fecond:
So that he was by the lawes right lawfull heire to the
    kingdome,
Which Edward did ataine by force, and partly by wifdome.
Henry the fourth did ufurpe, and put downe wrongfuly
    Richard,
Second king by name, at Pomfret flaine by the coward
Sir Pierce of Exton ; who ftrake him downe, as a butcher
Striketh an ox on his heade. Wo worth fo fhameful a
    monfter!
This trecherus bludy Duke did bring eight tal men in
    harneffe,
Each man a bill in his hand, like thieves, to murder his
    Highneffe ;
Who, with a bill that he got by force, did manfuly withftand*
Thofe Machavile hypocrites (for he kild foure men with his
    owne hand)
Till that he was ftruck down by the knight ; who leapt in
    a chay-er,
Like cravenus coward, to repofe himfelf from a daunger.

* Grafton, fol. 412, Hen. 4.

The second Booke of the tyranny and
uſurpation of king Richard : and how king Henry the ſeaventh, when he was Earle of Richmond, was preſerved in his time.

A praier.

I (he, that here doth apeale to the ſacred ſeate of a kingly,
Kingly tribunall throne, of a King celeſtial only,
Only the King of kings, the triumphant Lord God imortall,
Three perſons, one God, deifi'd with glory coequall)
Humbly before thee, my God, that King, and Lord God of heaven,
Wholly my-ſelfe proſtrate: give eare, O Lord, to me, liſten :
Sanctify me by thy grace, and juſtify me by thy mercy,*
For by the grace of God comes our ſalvation only.
Graunt that I may paraphraſe, ſtout Henries glory to publiſh,
And to promulgat abroad King Richards tyrrany diveliſh.

I he, that only before (in Romane rythmery verſes)
Did modulate, with a thinne oten pype, fortunat Henries
Flight that he made to the Duke, with his uncle there in a ſafety
Both to remaine for a time, till time ſhould proove to be friendly.
Which was a worke of thanks: But now, now, murtherus horror,

* Ephe. 2, 5, 8.

And Machavile ſtratagemes I recorde, of a lewde malefactor,
That did uſurpe as a king, that killed his own very brethren,
Murdered his nephues wife, and many peeres, on a ſudden,
Mournefuly, Muſe, manifeſt the deteſted deedes of a tyrant,
Monſter of all mankinde, whoſe ſinnes to the world ar aparant:
With ſalt watery teares this wofull tragedy penfill:
Teares, from a ſabel penne of direfull ebony, diſtill.
I to the clowdes ſeeke not to mount, like Icarus, in ſky;*
Nor, like proud Phaëton, with a minde preſume to be 'lofty.
Witty Thales maiden, that ſawe him looke up on heaven,
And in a ditch to decline: he is wel ſerv'd, quoth the maiden,
For that he looked aloft when he ſhould have lookt on his owne feete.
Looke not aloft, ſily Muſe, but ſhew thy ſelfe to be diſcreet.
Here do I mean to declare (O Queene) how ſhamefuly Richard
That Duke of Gloſter (but a younger brother of Edward,
Lately the king) did ataine to the crowne, and dignity regal.
Trewly my minde doth abhorre that I ſhould here make the recitall,
What Machavile policies, what ſhifts, what crafty devices,
What tyranus ſtratagemes he devis'd, to crucifie princes.
Firſt of all, here to beginne: he ſtab'd and kill'd with a dagger
Henry the ſixt, when he was ſafe kept (as a priſoner) in Tower,†
For that he conſidered King Henries life was an hindr'ance

* Ovid. Poeticè.   † Grafton, fol. 713, Edw. 4.

Both to the king and him, by the which they wanted
　　asurance;
Therefore he did this fact, his brother firmly to settel
In throne of regiment (whose state he knew to be fickel)
For that he knew that he might, when a sure foundation is
　　laide,
Build as he would himselfe. Can a building stand that is
　　unstaid?
Like as a hungry lyon (ramping) will seeke to devow-er
Every beast that he meetes, til he hath ful apeased his
　　hunger,*
So this vile bludy Duke their deathes did wilfuly conspire,†
Which did opose themselves that he might not ataine to
　　this empire.‡
For greedy thirst of gould, and fervent love of a kingdome,
All felo mates doth abhor; there faith is found very seldom.
Like as a weak patient that lyes sore sick of a dropsy§
Drinkes yet is alwaies dry, so that no liquor his hasty,
Or greedy, thirst can alay: so minds that proudly desi-er
Imperiall regiment, still thirst and long for an empyre.‖
Next he, the Duke of Clarence (his brother) caus'd in a
　　malmsey
Butte to be drown'd, as a duke (thought guiltlesse) found to
　　be guilty;
Immagining that he might then sooner ataine to the
　　kingdom,
When that he was put away. For he div'd each drift to
　　the bottom.
Like Auroras birde, that fluttereth up to the welkin,¶

　　* Similie.　　† Sentence.　　‡ Nulla fides, regni sociis, &c.
　　§ Similie.　　‖ Grafton, fol. 781 & fol. 719, Edw. 5.　　¶ Similie.

Soareth aloft higher then a groffe mans fight can imagine ;
So this proud greedy duke (whofe minde fo lofty did afpire)
Reached a thought higher than meane wits thought to this empire.
O what a vile perilus ferpent, what a cormoran helhound,*
Is cruell ambition, which feekes mans glory to confound !
For mindes infatiate wil atempt ftill, ftill to be higheft ;
Firft to be greatly prefered ; next equall ; then to be chiefeft.
Ambitius wifdome comes not from above, but is earthly,
Senfual, and divelifh, contentius, and ful of envy ;†
But fapience from above is gentel, merciful, harmeleffe,
Wrongfully not judging, but void of hypocrifie doubtleffe.
Now to proceede, as I meant.
King Edward, when he knew that he was fo fpitefuly drowned,
His fory misfortune and lewd luck greatly repented :
For when as other lords would fpeake for a lewde fory perfon
(Humbly befeaching him that he would vouchfafe him a parfon)
Sadly the king would fay, many times, O brother unhappy !
For whom no body would once feeme to requeft any mercy :
But many men do repent when it is too late to redreffe it.
That privy vile bludy faɕt that he did fo fhamefuly permit
Strake a remorfe in his hart,
Surely the more that a mind is clogd with a grevius offence,
More dolor and anguifh doth torment daily the confcience.
Sundry report divers reafons of their privy mallice
Fiercely revived againe ; each caufe yet prov'd but a furmife.

* Sentence.   † See James 3, v. 16, 17.

For why ? The King and Queene fufpected a prophecie
    fore-tould,*
Which they immagined would prove to be true ; that a G
    fhould
(Thought to be George Clarence) their nobil progeny
    fupplant :
Which foon was verify'd and prov'd to be true by the tyrant,
That Duke of Glofter, when he was proclaim'd a Protector,
Who to the Kings children did prove their fole malefactor.
O fond fufpicion of mindes ! Who can the characters
Of future happes foretell fet downe by celeftial orders ?
Like as a cockes crowing, or crackling flame of fy-er,
Daunteth a lufty lyon, which flies for feare of a daunger :
So doth a fufpition, conceiv'd by the bruit of a rumor,
Breed in a princes mind, but an inward feare, but a terror.
Some did afirme this Duke fhould match with Mary, the
    daughter
Of Charles Duke Burgon, which Edward daily did hinder ;
Which was a griefe to the Duke, as a fore that feftereth
    inward,
For that his owne brother fo dealt that apeard to be
    for-ward.
Thirdly, the caufe was aledg'd, that this Duke, George, had
    a fervant
Wrongfuly condemned, that fhould as a forcerer enchant
Their regall perfons and their pofterity. Wherefore,
This Duke complayning to the King, was araign'd as a
    traytour ;
With fory wordes who revyl'd, and ftill did murmur againft
    them :

* Grafton, fol. 741, Edw. 4.

Whereby the King, in a rage, this Duke did speedily
    condemne.
There is a time for a man both where and when to do
    wisely;
As did apeare by the Duke, who prov'd too daungerous
    hasty.
Silence seldom ofendes, large speach oft stirreth up anger.*
That wity grave Socrates his schollers charg'd to remember†
Three speciall documents: to be shamefast, wise, to be silent;
Most requisite for them, that they may prove to be prudent:
For let a man see much, let him heare, and say but a littel,
For littel meddling doth seldom bring any troubel.‡
As litel hoat sparkles many times do kindel a fy-er§
Great, fierce and violent; so lewd speech stirreth up anger
Sore, sharpe, and vehement: and as fire forcibly great
    streames
Upflaming spreadeth, so lewd wordes enmitie by meanes
Endamaging disperse. And as fire quenched is hardly‖
Till that it hath burned to the full, and that very fiercely,
Whose force doth ruinate, burne and consumeth in ashes
Great, large, huge tenements, faire, fine, and sumptuus
    houses;
Semblabel (in like sort) is an anger merciles, ardent,
Continuing vehement; whose madde rage and fury fervent
Doth townes depopulate, subverteth flatly the citties,
Upturneth castels, murdreth kinges, and many princes
Stout, wise and valiaunt. What is it, but mischievus Envy
Cankereth up in her hart? To do wrong she practiceth
    only,

    * Sentence.   † Maxim. Serm.   ‡ Proverbes.   § Similie.
                         ‖ Similie.

64 *The preservation of K. Henry the seaventh,*

Which she delights most in. With pride she jettes as a copesmate,
Immagining vengeance. Wo worth so spiteful [a] brewbate!
Better a staf that bendes than a staf that breaketh asunder;*
Better a man patient than a man that stirreth up anger.†
No wrath so vehement as brothers enmity; whose rage,‡
Fiercely revived againe, what man may possibil asswage?
As for an exampel: since Typhon killed Osyris,
Romulus also Remus, Cambises wrongfully Smerdis.

TO HER MAJESTIE.

Here I desist for a time, O Queene! For like an abortive
Droupeth afore he be ripe, so my booke may prove but offensive,§
If that he passe to the print, yet my poore skill hath adornist
That, that I meane to deline. Soft fyre makes malt to be sweetest.‖
And God graunt thee to rule as a joyful prince to thy peepil,
Princely so long to live, as an hart, as an oke, or a woosel.
If so be your Highnes this verse and history fancy,
Then will I gladly proceed, els not; for I count it a folly.

Here is a Book that I made, which pagan Jove in his anger,
Nor steele shall outweare, nor time authentical, ever.¶

THE AUTHOR TO HIS MUSE.

Here let us harbor a while: thinges ar to be done in a measure;
Every tyde hath an ebbe; paines past to recount is a pleasure.

* Similie.   † Sentence.   ‡ Sentence.   § Similie.
‖ Proverbe.   ¶ Jam opus exegi, &c.

Glory to God, God above! which was God from the be-
> ginning,
Which is, which fhal be our Lord eternal abiding.

Sereniffimæ Reginæ.
En meliora canam, fi placant carmina, Princeps:
Sin tibi difpliceant, hic murus aheneus efto.

Certaine Latine verfes, that were made long fince by one Doctor Bufte, a phifitian, in commendation of the Queenes Majefty, when fhe came to Oxford.

Juno, Minerva, Venus, nemerofæ vallibus Idæ,
Judicium formæ dum fubiere fuæ,
Juno jactat opes. Quid tum? Prudentior illis
Eft Pallas; Pallas haud opulenta tamen.
Inter formofas, fi tu Dea forte fuiffes,
Vicifti reliquas, O Dea, quarta Deas.
Quam Juno jeuna foret! Quam pallida Pallas!
Quam Dea vana Venus! Quam Dea fola fores!
Sit Venus alma viris; regni virtutis egena eft.
Omnia funt tua: tu Juno, Minerva, Venus.

Tranflated into Englifh Hexameters and Pentameters, verfe for verfe.

Juno, Minerva, Venus, in vales of wodded hil Ida,
Whyles, which was fayreft, they did agree to be try'd,
Juno fhe brag'd of wealth. What then? Then thought to
> be wifeft
Was Pallas; Pallas was not a wealthy godeffe.
If that among thofe fair godefes thou, fair godes, hadft ben,
Thou hadft furpaft them (there, as a fourth godes) all.

Juno, fhe how jejune! How pale had Pallas apeared!
And Venus how vainelike! Thou then an only godeffe.
Let Venus all men pleafe, yet throne of vertue fhe wanteth.
All thinges are thine; thou Juno, Minerva, Venus.

And Saphickes in Englifh I have made thus:

Godly Queene Princeffe prefident remayneth
Only our fortreffe, refident apeareth,
Duly like Empreffe pre'minent requireth
          All us apointed,
Stoutly with bouldnes provident, to venter
Bouldly foes fiercenes violent to conquer,
Manly with ftoutnes diligent defend her,
          Which is anoynted.

[FINIS.]

INTRODUCTION.

WE have here reprinted two of old Thomas Churchyard's Poems —the first utterly unknown, but of little worth excepting in a historical point of view—the second, the most popular piece that he ever wrote, and which originally, and in a shorter form, made its appearance in "The Mirror for Magistrates," a well-known series of supposed autobiographical productions in verse, first published in 1559, and again, with Sackville's famous "Induction," in 1563.

The "Wished Reformation of wicked Rebellion" was put forth at the period of the breaking out of the insurrection in Ireland, which Robert Earl of Essex was sent to subdue. Two poems, the "Fortunate Farewell" of the Earl of Essex, and the "Welcome Home" of the same nobleman, have been included in all the lists of Churchyard's productions; but the "Wished Reformation of wicked Rebellion," which necessarily preceded them, has not even been mentioned. The writer never displayed any striking powers of imagination or happiness of invention; and in the later part of his career (failing, perhaps, other attractions) he endeavoured to draw attention to his labours by the adoption of a very peculiar system (if system it can be called in which no established principle seems to have been observed) of spelling and punctuation, both of which are continued in the reproduction in the hands of the reader. Having been born at

Shrewsbury about 1520, Churchyard was, probably, in his seventy-eighth year when the tract (of only four leaves) appeared, and he died six years afterwards.

His "Tragedy of Shore's Wife" (not a drama, although the subject was dramatised late in the reign of Elizabeth) had been known for more than thirty years before it was enlarged and altered as it appears in the following pages. In 1593, its author gave to it his latest improvements, and it was then made to form a separate tract in "Churchyard's Challenge," a collection of poems which the author "challenged" as his own, although he complained that his enemies had, in several instances, denied the paternity. Such had especially been the case with his "Shore's Wife;" but in the year following its reappearance in 1593, it was warmly applauded by no less a critic than Thomas Nash, who, among other points, thus addressed Churchyard in the Epistle before "Christ's Tears over Jerusalem:" " I love you unfeignedly and admire your aged Muse, that may well be grand-mother to our grand-eloquentest Poets of this present. *Sanctum et venerabile vetus omne Poema.* Shore's Wife is young, though you be stept in years: in her shall you live when you are dead."

We doubt whether the modern reader will accord entirely in Nash's eulogy, which was, perhaps, more highly spiced, because Gabriel Harvey had done his best to detract from the old poet's merits. Besides the peculiarity of spelling, especially in the "Wished Reformation," Churchyard purposely, and obviously, set grammatical concords at defiance: the verb and its nominative often disagree.

J. P. C.

A

WISHED REFORMACION

OF

WICKED REBELLION.

Newly fet foorth by

Thomas Churchyard

Esquier.

IMPRINTED AT LONDON
by Thomas Efte, dwelling in
Alderfgate ftreete.
1598.

To all the right noble of birth or
mynd, with the true hartted Gentlemen and
loyall fubjects of England, Thomas Churchyard wifheth hevenly happineffe, with
worldly honour, reft, peace and
parfait felicite.

MOEST worthy, vertuos, honorable, and well difpofed people of all degrees, whoes goodnes and wifdom I dowt not, but have offtten ballanced in breft the terryble trobuls and broyls that trefon and rebellion hath broght to many quyet kingdoms by parrelos practifes, proud attempts, and feditios diforders, a foer peftilent ficknes that breeds many dangeros deffects in a publyck ftaet. If thear wear no other prefident, make Ierland an example; what curfed callamitees aer fet a broetch by theas wicked and unwelcom cawfis, canckers in a common weall, blayns and botchis in a found body, and gnawing worms and caetter pillars to every honeft hart. If a wyes world accownts theas rotten byells no better, how fhuld a true wrytter give them any better naem? Wherefore I pray you with pacyence and fweet confitheracion (and no fowre fenffuer) read what followeth in mield manner of vers, albeit fomwhat byetting the gawlls of fuch, whoes wounds cannot bee healed but by fom fharp and ferching medfon : thear is ment, by the wryttars good will, a fodayn wifhed reformacion of wicked rebellion, and over great boldnes that fhuld maek them bloefh that aer actters and doers in theas tragecall commedies and mizerable pagants, I crave but your good juegments and layzar to loek with frindly eyes on the verfis that wear well ment and lovingly offred.

THOMAS CHURCHYARD.

A wished reformacion of wicked rebellion.

GOOD men wear glad at Gods great glorie feen
(By fpefhall grace) on Englands joy to fhyen,
Which grace prezarvd our quinttefenffed Queen,
That fkaeped faef from fkaeth throw power devien.
O falls forfworn, what ear you aer, give place
To mightty Jovs Lieftenant heer on earth!
O haetfull flock of traytors, heid your face
From rightfull kings and queens well boern by byrth!
Fy, tretcheros trafh, that wind will blo a way;
Pluck up your fight, and fee your own decay!

Have you not hard how birds of theayr difcloes
Fowll treafons oft, and brings traytors to fhaem?
His confhence doth condemp him whear hee goes,
That feeks to torn a kingdom out of fraem;
Cowncell a broed, and bad device at hoem,
Ritches ill won, and gold that enmies give,
Baerfoet lyek freers to wrangling Roem may roem;
In England long heer may no traytors live.
O Jezuwits! can you your felves efkues,
Whan Jhefus naem and docttrin you abues?

Hee preached peace, you fow difcord and war,
All duety done to Sezar Cryft dyd lyek;
But you in rage and errors run fo far,
Yee care not whom yee poyfon, kill, or ftryek:
A fhameleffe fwarm off Seminaries now,
Difguifd lyek dogges that whine beefore they bite,
Fills every towne with truthleffe traytors throw,
Whoes words, lyke fwords, are ready drawne to fmite;
But blo of axe comes oft ere they bee waer,
And ftryeks of head, and leaves the body baer.

All fpeeds a lyek, and all comes to one end;
Hee dyes to day, next moern his fellow goes:
No warning farves, nor may the mifchiefe mend,
So faft and far the floods of folly floes.
Runs ore the brym beeyond obedience bounds,
Tears up great trees, and throwes good houfes downe,
Harms common weales, maeks cuerles foers and wounds,
And cuts them off that ought farve prince and crowne.
What win you then, when lyves of many a man
Are fpilt and loft, fince you theas broyls beganne?

To ryed in poeft from Spayne to Tybron ftreight
Is fure a knack of coofnaeg in a coerd.
Some fwyngars fay, hanging is but a fleight,
Yet drawing fuer, and quartring is aboerd
Of honeft harts. Fy, helhounds! hunt no moer
Among true men, your haunt is foen efpyed:
To bee truft up, and get no thank therfoer,
Is boldneffe great, fo lyek a traytor tryed.
O England! wayll the baebs boern in thy woem,
Who never brings no better fruet from Roem.

Of Wicked Rebellion.

Poyfons do mutch, but murthers fmell the fmoek,
(A fit perfuem for Plutoes fellows all)
They are fent ore, under a cunning cloek,
To fhrowd a plaeg that one fome fhoulders fall.
The Sacrament, firft, traytors muft receive
To doo fowll deeds. Is that relygion good?
Fy on that fayth that fhall mans fowll difceave
By bold attempts, and bathing hands in blood!
Without efkues theas faults muft fuffer blaem,
(In fecret fayd) aut com to open fhaem.

Treafons do end with plaegs and fkorgis great,
A juft reward for wilfull fowll offence:
Than, what is won by bloddy angers heat?
As Judas fold our Chrift for thirtty pens,
Hee hangd himfelf for doing fuch a deed:
The law loeks well on all thofe divlifh drifts
Which coms to nought, for ftrangly ftill they fpeed
That wold gro great by cruell fhaemles fhifts:
Death, hell, and fier at heells doth follow thofe
That from the prince and ftaet a gadding goes.

No kingdom fhoes fo many rebells yet,
Althoguh a Freer in France wold fellows have;
Yee run to far with over weening wit,
For traytors wants the powre to powll and fhave,
Or cut our throets, fharp razors how you may.
Tiem tells us taells of all your practyes throw,
Then fly hens, foells, your deeds do you beewray:
Fowll murther brings your naems in queftion now,
Efcaep is noen, but only throw the pyeks,
For all the world your doings mutch miflyeks.

Kill oen, kill all; kill all, firſt hang your felvs,
So all is faeff, for hee that all doth fee
Loeks down on thoes that dayly digs and delvs,
To fave from harms all fuch as harmles bee:
So, on thoes props that holds up publyek ſtaet
Hee loeks, and doth thearin as hee doth pleas,
And for a pawne hee givs you all check maet,
Boern heer at hoem, or bred beeyond the feas.
Than, think on all you wiſh to overthrow,
So is your fall moer neerar than you know.

For as you wiſh a change for hired caufe,
So evry ſtaet haets thoes that traytors bee;
No frinds you find in common world or lawfe,
Whear conſtant fayth your changing minds may fee.
Think you our world loves traytors half fo well,
That children, wievs, and goods they do forget?
And will loes land and houfis whear they dwell,
And roet up all, untyemly twigs to fet?
Goe, bloody brood, hatcht up in rebell rowt,
Hyed heads in hoells, elfe world will find you out.

God may convert vyell men from vicyous arts,
Reform the mind, the body vertuous grows;
When ſhaem maeks bluſh the face that playes bad parts,
God's grace will work moer goodneffe then man knoes:
Ill lyef foer thought fils hart with hoep and grace,
Repentance brings fweet reſt and bleffings boeth;
Obedience fraems a confcience in good cace,
True feare and love delights in loyall troeth;
But who feeks blood in blood ſhall glotted bee,
And his own end by blood ſhall quickly fee.

Of Wicked Rebellion.

I can but wifh the wicked wear reform'd,
And all the ruft and kancker fkowred clean;
If no, bee fure thear madneffe will bee worm'd,
And troblos tongs bee tawght to fing a mean.
Thear poyfonings aer reveald by thear own crue,
Thear treafons hath no powre to paffe unknown;
Sedifhoes books and fawfy lybels nue,
In fier and flaem aer utterly oerthrown;
Themfelves in doubt of death and daunger ftill,
Under Gods wrath, and rightfull princes will.

Finis qd.   *Thomas Churchyard.*

THE TRAGEDIE

OF

SHORES WIFE.

*Much augmented, with divers new
Additions.*

By Thomas Churchyard.

LONDON.
Printed by John Wolfe.
1593.

To the right honorable the Lady
Mount Eagle and Compton, wife to the
right honourable the Lord of Buck-
hurſts ſon and heire.

GOOD Madame, for that the vertuous and good Ladie Carie, your ſiſter, honourablie accepted a diſcourſe of my penning, I beleeved your Ladiſhip would not refuſe the like offer, humbly preſented and dutifully ment, I bethought me of a Tragedie that long laye printed and many ſpeake well of, but ſome doubting the ſhallowneſſe of my heade (or of meere mallice diſdaineth my doeings) denies me the fathering of ſuche a worke, that hath won ſo much credit; but as ſure as God lives, they that ſo defames me, or doth diſable me in this cauſe, doth me ſuch an open wrong, as I would be glad to right with the beſt blood in my body, ſo he be mine equall that moved ſuch a quarrell: but mine old yeares doth utterly forbid me ſuch a combat, and to contend with the malicious, I think it a madneſſe; yet I proteſt before God and the world the penning of Shore's wife was mine, deſiring in my hart that all the plagues in the worlde maie poſſeſſe me, if anie holpe me either with scrowle or councell to the publishing of the invencion of the fame Shores wife. And to show that yet my spirits faile me not in as great matters as that, I have augmented her Tragedie, I hope in as fine a forme as the first impression thereof, and hath sette forth some more Tragedies and tragicall discourses no whit inferior, as I trust, to my first worke; and, good madame, because Rosimond is so excellently sette forth (the actor whereof I honour) I have somewhat beautified my Shore's wife, not in any kind of emulation, but to make the world knowe my device in age is as rife and reddie, as my disposition and knowledge was in youth. So having chosen a noble personage to be a patrone to support poore Shores wifes Tragedie againe, I commend all the verses of her (olde and newe) to your good Ladishhips judgment, hoping you shall lose no honour in the supportation of the same, because the true writer thereof with all humblenesse of mind and service presents the Tragedie unto your honourable censure, wishing long life and encrease of vertues fame to make your Ladishhips daies happie.

T. Churchyard.

Heere followes the Tragedie of Shores
wife, much augmented with divers new aditions.

AMONG the reſt by fortune overthrowne,
  I am not leaſt that moſt may waile her fate:
My fame and brute abroade the world is blowne:
Who can forget a thing thus done ſo late?
My great miſchance, my fall, and heavy ſtate
Is ſuch a marke, whereat each tongue doth ſhoote,
That my good name is pluckt up by the roote.

This wandring world bewitched me with wiles,
And won my wits with wanton ſugred joyes:
In Fortunes freakes who truſts her when she ſmiles
Shall find her falſe and full of fickle toyes.
Her triumphs all but fills our eares with noyſe,
Her flattering giftes are pleaſures mixt with paine,
Yea, and all her words are thunders threatning raine.

The fond deſire that we in glorie ſet
Doth thirle our hearts to hope in ſlipper hap;
A blaſt of pompe is all the fruite we get,
And under that lies hid a ſodaine clap.
In ſeeking reſt unwares we fall in trap:
In groping flowres with nettles ſtung we are;
In labring long we reape the crop of care.

Oh darke deceite with painted face for tho!
Oh poyſned baite that makes us eager ſtill!
Oh fained friend, deceiving people ſo!
Oh world, of thee we cannot ſpeake too ill!
Yet fooles we are that bend ſo to thy ſkill.
The plague and ſcourge that thouſands daily feele
Should warne the wyfe to ſhun thy whirling wheele.

But who can ſtop the ſtreame that runnes full ſwift,
Or quench the fire that crept is in the ſtraw?
The thirſty drinkes, there is no other ſhift,
Perforce is ſuch that neede obayes no lawe.
Thus bounde we are in worldly yokes to drawe,
And cannot ſtay nor turne againe in time,
Nor learne of thoſe that fought too high to clime.

My ſelfe for proofe, loe! here I now appeare
In womans weede, with weeping watred eyes,
That bought her youth and her delights full deare,
Whoſe lewd reproch doth ſound unto the ſkies,
And bids my corſe out of the ground to riſe,
As one that may no longer hide her face,
But needes muſt come and ſhewe her piteous caſe.

The ſheete of ſhame wherein I shrowded was
Did move me oft to plaine before this day,
And in mine eares did ring the trompe of braſſe,
Which is defame, that doth each thing bewray:
Yea, though full dead and low in earth I lay,
I heard the voyce, of mee what people ſaide,
But then to ſpeake, alas! I was affraide.

Shores Wife.

And nowe a time for me I fee preparde.
I heare the lives and falls of many wights;
My tale therefore the better may be heard,
For at the torch the little candle lights:
Where Pageants be, fmale things fill out the fights.
Wherefore give eare, good Churchyard; doe thy beft
My Tragedy to place among the reft.

Becaufe the truth fhall witnes well with thee,
I will rehearfe in order as it fell,
My life, my death, my dolefull deftene,
My wealth, my woe, my doing every deale;
My bitter bliffe, wherein I long did dwell:
A whole difcourfe, by me Shores wife by name,
Now fhalt thou heare, as thou hadft feene the fame.

Of noble blood I cannot boaft my byrth,
For I was made out of the meaneft moulde:
Mine heritage but feven foote of th' earth,
Fortune ne gave to me the gifts of gold;
But I could brag of nature, if I would,
Who fild my face with favour frefh and faire,
Whofe beautie fhon like Phœbus in the ayre.

My beautie blafd like torch or twinckling ftarre,
A lively lamp that lends darke world fome light:
Faire Phœbus beames fcarfe reacheth halfe fo farre
As did the rayes of my rare beautie bright.
As fummers day exceedes blacke winters night,
So Shores wives face made foule Browneta blufh,
As pearle ftaynes pitch, or gold furmounts a rufh.

The damaſke roſe, or Roſamond the faire,
That Henry held as deere as jewells be,
Who was kept cloſe in cage from open ayre,
For beauties boaſt could ſcarſe compare with me.
The kindly buds and bloſſomes of brave tree
With white and red had deckt my cheekes ſo fine,
There ſtood two balles like drops of claret wine.

The beaten ſnow, nor lily in the field,
No whiter ſure then naked necke and hand:
My lookes had force to make a lyon yeeld,
And at my forme in gaze a world would ſtand.
My body ſmall, framd finely to be ſpand,
As though dame Kind hap ſworne in ſolemne ſort
To ſhrowd herſelfe in my faire forme and port.

No part amiſſe when nature tooke ſuch care
To ſet me out as nought ſhould be awry,
To forniſh forth (in due proportion rare)
A peece of worke ſhould pleaſe a princes eie.
O, would to God that boaſt might prove a lie!
For pride youth tooke in beauties borrowde traſh
Gave age a whippe, and left me in the laſh.

My ſhape, ſome ſaide, was ſeemely to each ſight,
My countenance did ſhewe a ſober grace;
Mine eies in lookes were never proved light,
My tongue in wordes was chaſt in every caſe:
Mine eares were deafe, and would no lovers place,
Save that, alas! a prince did blot my browe:
Loe! there the ſtrong did make the weake to bowe.

Shores Wife.

The majeſtie that kings to people beare,
The ſtately port, the awefull cheere they ſhewe,
Doth make the meane to ſhrinke and couch for feare,
Like as the hounde that doth his maiſter know.
What then? Since I was made unto the bowe,
There is no cloake can ſerve to hide my fault,
For I agreede the fort he ſhould aſſault.

The eagles force ſubdues ech bird that flies:
What metell may reſiſt the flaming fire?
Doth not the ſun daſill the cleereſt eyes,
And melt the yſe and make the froſt retyre?
Who can withſtand a puiſſant kings deſire?
The ſtiffeſt ſtones are perced through with tooles,
The wiſeſt are with princes made but fooles.

Yf kinde had wrought my forme in common frames,
And ſet me forth in colours blacke and browne;
Or beautie had beene parcht in Phœbus flames,
Or ſhamefaſt waies had pluckt my feathers downe,
Then had I kept my fame and good renowne:
For natures gifts were cauſe of all my griefe.
A pleaſant pray entiſeth many a theefe.

Thus woe to thee that wrought my peacocks pride
By cloathing me with natures tapeſtry!
Woe worth the hewe wherein my face was dyde,
Which made me thinke I pleaſed every eie!
Like as the ſtarres make men beholde the ſkye,
So beauties ſhowe doth make the wiſe full fond,
And brings free hearts full oft in endleſſe bond.

But cleere from blame my frends can not be found:
Before my time my youth they did abuse.
In mariage yoke a prentise was I bound
When that meere love I knewe not how to use.
But wel away! that cannot me excuse.
The harme is mine, though they devisde my care,
And I must smart, and set in slaunderous snare.

Yet giue me lieve to pleade my cause at large.
Yff that the horse doe run beyonde his race,
Or any thinge that keepers have in charge
Doe breake their course where rulers may take place,
Or meate be set before the hungries face,
Who is in fault? th' offender, yea or no?
Or they that are the cause of all this woe.

Note well what strife this forced mariage makes,
What lothed lives doe come where love doth lacke,
What scratching briers doe growe upon such brakes,
What common weales by it are brought to wracke;
What heavy loade is put on patients backe,
What strange delights this branch of vice doth breed,
And marke what graine springs out of such a seede.

Compell the hauke to sit that is unmande,
Or make the hounde unraind to drawe the deere,
Or bring the free against his will in band,
Or move the sad a pleasant tale to here,
Your time is lost and you no whit the nere:
So love ne learnes of force the knot to knit,
She serues but those that feeles sweete fancies fit.

The less defame redounds to my dispraise;
I was intiste by traines and trapt by trust:
Though in my force remained yeas and nayes
Unto my friends, yet needes consent I must
In every thing, yea, lawfull or unjust.
They breake the bowes and shake the tree by sleight,
And bend the wand that mought have growne full straight.

What helpe is this? the pale once broken downe,
The deere must needes in danger run astray:
At me therefore why should the world so frowne?
My weaknes made my youth a princes pray.
Though wisdome should the course of nature stay,
Yet try my case, who list, and they shall prove
The ripest wits are soonest thralls to love.

What neede I more to cleere my selfe so much?
A king me wan and had me at his call:
His royall state, his princely grace was such,
The hope of will that women seeke of all;
The ease and wealth, the gifts which were not small
Beseeged me so strongly round about,
My powre was weake: I could not holde him out.

Duke Hanniball in all his conquest great,
Or Cæsar yet, whose triumphes did exceed,
Of all their spoyses, which made them toyle and sweate,
Were not so glad to have so rich a meede
As was this Prince when I to him agreede,
And yeelded me a prisner willingly,
As one that knew no way away to fly.

The nightingale, for all his merry voyce,
Nor yet the larke that ftill delights to fing,
Did neuer make the hearers fo rejoyce,
As I with wordes have made this worthy king :
I neuer jarde, in tune was euery ftring :
I tempred fo my tongue to pleafe his eare
That what I faid was currant every where.

Sweete are the fongs that merry night-crow finges,
For many parts are in thofe charming notes;
Sweete are the tunes and pipes that pleafeth kings;
Sweete is the love wherein great lordings dotes ;
But fweetft of all is fancie where it flotes,
For throwe rough feas it fmoothy fwimmes away,
And in deepe flouds where fkulles of fifhe doe play.

And where love flides it leaves ne figne nor fhowe
Where it hath gon, the way fo fhuts againe.
It is a fport to heare the fine night-crow
Chaunt in the queere upon a pricke fong plaine :
No muficke more may pleafe a princes vaine
Then defcant ftrange and voice of favrets breeft
In quiet bower, when birds be all at reft.

No fuch comfort as plaine two parts in one,
Whofe rare reports doth carry cunning clean :
Where two long loves and lives in joy alone
They fing at will the treble or the meane.
Where muficke wants the mirth not worth a beane.
The king and I agreed in fuch concorde,
I ruld by love, though he did raigne a lord.

I joynd my talke, my jeſtures and my grace
In wittie frames that long might laſt and ſtand,
So that I brought the king in ſuch a caſe
That to his death I was his chiefeſt hand.
I governd him that ruled all this land :
I bare the ſword, though he did weare the crowne ;
I ſtrake the ſtroke that threwe the mightie downe.

If juſtice ſaid that judgement was but death,
With my ſweete wordes I could the king perſwade,
And make him pauſe, and take therein a breath
Till I with ſuite the fautors peace had made :
I knewe that way to uſe him in his trade ;
I had the art to make the lyon meeke ;
There was no point wherein I was to feeke.

I tooke delight in doying each man good,
Not ſcratting all my ſelfe, as all were mine,
But lookt whoſe life in neede and danger ſtoode,
And thoſe I kept from harme with cunning fine.
On princes traine I alwayes caſt mine eine ;
For lifting up the ſervants of the king
I did throwe court my ſelfe in favour bring.

I offered ayde before they ſued to me,
And promiſd nought but would performe it ſtreight ;
I ſhaked downe ſweete fruit from top of tree,
Made apples fall in laps of men by ſleight.
I did good turnes whiles that I was in height,
For feare a flawe of winde would make me reele,
And blowe me downe when Fortune turnd his wheele.

I fild no chefts with chynks to cherifh age,
But in the harts of people layde my gold;
Sought love of lord, of maifter and of page,
And for no bribbe I never favour folde.
I had enough, I might doe what I would,
Save, fpend, or give, or fling it on the ground:
The more I gave, the more in purfe I found.

Yf I did frowne, who then durft looke awry?
Yf I did fmile, who would not laugh outright?
Yf I but fpake, who durft my wordes denye?
Yf I purfude, who would forfake the flight?
I meane, my powre was knowne to every wight.
On fuch a height good hap had built my bowre,
As though my fweete fhould nere have turnd to fowre.

My husband then, as one that knewe his good,
Refufde to keepe a princes concubine,
Forfeeing the end, and mifchiefe as it ftood,
Againft the king did never much repine.
He fawe the grape whereof he dranke the wine:
Though inward thought his hart did ftill torment,
Yet outwardly he feemde he was content.

To purchafe praife and win the peoples zeale,
Yea, rather bent of kind to doe fome good,
I ever did upholde the common weale:
I had delight to fave the guiltles blood:
Each futers caufe, when that I underftood,
I did prefer, as it had beene mine owne,
And helpe them up that might have beene orethrowne.

Shores Wife.

My powre was preſt to right the poore mans wrong,
My hands were free to give where neede required:
To watch for grace I never thought it long;
To doe men good I neede not be deſired;
Nor yet with giftes my hart was never hyred,
But when the ball was at my foote to guide,
I playde to thoſe that Fortune did abide.

My want was wealth, my woe was eaſe at will;
My robes were rich and braver then the ſunne:
My fortune then was far above my ſkill,
My ſtate was great, my glaſſe did ever runne.
My fatall threed ſo happely was ſpunne
That then I ſate in earthly pleaſures clad,
And for the time a goddeſſe place I had.

But I had not ſo ſoone this life poſſeſt,
But my good hap began to ſlide aſide,
And Fortune then did me ſo ſore moleſt,
That unto plaints was turned all my pride.
It booted not to row againſt the tide:
Mine oares were weake, my heart and ſtrength did faile;
The winde was rough, I durſt not beare a ſaile.

What ſteps of ſtrife belong to high eſtate!
The climing up is doubtfull to endure;
The feate it ſelfe doth purchaſe privy hate,
And honours fame is fickle and unſure,
And all ſhe brings is flowres that be impure,
Which fall as faſt as they doe ſprout and ſpring,
And cannot laſt, they are ſo vaine a thing.

We count no care to catch that we doe wiſh,
But what we win is long to us unknowen:
Till preſent paine be ſerved in our diſh,
We ſcarſe perceive whereon our griefe hath growen.
What graine proves well that is ſo raſhly ſowen?
If that a meane did meaſure all our deedes,
In ſteede of corne we ſhould not gather weedes.

The ſetled mind is free from Fortunes power:
They neede not feare who looke not up aloft;
But they that clime are carefull every hour,
For when they fall they light not very ſoft.
Examples hath the wifeſt warned oft,
That where the trees the ſmalleſt branches beare
The ſtormes doe blow, and have moſt rigour there.

Where is it ſtrong, but neere the ground and roote?
Where is it weake but on the higheſt ſprayes?
Where may a man ſo ſurely ſet his foote
But on thoſe bowes that groweth lowe alwayes?
The little twigs are but unſtedfaſt ſtayes,
Yf they breake not, they bend with every blaſt:
Who truſts to them ſhall never ſtand full faſt.

The winde is great upon the higheſt hilles,
The quiet life is in the dale belowe;
Who treades on yſe ſhall ſlyde againſt their wills;
They want no cares that curious artes doe knowe.
Who lives at eaſe, and can content him ſo
Is perfect wife, and ſets us all to ſchoole:
Who hates this lore may well be calde a foole.

Shores Wife.

What greater griefe may come to any life
Then after sweete to taste the bitter sowre,
Or after peace to fall at warre and strife,
Or after mirth to have a cause to lowre?
Under such props false Fortune buildes her bowre;
On sodaine change her flittering frames be set,
Where is no way for to escape the net.

The hasty smart that Fortune sends in spite
Is harde to brooke where gladnes we embrace;
She threatens not, but sodainely doth smite;
Where joy is most there doth she sorrow place.
But sure I think this is too strange a case
For us to feele such griefe amid our game,
And know not why untill we tast the same.

As erst I sayde, my blisse was turnd to bale:
I had good cause to weepe and wring my hands,
And showe sad cheere with countenance full pale,
For I was brought in sorrowes wofull bands:
A pirry came and set my ship on sands.
What should I hyde, and colour care and noy?
King Edward dyde, in whome was all my joy.

And when the earth received had his corse,
And that in tombe this worthy prince was layde,
The world on me began to showe his force:
Of troubles then my part I long assayde;
For they of whome I never was affrayde
Undid me most, and wrought me such despite,
That they bereft me of my pleasure quite.

Brought bare and poore, and throwne in worldes disgrace,
Holds downe the head, that never casts up eye;
Cast out of court, condemned in every place,
Condemnd perforce at mercies foote must lye.
Hope is but small when we for mercie crye:
The bird halfe dead that hauke hath fast in foote;
Lay heade on blocke, where is no other boote.

The rowling stone that tumbleth downe the hill
Fynds none to stay the furie of his fall;
Once under foote for ever daunted still:
One cruell blowe strikes cleane away the ball.
Left once in lacke feeles alwayes want of will:
A conquerd mind must yeeld to every ill:
A weake poore soule, that Fortune doth forsake
In hard extreames, from world her leave may take.

From those that fall such as doe rise and run;
The sound with sicke doe seldome long abide,
Poore people passe (as shadowes in the sun)
Like feeble fish that needes must followe tyde.
Among the rich a beggar soone is spied.
When weake Shores wife had lost her staffe of stay,
The halt and blind went limping lame away.

The poore is pincht and pointed at in deed,
As baited bull were leading to the stake.
Wealth findes great helpe, want gets no friend at neede:
A plaged wight a booteles mone may make.
A naked foole in street for colde may quake;
But colde or hot, when mischiefes comes a roe,
As falles the lot the backe beares of the bloe.

Prefarment paft the world will foone forget :
The prefent time is daily gazd upon.
Yf merchant rich from wealth doe fall in debt,
Small count is made of his good fortune gon.
We feede on flefh, and fling away the bone :
Embrace the beft, and fet the world afide,
Becaufe faire flowers are made of in their pride.

You yonglings, nowe, that vaine delights leads on
To fell chaft life for lewd and light defires,
Poore gaine is gote when rich good name is gon ;
Foule blot and fhame lives under trimme attires.
World foone cafts of the hackney horfe it hiers,
And when bare nagge is ridden out of breath,
Tibbe is turnd lofe to feed on barren heath.

Of flowers a while men doe gay pofes make ;
The fent once paft, adue dry withered leaves.
Love lafts not long prickt up for pleafures fake,
Straw little worth when corne forfakes the fheaves ;
A painted poft the gazers eie deceives,
But when foule fauts are found that bleard the fight,
The account is gon of girlls or gugawes light.

Young pooppies play fmall feafon lafts, you fee,
Old appifh fportes are quickly out of grace,
Fond wanton games will foone forgotten be ;
As fowre as crabbe becomes the fweeteft face.
There needes no more be fpoken of this cafe :
All earthy joyes by tract of time decayes ;
Soone is the glafe runne out of our good dayes.

My fall and facte makes proofe of that is fpoke,
Tels world to much of fhadowes in the funne,
Duft blowne with winde, or fimple proofe of fmoake
That flies from fire, and faft throwe aire doth run :
It ends with woe that was with joy begun :
It turnes to teares that firft began with fport ;
At length long paine finds pleafure was but fhort.

As long as life remaind in Edwards breft,
Who was but I ? who had fuch friends at call ?
His body was no fooner put in cheft,
But well was he that could procure my fall.
His brother was mine enemy moft of all,
Protector then, whofe vice did ftill abound,
From ill to worfe, till death did him confound.

He falfely fainde that I of counfell was
To poyfon him, which thing I never meant ;
But he could fet thereon a face of braffe
To bring to paffe his lewde and falfe intent,
To fuch mifchiefe this tyrants heart was bent.
To God ne man he never ftood in awe,
For in his wrath he made his will a lawe.

Lord Haftings bloud for vengeaunce on him cryes,
And many moe that were to long to name ;
But moft of all, and in moft woefull wife,
I had good caufe this wretched man to blame.
Before the world I fuffered open fhame :
Where people were as thicke as is the fand,
I pennance tooke with taper in my hand.

Shores Wife.

Each eye did ſtare and looke me in the face;
As I paſt by the rumours on me ran,
But pacience then had lent me ſuch a grace,
My quiet lookes were praiſd of every man.
The ſhamefaſt bloud brought me ſuch collour than,
That thouſands ſayde, that ſawe my ſober cheere,
It is great ruth to ſee this woman heere.

But what prevayld the peoples pitie there?
This raging wolfe would ſpare no guiltles blood.
Oh wicked wombe, that ſuch ill fruit did beare!
Oh curſed earth that yeeldeth forth ſuch mud!
The hell conſume all things that did thee good,
The heavens ſhut their gates against thy ſpreete,
The world tread downe thy glory under feete!

I aſke of God a vengeance on thy bones.
Thy ſtinking corps corrupts the aire, I knowe:
Thy ſhamefull death no earthly wight bemones,
For in thy life thy workes were hated ſo,
That every man did wiſh thy overthroe;
Wherefore I may, though parciall nowe I am,
Curſe every cauſe whereof thy body came.

Woe worth the man that fathered ſuch a childe!
Woe worth the howre wherein thou waſt begate!
Woe worth the breſts that have the world begylde
To noriſh thee, that all the world did hate!
Woe worth the Gods that gave thee ſuch a fate
To live ſo long, that death deſervde ſo oft!
Woe worth the chance that ſet thee up aloft!

Woe worth the day, the time, the howre and all
When fubjects clapt the crowne on Richards head!
Woe worth the lordes that fat in fumptuous hall
To honour him that princes blood fo fhead!
Would God he had bin boyld in fcalding lead,
When he prefumde in brothers feat to fit,
Whofe wretched rage ruld all with wicked wit!

Ye princes all and rulers everechone,
In punifhment beware of hatreds yre:
Before yee fcourge, take heede, looke well thereon,
In wraths ill will if malice kindle fyre,
Your harts will burne in fuch a hote defyre,
That in thofe flames the fmoke fhall dim your fight,
Yee fhall forget to joyne your juftice right.

You fhould not judge till things be well defcernd,
Your charge is ftill to maintaine upright lawes:
In confcience rules you fhould be throwly lernd,
Where clemencie bids wrath and rafhnes paufe,
And further faith, ftrike not without a caufe:
And when yee fmite, doe it for juftice fake,
Then in good part ech man your fcourge will take.

If that fuch zeale had movd this tyrants mind
To make my plague a warning for the reft,
I had fmall caufe fuch fault in him to finde:
Such punifhment is ufed for the beft.
But by ill will and powre I was oppreft:
He fpoylde my goods and left me bare and poore,
And caufed me to beg from dore to dore.

Shores Wife.

What fall was this! to come from princes fare
To watch for crumes among the blind and lame!
When almes were delt, I had an hungry fhare,
Becaufe I knewe not how to afke for fhame;
Till force and neede had brought me in fuch frame,
Than ftarve I muft, or learne to beg an almes,
With booke in hand to fay S. Davids Pfalmes.

Where I was wont the golden chaines to weare,
A payre of beads about my necke was wound;
A linnen cloth was lapt about my heare,
A ragged gowne that trailed on the ground;
A difh that clapt and gave a heavie found,
A ftaying ftaffe, and wallet therewithall,
I bare about as witneffe of my fall.

The fall of leafe is nothing like the fpring:
Ech eye beholdes the rifing of the funne,
And men admire the favour of a king,
And from great ftates growne in difgrace they run.
Such fodaine claps ne wit nor will can fhun,
For when the ftoole is taken from our feete,
Full flat on floore the body falls in ftreete.

I had no houfe wherein to hide my head,
The open ftreete my lodging was perforce;
Full oft I went all hungry to my bed,
My flefh confumde, I looked like a corfe.
Yet in that plight who had on me remorfe?
O God! thou knowfte my friends forfooke me than;
Not one holpe me that fuccred many a man.

They frownd on me that fawnd on me before,
And fled from me that followed me full faſt;
They hated me by whome I ſet much ſtore,
They knewe full well my fortune did not laſt;
In every place I was condemnde and caſt.
To pleade my cauſe at bar it was no boote,
For every man did tread me under foote.

Thus long I livd, all weary of my life,
Till death approcht and rid me from that woe.
Example take by me, both maide and wife;
Beware, take heede, fall not to folly ſo;
A mirrour make by my great overthroe:
Defye the world and all his wanton wayes,
Beware by me that ſpent ſo ill her dayes.

T. Churchyard.

INTRODUCTION.

WITH the exception of one other of Dekker's productions (which the editor may hereafter reproduce in its original but neglected shape) there is, perhaps, no tract in our language which contains so many and such curious illustrations of the language, opinions, and manners of our ancestors as the tract here reprinted. It is, from beginning to end, a species of prose allegory, but in all places extremely intelligible; and it exposes unsparingly the frauds, abuses, and vices prevalent in the metropolis soon after the demise of Elizabeth: " the seven deadly sins of London" are all pourtrayed in their turn; and if anything incongruous appear in the details supplied by the author, it must be attributed to the peculiar form he has chosen for the display of the severity of his reproof.

The literary and dramatic allusions are very remarkable, especially as regards Shakespeare; and severe as are Dekker's reflections upon all classes, he intermixes no personal matter, and assails no individual delinquents. One passage near the end is peculiarly noticeable as fixing the date of the original appearance of a woodcut broadside, the existence of which, in a single copy, is known in our day, and which is valuable upon all accounts, but most of all, as an early specimen of politico-religious caricature.

We are probably to take Dekker's assertion, that his effusion was the *opus septem dierum*, as a statement of fact. He was generally a struggler against poverty; and we may presume that such was the case in 1606, and that Nathaniel Butter, the stationer, who was generally the patron of needy and speedy authors, offered, or advanced to Dekker a sum of money, on condition that he produced his work by a certain day: the printer was Edward Allde, who was often employed on an emergency; and his battered type bears witness of the service it had gone through, while inaccuracies and bad workmanship shew the haste with which the piece was composed by the typographer, as well as written by the author. Considering it as only a week's labour, " The Seven Deadly Sins of London" is proof of the ready resources of Dekker, as well of his industry, in a very original species of composition. We are aware of nothing precisely like it in our language, either for invention, or for accuracy and vivacity of description. The aim of the writer was not, in this instance, to display his poetical powers; and he addressed himself to a class of readers, including the apprentices of the metropolis, who would be little able to estimate the merit of a work of higher genius, but would be ready purchasers of a production like that here reproduced. It is of the greatest rarity.

J. P. C.

THE
SEVEN DEADLY
Sinnes of London:

DRAWNE IN SEVEN SEVERALL COACHES THROUGH
THE SEVEN SEVERALL GATES OF
THE CITTIE

Bringing the Plague with them.

Opus septem Dierum.

THO: DEKKER.

AT LONDON

Printed by E. A. for Nathaniel Butter, and are
to be folde at his shop neere Saint
Austens gate.
1606.

To the worshipfull and very worthy
Gentleman Henry Fermor Efquire,
Clarke of the Peace for the
Countie of Middlefex.

I AM fory (deare fir) that in a time (fo abundant with wit) I fhold fend unto you no better fruit then the fins of a city: but they are not common (for they were never gathered till this yeare) and therefore I fend them for a rarity. Yet now I remember my felfe, they are not the finnes of a citie, but onely the picture of them; and a drollerie (or Dutch peece of Lantfkop) may fometimes bread in the beholders eye as much delectation as the beft and moft curious mafterpeece excellent in that art. Bookes being fent abroad after they are begotten into the world, as this of mine is, are in the nature of orphans; but being received into a gardianfhip (as I make no doubt but this fhall) they come into the happie ftate of adopted children. That office muft now be yours, and you neede not bee afhamed of it, for kings have beene glad to do them honour, that have beftowed such a never-dying honour uppon them. The benefite you fhall receive is this, that you fee the building up of a tombe (in your life time) wherein you are fure to lie, as that you cannot bee forgotten, and you read that very epitaph that fhal ftand over you, which by no envie can bee defaced, nor by any time worne out. I have made choife of you alone, to bee the onely patron to thefe my labours; by which word (onely) I chalenge to my felfe a kinde of dignitie; for there hath beene a generation of a fort of ftrange fellowes (and I thinke the race is not yet eaten out) who when a booke (of their owne) hath bin borne in the lawfull matrimonie of learning and induftrie, have bafely compelled it either, like a baftard, to call a great many father (and to goe under all their names) or elfe (like a common fellow at a feffions) to put himfelfe (as they tearme it) upon twelve godfathers. In which cafe (contrarie to all law) the foreman is moft dishonoured. That art of *fkeldring* I ftudie not: I ftand upon ftronger bases. The current of a mans reputation being divided into fo manie rivolets muft needes grow weake. If you give intertainment to this in your beft affection, you will binde me (one day) to heighten your name, when by fome more worthy columne (by me to be erected) I fhall confecrate that and your felfe to an everlafting and facred memorie.

Moft affectionately defirous to be yours:

THO. DEKKER.

READER,

IT is an ordinarie cuftome (for us that are bookifh) to have a bout with thee, after wee have done with a patron, as for fchollers (in the noble fcience) to play at the woodden rapier and dagger, at the ende of a maifters prize. In doing which we know not upon what fpeeding points wee runne, for you (that are readers) are the moft defperate and fowleft players in the world: you will ftrike when a mans backe is toward you, and kill him (if you could for fhame) when he lies under your feete. You are able (if you have the tokens of deadly ignorance and boldnes at one time upon you) to breede more infection in Pauls Church-yard then all the bodies that were buried there in the Plague-time, if they had beene left ftill above ground. You ftand fomtimes at a ftationers ftal, looking fcurvily (like mules champing upon thiftles) on the face of a new booke, bee it never fo worthy, and goe (as il favouredly) mewing away. But what get you by it? The bookefeller ever after, when you paffe by, pinnes on your backes the badge of fooles to make you be laught to fcorne, or of fillie carpers to make you be pittied. Conradus Gesner never writ of the nature of fuch ftrange beafts as you are; for where as we call you *Lectores*, readers, you turne your felves into *Lictores*, executioners and tormenters. I wold not have him that writes better than I to read this, nor him that cannot do fo well to raile; or if hee cannot chufe but raile, let him doe it to my face: otherwife (to me being abfent) it is done cowardly; for *Leonem mortuum mordent etiam catuli:* cats dare fcratch lions by the face when they lie dead, and none but colliers will threaten a Lord Maior when they are farre enough from the cittie. I have laide no blockes in thy way: if thou findeft

ftrawes (*Vade, vale*) *cave*

ne titubes.

The names of the Actors in this old Enterlude of Iniquitie.

1 Politike Bankeruptifme	
2 Lying	
3 Candle-light	Seven may eafily play
4 Sloth	this, but not without a
5 Apifhneffe	Divell.
6 Shaving	
7 Crueltie	

THE INDUCTION TO THE BOOKE.

I FINDE it written in that Booke where no untruthes can be read; in that Booke whofe leaves shall outlaft sheetes of braffe, and whofe lines leade to eternity; yea, even in that Booke that was pend by the beft Author of the beft wifedome, allowed by a Deity, licenfed by the Omnipotent and published (in all languages to all nations) by the greateft, trueft and onely Divine, thus I finde it written: that for finne angels were throwne out of heaven; for finne the firft man that ever was made was made an outcaft: he was driven out of his living that was left unto him by his Creator. It was a goodlier living than the inheritance of Princes: he loft Paradice by it (he loft his houfe of pleafure): hee loft Eden by it, a garden where Winter could never have nipt him with cold, nor Summer have fcorcht him with heate. He had there all fruits growing to delight his tafte, all flowers flourishing to allure his eye, all birds finging to content his eare: he had more than he could defire; yet becaufe he defired more than was fit for him, he loft all. For finne all thofe buildings which the great workemafter of the world had in fixe dayes rayfed were fwallowed at the firft by waters, and shall at laft be confumed in fire. How many families hath this leviathan devoured! how many citties! how many kingdoms!

Let us awhile leave the kingdomes, and enter into citties:

Sodom and Gomorrah were burnt to the ground with brimſtone that dropt in flakes from heaven: a hot and dreadfull vengeance. Jeruſalem hath not a ſtone left upon another of her firſt glorious foundation: a heavy and fearfull downefall. Jeruſalem, that was Gods owne dwellinghouſe: the ſchoole where thoſe Hebrew lectures, which he himſelfe read, were taught: the very nurſery where the Prince of Heaven was brought up: that Jeruſalem whoſe rulers were princes, and whoſe citizens were like the ſonnes of kings: whoſe temples were paved with gold, and whoſe houſes ſtood like rowes of tall cedars: that Jeruſalem is now a dezert: it is unhallowed and untrodden: no monument is left to shew it was a citty, but onely the memoriall of the Jewes hard-hartednes in making away their Saviour. It is now a place for barbarous Turks, and poore deſpiſed Grecians: it is rather now (for the abominations committed in it) no place at all.

Let us hoyſt up more ſayles and lanch into other ſeas, till we come in ken of our owne countrey. Antwerp (the eldeſt daughter of Brabant) hath falne in her pride; the citties of rich Burgundy in theyr greatnes; thoſe ſeventeene Dutch virgins of Belgia (that had kingdomes to theyr dowries, and were worthy to be courted by nations) are now no more virgins: the ſouldier hath deflowred them, and robd them of theyr mayden honor: warre hath ſtill uſe of their noble bodyes, and diſcovereth theyr nakednes like proſtituted ſtrumpets. Famine hath dryed up the freſh bloud in theyr cheekes, whilſt the peſtilence digd up theyr fields, and turned them into graves. Neither have theſe puniſhments bin layd upon them onely, for bloud hath bin alſo drawne of their very next neighbours. France lyes yet panting under the blowes which her owne children have given her. Thirty yeres together fuffred fhe her bowels to be torne out by thofe that were bred within them: fhe was full of princes, and faw them lye mangled at her feete: fhe was full of people and faw in one night a hundred thoufand maffacred in her ftreetes: her kings were eaten up by civill warres, and her fubjects by fire and famine. O gallant monarchy! what hard fate hadft thou, that when none were left to conquer thee, thou fhouldft triumph over thy felfe. Thou haft wynes flowing in thy veynes, but thou madeft thy felfe druncke with thine owne bloud. The Englifh, the Dutch, and the Spanifh ftoode aloofe and gave ayme, whilft thou fhotft arrowes upright that fell upon thine owne head, and wounded thee to death. Wouldft thou (and the reft) know the reafon why your bones have bin bruzed with rods of iron? It was becaufe you have rifen in arch-rebellion againft the Supremeft Soveraigne: you have bin traytors to your Lord, the King of heaven and earth, and have armed your felves to fight againft the Holy Land. Can the father of the world meafure out his love fo unequally that one people (like to a mans yongeft child) fhould be more made of than all the reft, being more unruly than the reft?

O London! thou art great in glory, and envied for thy greatnes: thy towers, thy temples and thy pinnacles ftand upon thy head like borders of fine gold, thy waters like frindges of filver hang at the hemmes of thy garments. Thou art the goodlieft of thy neighbors, but the proudeft, the welthieft but the moft wanton. Thou haft all things in thee to make thee faireft, and all things in thee to make thee fouleft; for thou art attir'de like a bride, drawing all that looke upon thee to be in love with thee, but there is much harlot in thine eyes. Thou fitſt in thy gates heated with wines, and in thy chambers with luſt. What miſeries have of late overtaken thee! yet (like a foole that laughs when hee is putting on fetters) thou haſt bin merry in height of thy misfortunes. She (that for almoſt halfe a hundred of yeeres) of thy nurſe became thy mother, and layd thee in her boſome, whoſe head was full of cares for thee, whilſt thine ſlept upon ſofter pillowes than downe : ſhe that wore thee always on her breſt as the richeſt jewell in her kingdome ; who had continually her eye upon thee, and her heart with thee; whoſe chaſte hand clothed thy rulers in ſcarlet, and thy inhabitants in roabes of peace, even ſhe was taken from thee, when thou wert moſt in feare to loſe her ; when thou didſt tremble (as at an earth-quake) to thinke that bloud ſhould runne in thy channels, that the canon ſhould make way through port-cullifes, and fire rifle thy wealthy houſes, then, even then, wert thou left full of teares, and becamſt an orphan. But, behold! thou hadſt not ſat many howres on the banks of ſorrow, but thou hadſt a loving father that adopted thee to be his owne : thy mourning turnd preſently to gladnes, thy terrors into triumphs. Yet, left this fulneſſe of joy ſhould beget in thee a wantonnes, and to try how wiſely thou couldſt take up affliction, ſick-nes was ſent to breathe her unholſome ayres into thy noſthrils, ſo that thou, that wert before the only gallant and minion of the world, hadſt in a ſhort time more diſeaſes (then a common harlot hath) hanging upon thee : thou ſuddenly becamſt the by-talke of neighbors, the ſcorne and contempt of nations.

[sidenote: Qu. Elizabeths death.]

[sidenote: King James his coronation.]

The Induction to the Booke.

Heere could I make thee weepe thy felfe away into waters by calling backe thofe fad and difmall houres wherein thou confumedft almoft to nothing with fhrikes and lamentations in that *Wonderfull Yeere* when thefe miferable calamities entred in at thy gates, flaying 30,000 and more, as thou heldft them in thine armes; but they are frefh in thy memory, and the ftory of them (but halfe read over) would ftrike fo coldly to thy heart, and lay fuch heavy forrow upon mine *(Namque animus meminiffe horret, luctuque refugit)* that I will not be thine and my owne tormentor with the memory of them. How quickly, notwithftanding, didft thou forget that beating! The wrath of him that fmot thee was no fooner (in meere pitty of thy ftripes) appeafed, but howrely (againe) thou wert in the company of evill doers, even before thou couldft finde leyfure to afke him forgivenes.

A booke fo called, written by the author, defcribing the horror of the Plague in 1602, when there dyed 30578 of that difeafe.

Ever fince that time hath hee winckt at thy errors, and fuffred thee (though now thou art growne old, and lookeft very ancient) to goe on ftill in the follyes of thy youth: he hath ten-fold reftor'de thy loft fonnes and daughters, and fuch fweete lively frefh colours hath he put upon thy cheekes, that kings have come to behold thee, and princes to delight théir eyes with thy bewty. None of all thefe favours (for all this) can draw thee from thy wickednes. Graces have powrd downe out of heaven uppon thee and thou art rich in all things, faving in goodnes; fo that now once againe hath he gone about (and but gone about) to call thee to the dreadfull barre of his judgement. And no marvaile; for whereas other citties (as glorious as thy felfe)

King of England and Chriftierne King of Denmarke.

and other people (as deare unto him as thine) have in his indignation bin quite taken from the face of the earth, for some one peculiar sinne, what hope hast thou to grow up still in the pride of thy strength, gallantnes and health, having seven deadly and detestable sinnes lying night by night by thy lascivious sides?

O thou beawtifullest daughter of two united monarchies! from thy womb received I my being, from thy brests my nourishment; yet give me leave to tell thee that thou hast seven divels within thee, and till they be cleane cast out the arrowes of pestilence will fall upon thee by day, and the hand of the invader strike thee by night. The sunne will shine, but will not be a comfort to thee, and the moone looke pale with anger when she gives thee light. Thy lovers will disdayne to court thee: thy temples will no more send out divine oracles: Justice will take her flight and dwell else-where; and that desolation, which now for three yeeres together hath hovered round about thee, will at last enter, and turne thy gardens of pleasure into church-yards, thy fields that served thee for walks into Golgotha, and thy hye built houses into heapes of dead mens sculs. I call him to witnes, who is all truth; I call the cittizens of heaven to witnes, who are all spotlesse, that I slander thee not in saying thou nourisheft seven serpents at thy brests that will destroy thee. Let all thy magistrates and thy officers speake for me: let strangers that have but seene thy behaviour be my judges: let all that are gathered under thy wings, and those that sleepe in thy bosome give their verdict upon me: yea, try me (as thy brabblings are) by all thy petit and graund jurors, and if I belye thee, let my country (when I expire) deny me her common blessing, buriall. Lift up therefore thy head (thou mother of fo many people): awaken out of thy dead and dangerous flumbers, and with a full and fearleffe eye behold thofe feven monfters that with extended jawes gape to fwallow up thy memory; for I will into fo large a field fingle every one of them, that thou and all the world fhall fee their uglineffe, for by feeing them thou mayft avoyd them, and by avoyding them be the happieft and moft renowned of citties.

POLITICK BANKRUPTISME
OR
THE FIRST DAYES TRIUMPH OF THE FIRST SINNE.

IT is a cuſtome in all countries, when great perſonages are to be entertained, to have great preparations made for them; and becauſe London diſdaines to come ſhort of any city, either in magnificence, ſtate or expences on ſuch an occaſion, ſolemne order was ſet downe, and ſeven ſeverall ſolemne dayes were appointed to receive theſe ſeven potentates; for they carry the names of princes on the earth, and wherefoe're they inhabit, in a ſhort time are they lords of great dominions.

The firſt dayes triumphs were ſpent in meeting and conducting Politick Bankruptiſme into the freedome; to receive whom the maſter, the keepers and all the priſoners of Ludgate, in their beſt clothes, ſtood moſt officiouſly readie: for at that gate his Deadlineſſe challenges a kind of prerogative by the cuſtome of the citie, and there loves he moſt to be let in. The thing they ſtood upon was a ſcaffold erected for the purpoſe, ſtuck round about with a few greene boughes (like an alehouſe booth at a fayre) and covered with two or three threed-bare carpets (for priſoners have no better) to hide the unhandſomenes of the carpenters worke: the boughes with the very ſtrong breath that was preſt out of

The maner how Bank-ruptiſme is en-tertained, and at what gate.

the vulgar, withered and like Autumnian leaves dropt to the ground, which made the broken Gentleman to haften his progreffe the more, and the rather, becaufe Lud and his two fonnes ftood in a very cold place, waiting for his comming. Being under the gate there ftood one armed with an extemporall fpeech to give him the onfet of his welcome. It was not (I would you fhould well know) the clarke of a country parifh, or the fchoolemafter of a corporate towne, that every yeere has a faying to Mafter Maior; but it was a bird pickt out of purpofe (amongft the Ludgathians) that had the bafeft and lowdeft voice, and was able in Terme time, for a throat, to give any prifoner great ods for the boxe at the grate.

This organ-pipe was tunde to rore for the reft, who with a hye found and glib delivery made an encomiaftick paradoxicall oration in praife of a prifon, proving that captivity was the only bleffing that could happen to man, and that a Politick Bankrupt (becaufe he makes himfelfe for ever by his owne wit) is able to live in any common wealth, and deferves to go up the ladder of promotion, when five hundred fhallow-pated fellowes fhall be turnd off. The poore orator having made up his mouth, Bankruptifme gave him very good words and a handful or two of thanks, vowing he would ever live in his debt. At which all the prifoners, rending the ayre with fhouts, the key was turnd, and up (in ftate) was he led into King Luds houfe of Bondage, to furvey the building, and to take poffeffion of the lodgings; where he no fooner entred, but a lufty peale of welcomes was fhot out of kannes in ftead of canons, and though the powder was exceeding wet, yet off they went thick and threefold. The day was

<small>Solamen mife-
ris focios habu-
iffe doloris.</small>

proclaymed holiday in all the wardes; every prifoner fwore if he would ftay amongft them, they would take no order about their debts, becaufe they would lye by it too; and for that purpofe fwarmd about him like bees about comfit-makers, and were drunke according to all the learned rules of Drunkennes, as *Upfy-freeze, Crambo, Parmizant,* etc., the pimples of this ranck and full-humord joy rifing thus in their faces, becaufe they all knew that, though he him-felfe was broken, the linings of his bags were whole; and though he had no confcience (but a crackt one) yet he had crownes that were found. None of all thefe hookes could faften him to them: he was (like their clocks) to ftrike in more places than one, and though he knew many citizens hated him, and that if he were encountred by fome of them, it might coft him deare, yet under fo good a protec-tion did he go, (as he faid) becaufe he owed no ill will even to thofe that moft fought his undoing; and therefore tooke his leave of the houfe with promife to be with them or fend to them once every quarter at the leaft. So that now, by his wife inftructions, if a puny were there amongft them, he
<small>Mifery makes men cunning.</small> might learne more cafes and more quiddits in law within feven dayes, than he does at his Inne in fourteene moneths.

The Politician, beeing thus got into the citie, caries him-felf fo difcreetly that he fteales into the hearts of many. In words is he circumfpect, in lookes grave, in attire civill, <small>His qualities.</small> in diet temperate, in company affable, in his affaires ferious; and fo cunningly dooes he lay on thefe colours, that in the end he is welcome to, and familiar with the beft. So that now there is not any one of all the twelve Companies in which (at one time or other) there are not thofe that have forfaken their owne Hall to be free of his: yea, fome of your beft fhop-keepers hath he inticed to fhut themfelves up from the cares and bufinefs of the world to live in private life; nay, there is not any great and famous ftreete in the city wherein there hath not (or now doth not) dwell fome one or other that hold the points of his religion. For you muft underftand that the Politick Bankrupt is a harpy that lookes fmoothly, a hyena that enchants fubtilly, a mermaid that fings fweetly, and a cameleon that can put himfelfe into all colours. Sometimes hee's a Puritane; he fweares by nothing but "indeede," or rather does not fweare at all, and wrapping his crafty ferpent's body in the cloake of religion, he does thofe acts that would become none but the Divell. Sometimes hee's a Proteftant and deales juftly with all men till he fee his time, but in the end he turnes Turke. Becaufe you fhall beleeve me, I will give you his length by the fcale, and anatomize his body from head to foote. Heere it is.

His difguifes.

Whether he be a tradefman, or a marchant when he firft fets himfelfe up, and feekes to get the world into his hands (yet not to go out of the City), or firft talks of countries he never faw (upon the Change), he will be fure to keepe his dayes of payments more truly than lawyers keepe their termes, or than executors keepe the laft lawes that the dead injoyned them to, which even infidels themfelves will not violate: his hand goes to his head to his meaneft cuftomer (to expreffe his humilitie): he is up earlier then a fargeant, and downe later then a conftable to proclaime his thrift. By fuch artificiall wheeles as thefe he winds himfelfe up into the height of rich mens favors, till he grow rich himfelfe, and when he fees that they dare

His policy.

build on his credit, knowing the ground to be good, he takes upon him the condition of an affe to any man that will loade him with gold, and ufeth his credit like a fhip freighted with all forts of merchandize by ventrous pilots; for after he hath gotten into his hands fo much of other mens goods or money as will fill him to the upper deck, away he fayles with it, and politickly runnes himfelfe on ground to make the world beleeve he had fufferd fhip-wrack. Then flyes he out like an Irifh rebell, and keepes aloofe hiding his head when he cannot hide his fhame; and though he have fethers on his back puld from fundry birds, yet to himfelfe is he more wretched then the cuckoo in winter, that dares not be feene. The troupes of honeft citizens (his creditors) with whom he hath broken league and hath thus defyed, mufter themfelves together, and proclaime open warre: their bands confift of tall yeomen that ferve on foot, commanded by certaine fargeants of their bands, who for leading of men are knowne to be of more experience than the beft Low-countrey Captaines. In ambufcado do thefe lye day and night, to cut off this enemy to the City, if he dare but come downe. But the Politick Bankrupt barricadoing his fconce with double locks, treble dores, invincible bolts and pieces of timber, four or five ftoryes hye, victuals himfelfe for a moneth or fo, and then, in the dead of the night, marches up higher into the country with bag and baggage. Parlies then are fummond, compofitions offred, a truce is fometimes taken for three or four yeeres, or (which is more common) a dis-honorable peace (feeing no other remedy) is on both fides concluded, he (like the States) being the only gayner by fuch civill warres, whilft the citizen that is the lender is the loſer: *Nam crimine ab uno diſce omnes:* looke how much he ſnatche from one mans ſheafe hee gleanes from every one, if they bee a hundred.

The victory being thus gotten by baſenes and trechery, back comes he marching with ſpred colours againe to the City, advances in the open ſtreete as he did before, ſels the goods of his neighbor before his face without bluſhing: he jets up and downe in his ſilks woven out of other mens ſtocks, feeds deliciouſly upon other mens purſes, rides on his ten pound geldings in other mens ſaddles, and is now a new man made out of wax; that's to ſay, out of thoſe bonds whoſe ſeales he moſt diſhoneſtly hath canceld. O velvet garded theeves! O yea-and-by-nay cheaters! O grave and right worſhipfull couzeners!

What wretchednes is it by ſuch ſteps to clime to a counterfetted happines! So to be made for ever is to be utterly undone for ever: ſo for a man to ſave him ſelfe is to venture his own damnation; like thoſe that laboring by all meanes to eſcape ſhipwrack, do afterwards deſperatly drown themſelves. But, alas! how rotten at the bottom are buildings thus raiſd! How ſoone do ſuch leaſes grow out of date! The third houſe to them is never heard of. What ſlaves then doth mony (ſo purchaſt) make of thoſe who by ſuch wayes thinke to find out perfect freedome! But they are moſt truly miſerable in midſt of their joyes; for their neighbors ſcorne them, ſtrangers point at them, good men neglect them; the rich man will no more truſt them; the begger in his rags upbraydes them. Yet, if this were all, this all were nothing. O thou that on thy pillow (lyke a ſpider in his loome) weaveſt miſchevous nets, beating thy braynes, how by caſting downe others to raiſe up thy ſelfe!

Then Politick Bankrupt, poore rich man, then ill-painted foole, when thou art to lye in thy laſt inne (thy loathſome grave) how heavy a loade will thy wealth bee to thy weake corrupted conſcience! Thoſe heapes of ſilver, in telling of which thou haſt worne out thy finger's ends, will be a paſſing bell tolling in thine eare, and calling thee to a fearefull audit. Thou canſt not diſpoſe of thy riches, but the naming of every parcell will ſtrike to thy heart, worſe then the pangs of thy departure: thy laſt will at the laſt day will be an inditement to caſt thee; for thou art guilty of offending thoſe two lawes (enaƈted in the Upper Houſe of Heaven) which direƈtly forbid thee to ſteale, or to covet thy neighbors goods.

But this is not all neither; for thou lyeſt on thy bed of death, and art not cared for: thou goeſt out of the world, and are not lamented: thou art put into the laſt linen that ever thou ſhalt weare (thy winding ſheete) with reproch, and art ſent into thy grave with curſes: he that makes thy funerall ſermon dares not ſpeake well of thee, becauſe he is aſhamed to belye the dead; and upon ſo hatefull a fyle doeſt thou hang the records of thy life, that even when the wormes have peckt thee to the bare bones, thoſe that goe over thee will ſet upon thee no epitaph but this—*Here lyes a knave.*

Alack! this is not the worſt neither: thy wife being in the heate of her youth, in the pride of her beawty, and in all the bravery of a rich London widow, flyes from her neſt (where ſhe was thus fledg'd before her time) the City, to ſhake off the imputation of a bankrupts wife, and perhaps marries with ſome gallant: thy bags then are emptied to hold him up in riots: thoſe hundreds which thou ſubtilly tookſt up upon thy bonds do ſinfully ſerve him to pay taverne bills, and what by knavery thou gotſt from honeſt men is as villanouſly ſpent upon pandars and whores. Thy widow, being thus brought to a low ebbe, grows deſperat, curſes her birth, her life, her fortunes; yea, perhaps, curſes thee when thou art in thy everlaſting ſleepe, her conſcience perſwading ſtrongly that ſhe is puniſhed from above for thy faults; and being poore, friendleſſe, comfortleſſe, ſhe findes no meanes to raiſe her ſelfe but by *falling*, and therefore growes to be a common woman. Doth not the thought of this torment thee? She lives baſely by the abuſe of that body to maintaine which in coſtly garments thou didſt wrong to thine owne ſoule: nay, more to afflict thee, thy children are ready to beg their bread in that very place where the father hath ſat at his dore in purple, and at his boord like Dives, ſurfeting on thoſe diſhes which were earned by the ſweat of other men browes. The infortunate marchant, whoſe eſtate is ſwallowed up by the mercileſſe ſeas, and the provident tradeſman, whom riotous ſervants at home, or hard-harted debtors abroad undermine and overthrow, blotting them with the name of bankrupts, deſerve to be pittied and relieved, when thou that haſt cozend even thine owne brother of his birth-right, art laught at, and not remembred but in ſcorne when thou art plagued in thy generation.

Be wiſe, therefore, you grave and wealthy cittizens; play with theſe whales of the ſea, till you eſcape them that are devourers of your merchants: hunt theſe Engliſh wolves to the death, and rid the land of them; for theſe are the rats that eate up the proviſion of the people: theſe are the grashoppers of Egypt, that ſpoyle the corne-fields of the husbandman, and the rich mans vineyards : they will have poore Naboths piece of ground from him, though they eate a piece of his heart for it. Thefe are indeede (and none but thefe) the Forreners that live without the freedome of your city better than you within it : they live without the freedome of honefty, of confcience and of Chriftianitie. Ten dicing-houfes cheate not yong gentlemen of fo much mony in a yeare as thefe do you in a moneth. The theefe that dyes at Tyburne for a robbery is not halfe fo dangerous a weede in a common-wealth as the Politick Bankrupt: I would there were a Derick to hang him up too!

The Ruffians have an excellent cuftome : they beate them on the fhinnes that have mony and will not pay their debts : if that law were well cudgeld from thence into England, barbar-furgeons might in a few yeeres build up a hall for their Company larger then Powles, only with the cure of Bankrupt broken-fhinnes.

I would faine fee a prize fet up, that the welted ufurer and the Politick Bankrupt might rayle one againft another for it : ô, it would beget a riming comedy ! The challenge of the Germayne againft all the mafters of the Noble Science would not bring in a quarter of the money ; for there is not halfe fo much love betweene the iron and the loadftone, as there is mortall hate betweene thofe two furies. The ufurer lives by the lechery of mony, and is bawd to his owne bags, taking a fee that they may ingender. The Politick Bankrupt lives by the gelding of bags of filver. The ufurer puts out a hundred pound to breede, and lets it run in a good pafture (thats to fay, in the lands that are mortgag'd for it) till it grow great with foale, and bring forth ten pound more. But the Politick Bankrupt playes the alchimift, and having taken a hundred pound to multiply it, he keepes a puffing and a blowing, as if he would fetch the philofophers ftone out of it, yet melts your hundred pound fo long in his crufibles, till at length he either melt it cleane away, or (at the leaft) makes him that lends it thinke good, if every hundred bring him home five with principall and intereft.

You may behold now in this perfpective piece which I have drawne before you, how deadly and dangerous an enemy to the ftate this Politick Bankrupt hath bin, and ftill is. It hath bin long enough in the Citty, and, for any thing I fee, makes no great hafte to get out. His triumphs have bin great, his entertainment rich and magnificent: he purpofes to lye here as Lucifers Legiar: let him therefore alone in his lodging (in what part of the Citty foever it be) toffed and turmoyled with godleffe flumbers, and let us take up a ftanding neere fome other gate to behold the entrance of the Second Sinne. But before you go, looke upon the chariot that this Firft is drawne in, and take fpeciall note of all his attendants.

The habit, the qualities and the complexion of this embaffador fent from hell are fet downe before. He rides in a chariot drawne upon three wheeles, that run fafteft away when they beare the greateft loades. The bewty of the chariot is all in-layd work, cunningly and artificially wrought, but yet fo ftrangely, and of fo many feverall-fafhioned pieces (none like another) that a found wit would miftruft they had bin ftolne from fondry worke-men. By this prowd counterfet ran two pages; on the left fide Confcience, raggedly attirde, ill-fac'd, ill-coloured and misfhapen in body. On the right fide runs Beggery, who, if he out-live him, goes to ferve his children. Hipocrify drives the chariot, having a couple of fat well-coloured and lufty coach-horfes to the eye, cald Covetoufnes and Cofenage, but full of difeafes, and rotten about the heart. Behind him follow a crowd of tradefmen and merchants, every one of them holding either a fhop-booke or an obligation in his hand, their fervants, wives and children ftrawing the way before him with curfes; but he carelefly runnes over the one, and out-rides the other; at the tayle of whom (like the pioners of an army) march troop-wife, and without any drum ftruck up, becaufe the leader can abide no noife, a company of old expert farjeants, bold yeomen, hungry baylifs, and other brave martiall men, who, becaufe (like the Switzers) they are well payd, are ftill in action, and oftentimes have the enemy in execution, following the heeles of this citty-conqueror fo clofe, not for any love they owe him, but only (as all thofe that follow great men do) to get mony by him. We will leave them lying in ambufh, or holding their courts of gard, and take a mufter of our next regiment.

2. LYING

OR

THE SECOND DAYES TRIUMPH.

When it came to the eares of the finfull Synagogue how the rich Jew of London (Barabbas Bankruptifme), their brother, was receyved into the Citty, and what a lufty reveler he was become, the reft of the fame progeny (being 6 in number) vowd to ride thither in their greateft ftate, and that every one fhould challenge to himfelfe (if he could enter) a feverall day of Tryumph, for fo he might doe by their owne cuftomes. Another, therefore, of the broode being prefently aptly accouftred and armed *cap-a-pe* with all furniture fit for fuch an invader, fets forward the very next morning, and arriv'de at one of the gates before any of the porters eyes were unglewd. To knocke hee thought it no policy, becaufe fuch fellowes are commonly moft churlifh when they are moft intreated, and are key-cold in their comming downe to ftrangers, except they be brybed: to ftay there with fuch a confufion of faces round about him, till light fhould betray him, might call his arrivall, being ftrange and hidden, into queftion: befides he durft not fend any fpy he had to liften what newes went amongft the people, and whether any preparation were made for him, or that they did expect his approche; becaufe indeede there was not any one of the damned crewe that followed his tayle whom he durft truft for a true word. He refolves, therefore, to make his entrance not by the fword, but by fome fleyght, what ftorme or fayre weather foever fhould happen.

And for that purpofe taking afunder his charriot (for it ftood altogether like a Germane clock, or an Englifh jack or turne-fpit upon fkrewes and vices) he fcatters his troops upon the fields and hye-way into fmall companies, as if they had bene Irifh beggers, till at laft efpying certayne colliers with carts moft finfully loaden for the Citty, and behind them certayne light country horfe-women ryding to the markets, hee mingled his foote-men carelefly amongft thefe, and by this ftratagem of coales bravely thorow Moore-gate got within the walles; where marching not like

a plodding grafyer with his droves before him, but like
a Citty-captayne with a company (as pert as taylours at
a wedding) clofe at his heeles (becaufe nowe they knewe
they were out of feare) he mufters together all the hackney-
men and horfe-courfers in and about Colman-ftreete.

No fooner had thefe fonnes and heyres unto horfe-fhooes
got him into their eyes, but they wept for joy to behold
him; yet, in the ende, putting up their teares into bottles
of hay, which they held under their armes, and wyping
their flubberd cheekes with wifpes of cleane ftrawe (pro-
vyded for the nonce) they harneffed the Grand Signiors
caroach, mounted his cavallery upon curtals, and fo fent
him moft pompoufly (like a new elected Dutch burgo-
mafter) into the citty.

He was lookt upon ftrangely by all whom he met, for at
the firft few or none knew him, few followed him, few bid
him welcome. But after hee had fpent heere a very little
peece of time, after it was voyc'd that Monfieur Mendax
came to dwell amongft them, and had brought with him
all forts of politick falfhood and lying, what a number of
men, women and children fell prefently in love with him!
There was of every trade in the citty, and of every profef-
fion fome that inftantly were dealers with him: for you
muft note that in a ftate fo multitudinous, where fo many
flocks of people muft be fed, it is impossible to have fome
trades to ftand, if they fhould not lye.

How quickly after the art of lying was once publiquely
profeft were falfe weights and falfe meafures invented!
And they have not fince done as much hurt to the inhabitants of citties as the invention of gunnes hath done to
their walles; for though a lye have but fhort legs (like a
dwarfes) yet it goes farre in a little time, *Et crefcit eundo*,

and at laſt prooves a tall fellow: the reaſon is that truth hath ever but one father, but lyes are a thouſand mens baſtards, and are begotten every where.

Looke up then (thou thy countryes darling) and behold what a develiſh inmate thou haſt intertained. The genealogy of truth is well knowne, for he was borne in heaven and dwels in heaven. Falſhood, then, and lying must of neceſſity come out of that hot country of hell from the line of devils; for thoſe two are as oppoſite as light and darknes. What an ungracious generation wilt thou mingle with thine, if thou draw not *this* from thee! What a number of unhappy and curſed children will be left upon thy hand! for Lying is father of Falſhood, and grandſire to Perjury. Frawd (with two faces) is his daughter, a very monſter: Treaſon (with haires like ſnakes) is his kinſeman, a very fury. How art thou incloſ'd with danger! The lye firſt deceives thee, and to ſhoote the deceit off cleanly, an oath (like an arrow) is drawne to the head, and that hits the marke. If a lye, after it is molded, be not ſmooth enough, there is no inſtrument to burniſh it but an oath. Swearing gives it cullor and a bright complexion: ſo that oathes are crutches upon which lyes (like lame ſoldiers) go and neede no other paſport. Little oathes are able to beare up great lyes; but great lyes are able to beate downe great families; for oathes are wounds that a man ſtabs into himſelfe; yea, they are burning words that confume thoſe who kindle them.

What fooles, then, are thy buyers and ſellers to be abuſed by ſuch hell hounds! Swearing and forſwearing put into their hands, perhaps, the gaines of a little ſilver, but like thoſe pieces which Judas received they are their deſtruction. Welth so gotten is like a tree set in the depth of winter: it prospers not.

But is it possible (thou leader of so great a kingdome) that heretofore so many bonfires of mens bodies should be made before thee in the good quarrell of truth, and that now thou shouldst take part with her enemy? Have so many triple-pointed darts of treason bin shot at the heads of thy princes, because they would not take truth out of thy temples, and art thou now in league with false witches that would kill thee? Thou art no traveler; the habit of lying, therefore, will not become thee: cast it off.

He that gives a soldier the lye lookes to receive the stab, but what danger does he run upon that gives a whole city the lye? Yet must I venture to give it thee. Let me tell thee, then, that thou doest lye with pride, and though thou art not so gawdy, yet art thou more costly in attiring thy selfe than the court, because Pride is the Queene of Sinnes: thou hast chosen her to be thy concubine, and hast begotten many daughters upon her body, as Vainglory, Curiosity, Disobedience, Opinion, Disdaine, &c. Pride, by thy lying with her, is growne impudent: she is now a common harlot, and every one hath use of her body. The Taylor call her his lemman: he hath often got her great with child of Phantasticallity and Fashions, who no sooner came into the world, but the fairest wives of thy tenants snatcht them up into their armes, layd them in their laps and to their brests, and after they had plaid with them their pleasure, into the country were those two children (of the Taylors) sent to be nurst up; so that they live sometimes there, but ever and anon with thee.

Thou doest likewise lye with Usury: how often hast thou

bin found in bed with her! How often hath fhe bin openly difgraced at the Croffe for a ftrumpet! yet ftill doeft thou keepe her company, and art not afhamed of it, becaufe you commit finne together, even in thofe houfes that have paynted pofts ftanding at the gates. What ungodly brats and kindred hath fhe brought thee! for upon Ufury haft thou begotten Extortion (a ftrong but an unmannerly child); Hardnes of Heart, a very murderer; and Bad Confcience, who is fo unruly that he feemes to be fent unto thee to be thy everlafting paine. Then, hath fhe fonnes in law, and they are all fcriveners: thofe fcriveners have bafe fonnes, and they are all common brokers: thofe brokers likewife fend a number into the world, and they are all common theeves.

All of thefe may eafily give armes; for they fetch their difcent from hell, where are as many gentlemen as in any one place in any kingdome.

Thou dooft lye with fundrye others, and committeft ftrange whoredomes, which by ufe and boldneffe growe fo common that they feeme to be no whoredomes at all. Yet thine owne abhominations would not appeare fo vilely, but that thou makeft thy buildings a brothelry to others; for thou fuffereft Religion to lye with Hipocrifie, Charitie to lye with Oftentation, Friendfhip to lye with Hollow-heartednes, the Churle to lye with Simony, Juftice to lye with Bribery, and, laft of all, Confcience to lye with everie one; fo that now fhee is full of difeafes. But thou knoweft the medicine for al thefe feavers that fhake thee: be, therfore, to thy felfe thine owne phifition, and by ftrong pilles purge away this fecond infection that is breeding upon the before it ftrike to the heart.

Falſhood and Lying thus have had their day, and, like almanackes of the laſt yeare, are now gon out: let us follow them a ſtep or two farther to ſee how they ride and then (if we can) leave them; for I perceive it growes late becauſe Candle-light (who is next to enter upon the ſtage) is making himſelf ready to act his comicall ſcenes. The chariot, then, that Lying is drawne in is made al of whet-ſtones: Wantonnes and Evil Cuſtome are his horſes: a foole is the coachman that drives them: a couple of ſwearing fencers ſometimes leade the horſes by the reynes, and ſometimes flouriſh before them to make roome. Worſhipfully is this Lord of Limbo attended, for knights themſelves follow at his heeles: mary, they are not poſt and poyre knightes, but one of the poſt; amongſt whoſe traine is ſhuffled in a company of ſcrambling ignorant petti-foggers, leane knaves and hungrie, for they live upon nothing but the ſcraps of the law, and heere and there (like a prune in white-broth) is ſtuck a ſpruice, but a meere prating unpractiſed, lawyers clarke all in blacke. At the tayle of all (when this goodly pageant is paſſed by) follow a crowde, of everie trade ſome, amongſt whome, leaſt we be ſmothered, and bee taken to bee of the ſame liſt, let us ſtrike downe my way. *Namque odi profanū vulgus.*

3. CANDLE-LIGHT

OR

THE NOCTURNALL TRYUMPH.

O, Candle-light! and art thou one of the curſed crew? Haſt thou bin ſet at the table of princes and noblemen?

Have all fortes of people doone reverence unto thee, and ftood bare fo foone as ever they have feene thee? Have theeves, traytors, and murderers been affraide to come in thy prefence, becaufe they knewe thee juft, and that thou wouldeft difcover them? And art thou now a harborer of all kindes of vices? Nay, dooft thou play the capitall Vice thy felfe?

Haft thou had fo many learned lectures read before thee, and is the light of thy underftanding now cleane put out, and have fo many profound fchollers profited by thee? Haft thou doone fuch good to univerfities, beene fuch a guide to the lame, and feene the dooing of fo many good workes, yet doeft thou now looke dimly, and with a dull eye upon al goodnes? What comfort have fickmen taken (in weary and irkfome nights) but onely in thee! Thou haft been their phifition and apothecary, and when the rellifh of nothing could pleafe them, the very fhadow of thee hath beene to them a reftoritive confolation. The nurfe hath ftilled her wayward infant, fhewing it but to thee. What gladnes haft thou put into mariners bofomes, when thou haft met them on the fea! What joy into the faint and benighted travailer when he has met thee on the land! How many poore handy-craftes men by thee have earned the beft part of their living! and art thou now become a companion for drunkards, for leachers, and for prodigalles! Art thou turnd reprobate? Thou wilt burn for it in hell; and fo odious is this thy apoftacy, and hiding thy felf from the light of the truth, that at thy death and going out of the world even they that love thee beft wil tread thee under their feete: yea, I, that have thus plaid the herald, and proclaimd thy good parts, wil now play the cryer and cal thee into open court to arraigne thee for thy mif-demeanors.

Let the world, therefore, underftand that this tallow-facde gentleman (cald Candle-light), fo foone as ever the funne was gon out of fight, and that darknes, like a thief out of a hedge, crept upon the earth, fweate till hee dropt agen with buftling to come into the Cittie. For having no more but one onely eye (and that fierie red with drinking and fitting up late), he was afhamed to be feene by day, knowing he fhould be laught to fcorne and hooted at. He makes his entrance, therefore, at Alderfgate of fet purpofe; for though the ftreete be faire and fpatious, yet few lightes in miftie evenings ufing there to thruft out their golden heads, he thought that the apteft circle for him to be raifed in, becaufe there his glittering would make greateft fhow.

What expectation was there of his comming! Setting afide the bonfiers, there is not more triumphing on Mid-fommer night. No fooner was he advaunced up into the moft famous ftreetes, but a number of fhops for joy beganne to fhut in: mercers rolde up their filkes and velvets: the goldfmithes drew back their plate, and all the Citty lookt like a private play-houfe, when the windowes are clapt downe, as if fome nocturnall or difmall tragedy were prefently to be acted before all the trades-men. But Cavaliero Candle-light came for no fuch folemnitie: no, he had other crackers in hand, to which hee watcht but his houre to give fire. Scarce was his entrance blown abroad, but the bankrupt, the fellon, and all that owed any money, and for feare of arrefts or juftices warrants had, like fo many fnayles, kept their houfes over their heads al the day before, began now to creep out of their fhels, and to ftalke up and down the ſtreets as uprightly and with as proud a gate as if they meant to knock againſt the ſtarres with the crownes of their heads.

The damaſk-coated cittizen that ſat in his ſhop both forenoone and afternoone, and lookt more ſowerly on his poore neighbors then if he had drunke a quart of vineger at a draught, ſneakes out of his owne doores and ſlips into a taverne, where, either alone or with ſome other that battles their money together, they ſo plye themſelves with penny pots, which (like ſmall-ſhot) goe off, powring into their fat paunches, that at length they have not an eye to ſee withall, nor a good legge to ſtand upon. In which pickle if anye of them happen to be juſtled downe by a poſt (that in ſpite of them will take the wall) and ſo reeles them into the kennell, who takes them up or leades them home? Who has them to bed, and with a pillow ſmothes this ſtealing ſo of good liquor, but that brazen-face Candle-light? Nay more, he intices their verie prentices to make their deſperate ſallyes out, and quicke retyres in (contrarie to the oath of their indentures) which are ſeaven yeares a ſwearing, onely for their pintes and away.

Tuſh! this is nothing. Yong ſhopkeepers that have but newly ventured upon the pikes of marriage, who are every houre ſhewing their wares to their cuſtomers, plying their buſineſſe harder all day then Vulcan does his anvile, and ſeeme better husbands than fidlers, that ſcrape for a poore living both day and night, yet even theſe, if they can but get Candle-light to ſit up all night with them in any houſe of reckning (that's to ſay in a taverne) they fall roundly to play the London prize, and that's at three ſeverall weapons, drinking, dauncing and dicing, their wives lying all that time in their beds sighing like widowes, which is lamentable, the giddie-braind husbands wasting the portions they had with them, which lost once they are (like maidenheades) never recoverable. Or, which is worse, this going bat-fowling a nights beeing noted by some wise yong man or other, that knowes how to handle such cases, the bush is beaten for them at home, whilest they catch the bird abroade; but what bird is it? The woodcocke.

Never did any cittie pocket up such wrong at the hands of one over whom she is so jealous and so tender that, in winter nights, if he be but missing and hide himselfe in the darke, I know not how many beadles are sent up and downe the streetes to crie him: yet you see there is more cause she should send out to curse him. For what villanies are not abroad so long as Candle-light is stirring? The serving-man dare then walke with his wench: the private puncke (otherwise called one that boords in London), who like a pigeon sits billing all day within doores, and feares to step over the thresholde, does then walke the round till midnight, after she hath beene swaggering amongst pottle pots and vintners boyes. Nay, the sober Perpetuana suited Puritane, that dares not (so much as by moone-light) come neere the suburb-shadow of a house where they set stewed prunes before you, raps as boldly at the hatch, when he knowes Candle-light is within, as if he were new chosen constable. When al doores are lockt up, when no eyes are open, when birds are silent in bushes, and beasts lie sleeping under hedges, when no creature can be smelt to be up, but they that might be smelt every night a streets length ere you come at them, even then doth this *Ignis fatuus* (Candle-light) walke like a fire-drake into sundrie corners. If you will not beleeve this, fhoote but your eye through the iron grates into the cellers of the vintners, there you fhall fee him hold his necke in a jin made of a clift hoope-fticke, to throttle him from telling tales, whileft they moft abhominably jumble together all the papifticall drinkes that are brought from beyond fea. The poore wines are rackt and made to confeffe anie thing: the Spanifh and the French meeting both in the bottome of the cellar, confpire together in their cups to lay the Englifhman (if he ever come into their company) under the boord.

To be fhort, fuch ftrange mad mufick doe they play upon their facke-buttes, that if Candle-light, beeing overcome with the fteeme of new fweete wines when they are at worke, fhoulde not tell them tis time to goe to bedde, they would make all the hogges-heads that ufe to come to the houfe to daunce the Canaries till they reeld againe. When the grape-mongers and hee are parted, hee walkes up and downe the ftreetes fquiring the old midwifes to anie houfe (verie fecretly) when any baftards are to be brought into the worlde. From them (about the houre when spirits walke and cats goe a goffipping) hee vifits the watch, where creeping into the beadles cothoufe (which ftandes betweene his legges that are lapt rounde about with peeces of rugge, as if he had newe ftrucke of[f] fhackles) and feeing the watchmen to nodde at him, hee hydes himfelfe prefently (knowing the token) underthe flappe of a gowne, and teaches them (by inftinct) how to fteale nappes into their heades, becaufe he fees all their cloakes have not one good nappe upon them; and uppon his warrant fnort they fo lowde that to thofe night-walkers (whofe wittes are up fo late) it ferves as a watch-worde to keepe out of the reach of their browne billes: by which meanes they never come to aun-fwere the matter before maifter Conftable, and the bench upon which his men (that fhoulde watch) doe fitte: fo that the Counters are cheated of prifoners, to the great dammage of thofe that fhoulde have their mornings draught out of the garnifh.

O Candle-light, Candle-light! to howe manie coftly facke-poffets and reare banquets haft thou beene invited by prentices and kitchen-maidens! When the bell-man, for anger to fpie (fuch a purloyner of cittizens goods) fo many, hath bounced at the doore like a madde man, at which (as if Robin Good-fellow had beene conjur'd amongft them) the wenches have falne into the handes of the greene-fickneffe, and the yong fellowes into colde agues, with verie feare leaft their maifter (like olde Jeronimo and Ifabella his wife after him) ftarting out of their naked bed fhould come downe (with a weapon in his hande), and this in his mouth, *What outcryes pull us from our naked bedde? Who calles?* &c., as the players can tell you. O Candle-light, howe haft thou ftuncke then, when they have popt thee out of their companye! Howe haft thou taken it in fnuffe, when thou haft beene fmelt out, efpecially the maifter of the houfe exclayming that by day that deede of darkneffe had not beene. One vennie more with thee, and then I have done.

How a many lips have beene worne out with kiffjng at the ftreet doore, or in the entry (in a winking blind evening)! How many odde matches and uneven mariages have been made there betweene young prentifes and there maifters daughters, whileft thou (O Candle-light) haft ftood watching at the ftaires head, that none could come ftealing downe by thee, but they muft be feene!

It appeares by thefe articles put in againſt thee, that thou art partly a bawd to diverfe loofe finnes, and partly a coozener; for if any in the cittie have badde wares lying deade uppon their handes, thou art better than *aqua vitæ* to fetch life into them, and to fend them packing. Thou fhalt, therefore, bee taken out of thy proude chariot and bee carted: yet firſt will wee fee what workmanfhip and what ftuffe it is made of, to the intent that if it bee not daungerous for a cittie to keepe any relique belonging to fuch a crooked faint, it may bee hung up as a monument to fhewe with what difhonour thou wert driven out of fo noble a lodging, to deface whofe buildings thou haft beene fo envious, that when thou haft beene left alone by any thing that would take fire, thou haft burnt to the ground many of her goodlieft houfes.

Candle-lights coach is made all of horne, fhaven as thin as changelinges are. It is drawne (with eafe) by two rats: the coachman is a chaundler, who fo fweats with yearking that he drops tallowe, and that feedes them as provender: yet are the lafhes that he gives the fqueaking vermine more deadly to them then all the rats baine in Bucklerf-burie. Painefulneffe and Studdy are his two lackeyes, and run by him: Darkneffe, Confpiracy, Opportunitie, Strata-gems, and Feare, are his attendants: hee's fued unto by diggers in mines, gravers, fchollers, mariners, nurfes, drunk-ards, unthriftes, and fhrode husbands: he deftroyes that which feedes him, and therefore, Ingratitude comes behinde all this, driving them before her. The next divel that is to be commaunded up is a very lazie one, and will be long in rifing: let us, therefore, unbinde this, and fall to other charmes.

4. SLOTH

OR

THE FOURTH DAYES TRYUMPH.

Man (doubtleſſe) was not created to bee an idle fellow, for then he ſhould be Gods vagabond: he was made for other purpoſe then to be ever eating as ſwine, ever ſleeping as dormiſe, ever dumb as fishes in the ſea, or ever prating to no purpoſe as birdes of the ayre: he was not ſet in the univerſall orchard to ſtand ſtill as a tree, and ſo to bee cut downe, but to be cut downe if he ſhould ſtand ſtill. And to have him remember this he carries certaine watches with larums about him, that are ever ſtriking; for all the inginous wheeles of the ſoule are continually going: though the body lye never ſo faſt bounde in ſlumbers, the imagination runnes too and fro; the phantaſie flyes round about, the vitall ſpirits walke up and downe; yea, the very pulſes ſhew activitie, and their hammers are ſtill beating, ſo that even in his very dreames it is whiſpered in his eare that he muſt be a dooing ſomething.

If hee had not theſe prompters at his elbowe, yet everie member of his body (if it could ſpeake) would chide him if they were put to no uſe, confidering what noble workmanſhip is beſtowed upon them. For man no ſooner gets upon his legges, but they are made ſo that either hee may run or goe? when he is weary they can give him eaſe by ſtanding ſtill: if he will not ſtand, the knees ſerve like hindges to bow up and downe, and to let him kneele. His armes have artificiall cordes and ſtringes, which ſhorten or flye out to their length at pleaſure. They winde about the bodye like a ſilver girdle, and being held out before, are weapons to defend it: at the end of the armes are two beautifull mathematicall inſtruments with five ſeverall motions in each of them, and thirtie other moving engines by which they ſtirre both. His head likewiſe ſtandes uppon three ſkrewes; the one is directly forward to teach him providence; the other two are on either ſide one, to arme him with circumſpection: how buſie are both the eyes to keepe danger from him everie way!

But admit hee had none of theſe wonderfull volumes to reade over, yet hee ſees the clowdes alwaies working; the waters ever labouring; the earth continuallye bringing foorth: he ſees the ſunne have a hye colour with taking paines for the day: the moone pale and ſickly with ſitting up for the night: the ſtarres muſtring their armyes togither to guard the moone; all of them, and all that is in the world ſerving as ſchoolemaiſters, and the world it ſelfe as Academ to bring up man in knowledge, and to put him ſtill into action.

How, then, dares this naſtie and loathſome ſin of Sloth venture into the citie amongſt ſo many people? Who doth he hope will give him entertainment? What lodging (thinks he) can be taine up where he and his heavy-headed company may take their afternoones nap ſoundly? for in every ſtreet carts and coaches make ſuch a thundring, as if the world ranne upon wheeles: at every corner men, women, and children meete in ſuch ſhoales that poſtes are ſette up of purpoſe to ſtrengthen the houſes, leaſt with juſtling one another they ſhould ſhoulder them downe. Beſides, hammers are beating in one place, tubs hooping in another, pots clincking in a third, water-tankards running at tilt in a fourth: heere are porters fweating under burdens; there marchants-men bearing bags of money; chapmen (as if they were at leape-frog) fkippe out of one fhop into another; tradefmen (as if they were dauncing galliards) are lufty at legges and never ftand ftill: all are bufie as countrie attorneyes at an Affizes. How, then, can Idlenes thinke to inhabit heere?

Yet the worfhipfull fir (that leades a gentlemans life and dooth nothing) though hee comes but flowly on (as if he trode a French march) yet hee comes, and with a great trayne at his tayle, as if the countrie had brought up fome fellon to one of our gayles: fo is hee convaide by nine or ten drowfie malt-men that lye nodding over their fackes, and even a mofte fleepie and ftill triumph begins his entrance at Bifhopfgate.

An armie of fubftantiall houfholders (mofte of them living by the hardneffe of the hand) came in battaile array, with fpred banners, bearing the armes of their feverall occupations to meete this cowardly Generall, and to beate him backe. But hee fummoning a parles hammered out fuch a ftrong oration in praife of Eafe that they all ftruck up their drums, flung up their round cappes (and as if it had beene another William the Conqueror) came marching in with him, and lodged him in the quieteft ftreete in the cittie, for fo his Lazineffe requefted.

Hee then prefently gave licenfes to all the vintners to keepe open houfe, and to emptye their hogsheads to all commers; who did fo, dying their grates into a drunkards blufh (to make them knowne from the grates of a prifon) leaft cuftomers should reele away from them, and hanging out new bushes, that if men at their going out could not fee the figne, yet they might not loofe themfelves in the bush. He likewife gave order that dicing-houfes and bowling alleyes should be erected, wherupon a number of poore handy-crafts-men, that before wrought night and day, made ftocks to themfelves of ten groates and crowns a peece, and what by betting, lurches, rubbers and fuch tricks they never tooke care for a good daies worke afterwards. For as Letchery is patron of al your fuburb colledges, and fets up vaulting-houfes and dauncing-fchooles; and as Drunkenneffe when it leaft can ftand does beft hold up alehoufes, fo Sloth is a founder of the almes-houfes firft mentioned, and is a good benefactor to thefe laft.

The Players prayed for his comming: they loft nothing by it: the comming in of tenne ambaffadors was never fo fweete to them as this our finne was: their houfes fmoakt everye after noone with ftinkards, who were fo glewed together in crowdes with the fteames of ftrong breath, that when they came foorth their faces lookt as if they had beene perboylde: and this comicall tearme-time they hoped for at the leaft all the fummer, becaufe tis given out that Sloth himfelfe will come and fit in the two-pennie galleries amongft the gentlemen to fee their knaveries and their paftimes.

But alas! if thefe were the foreft difeafes (thou nobleft city of the now nobleft nation) that Idlenes does infect thee with, thou haft phifick fufficient in thy felfe to purge thy bodie of them. No, no; hee is not flothfull, that is onelye lazie, that onelye waftes his good houres, and his filver in luxury and licentious eafe, or that onely (like a ſtanding water) does nothing but gather corruption : no, hee is the true ſlothfull man that does no good. And how many would crie *Guilty* unto thee, if this were there inditement ? Thy majeſtrates that (when they ſee moſt danger) put up the ſwordes that Juſtice hath guided to their loynes, and flie unto the countrie, leaving thee deſtitute of their counſell, they would crie guilty, they are ſlothfull.

Thy phiſitions that fearing to die by that which they live (ſicknes) doe moſt unkindely leave thee when thou art ready to lye upon thy death bed, they are ſlothfull; they would crie guilty. Thy great men, and ſuch as have been thy rulers, that being taken out of poore cradles, and nurſed up by thee, have fild their cofers with golde, and their names with honour, yet afterwards growing weary of thee (like mules having ſuckt their dammes) moſt ingratefully have they ſtolne from thee, ſpending thoſe bleſſings which were thine upon thoſe that no way deſerve them, are not theſe ſlothfull ? They would crie guiltye. There is yet one more whome I would not heare to crie guiltye, becauſe (of all others) I would not have them ſlothfull. O, you that ſpeake the language of angels, and ſhould indeed be angels amongſt us, you that have offices above thoſe of kinges, that have warrant to commaund princes, and controle them if they doe amiſſe; you that are ſtewards over the kings houſe of heaven, and lye heere as embaſſadors about the greateſt ſtate-matters in the world, what a diſhonour were it to your places that it ſhould bee knowne that you are ſloathfull! You are ſworne labourers to worke in a vineyard, which if you dreſſe not carefully, if you cut it not artificially, if you underprop it not wiſely when you ſee it laden, if you gather not the fruites in it when they bee ripe, but fuffer them to drop downe, and bee eaten by fwine, O, what a deere account are you to make to him that muft give you your hire! You are the beames of the fun that muft ripen the grapes of the vine, and if you fhine not cleerely he will eclipfe you for ever: your tongues are the inftruments that muft cut off rancke and idle fprigs, to make the bearing-braunches to fpred; and unleffe you keep them fharpe, and be ever pruning with them, he will caft you by, and you fhall be eaten up with ruft. The church is a garden, and you muft weede it: it is a fountaine and you muft keepe it cleere: it is her husbands jewell, and you muft pollifh it: it is his beft belooved and you muft keepe her chaft.

Many merchants hath this cittie to her fonnes, of al which you are the moft noble: you trafficke onely for mens foules, fending them to the Land of Promife, and to the heavenly Jerufalem, and receiving from thence (in exchange) the ritcheft commoditie in the world, your owne falvation. O, therefore, bee not you flothfull! for if, being chofen pilots, you fleepe and fo ftrike upon the rockes, you hazard your owne fhipwracke more then theirs that venture with you.

What a number of colours are here grounded to paint out Sloth in his uglines, and to make him loathed, whilft he (yawning, and his chin knocking nods into his breft) regardes not the whips of the moft crabbifh fatyriftes. Let us, therefore, looke upon his horfe-litter that he rides in, and fo leave him.

A couple of unfhodde affes carry it betweene them: it is all fluttifhly overgrowne with moffe on the outfide, and on the infide quilted through out with downe pillowes. Sleepe and Plenty leade the fore-affe : a purfie double chind Læna riding on a fumpter-horfe with provander at his mouth, and fhe is the litter-driver: fhee keepes two pages, and thofe are an Irifh beggar on the one fide, and one that fayes he has been a foldier on the other fide. His attendants are Sicknes, Want, Ignorance, Infamy, Bondage, Palenes, Blockifhnes, and Carelefnes. The retayners that wear his cloth are Anglers, Dumb Minifters, Players, Exchange-Wenches, Gamfters, Panders, Whores, and Fidlers.

APISHNESSE

OR

THE FIFT DAYES TRIUMPH.

Sloth was not fo flow in his march when hee entred the citie, but Apishneffe (that was to take his turne next) was as quick. Do you not know him? It cannot be read in any chronicle that he was ever with Henrie the eight at Bulloigne, or at the winning of Turwin and Turnay; for (not to belie the fweete gentleman) he was neither in the shell then, no nor then when Paules-fteeple and the weather-cocke were on fire; by which markes (without looking in his mouth) you may fafely fweare that hees but yong; for hees a feirfe dapper fellow, more light headed then a mufitian, as phantaftically attyred as a court jeafter, wanton in difcourfe, lafcivious in behaviour, jocond in good companie, nice in his trencher, and yet he feedes very hungerly on fcraps of fongs : he drinkes in a glaffe well, but vilely in a deepe French-bowle; yet much about the yeare when

Monfieur came in was hee begotten betweene a French tayler and an English court-feamfter. This Signior Joculento (as the divell would have it) comes prawnfing in at Cripplegate, and he may well doe it, for indeede all the parts hee playes are but con'd fpeeches ftolne from others, whofe voices and actions hee counterfeites, but fo lamely that all the cripples in tenne fpittle-houfes fhewe not more halting. The graver browes were bent againft him, and by the awfull charmes of reverend Authoritie would have fent him downe from whence he came, for they knew howe fmooth foever his lookes were there was a divell in his bofome. But hee, having the ftronger faction on his fide, fet them in a mutenie: *Sævitque animis ignobile vulgus:* the manie headed monfter fought as it had beene againft Saint George, won the gate, and then with fhowtes was the Gavefton of the time brought in. But who brought him in? None but richmens fonnes that were left well, and had more money given by will, then they had wit how to beftow it: none but prentices almoft out of their yeers, and all the tailors, haberdafhers and embroderers that could be got for love or money; for thefe were preft fecretly to the fervice by the yong and wanton dames of the citie, becaufe they would not be feene to fhewe their love to him themfelves.

Man is Gods ape, and an ape is Zani to a man, doing over thofe trickes (efpecially if they be knavifh) which hee fees done before him: fo that Apifhneffe is nothing but counterfetting or imitation; and this flower when it firft came into the citie had a prettie fcent, and a delightfull colour, hath bene let to run fo high, that it is now feeded, and where it fals there rifes up a ftinking weede.

For as man is Gods ape, ſtriving to make artificiall flowers, birdes, &c., like to the naturall, ſo for the ſame reaſon are women mens ſhee apes, for they will not bee behind them the breadth of a taylors yard (which is nothing to ſpeake of) in anie new-fangled upſtart faſhion. If men get up French ſtanding collers, women will have the French ſtanding coller too: if dublets with little thick ſkirts (ſo ſhort that none are able to ſit upon them) womens foreparts are thicke-ſkirted too. By ſurfetting upon which kinde of phantaſticall Apiſhneſſe in a ſhort time they fall into the diſeaſe of pride: pride is infectious, and breedes prodigalitie: prodigalitie after it has runne a little cloſes up and feſters, and then turnes to beggerie. Wittie was that painter, therefore, that when he had limned one of every nation in their proper attyres, and beeing at his wittes endes how to drawe an Englishman, at the laſt (to give him a quippe for his follie in apparell) drewe him ſtarke naked, with ſheeres in his hand, and cloth on his arme, becauſe none could cut out his fashions but himſelfe.

For an English-mans ſuite is like a traitors bodie that hath beene hanged, drawne and quartered, and is ſet up in ſeverall places: his codpeece in Denmarke; the collor of his duble[t] and the belly in France; the wing and narrow ſleeve in Italy; the ſhort waſte hangs over a Dutch botchers ſtall in Utrich; his huge floppes ſpeakes Spanish; Polonia gives him the bootes; the blocke for his head alters faſter then the feltmaker can fitte him, and thereupon we are called in ſcorne blockheades. And thus we that mocke everie nation, for keeping one faſhion, yet ſteale patches from everie one of them to peece out our pride, and are now laughing-stocks to them, becaufe their cut fo fcurvily becomes us.

This finne of Apifhneffe, whether it be in apparell or in diet, is not of fuch long life as his fellowes, and for feeing none but women and fooles keepe him companie, the one wil be afhamed of him when they begin to have wrinckles, the other when they feele their purfes light. The magiftrate, the wealthy commoner, and the aunciant cittizen difdaine to come neare him: wee were beft therefore take note of fuch things as are aboute him, leaft on a fuddaine hee flip out of fight.

Apifhneffe rides in a chariot made of nothing but cages, in which are all the ftrangeft out-landifh birds that can be gotten: the cages are ftucke full of parats feathers: the coachman is an Italian Mownti-banck who drives a fawne and a lambe, for they draw the gew-gaw in winter, when fuch beafts are rareft to be had: in fommer it goes alone by the motion of wheeles. Two pages in light coloured fuites, embrodered full of butterflies, with wings that flutter up with the winde, run by him, the one being a dauncing boy, the other a tumbler. His attendants are Folly, Laughter, Inconftancie, Riot, Niceneffe and Vainglorie: when his Court removes hee is followed by Tobacconifts, Shittlecock-makers, Feather-makers, Cob-web-lawne-weavers, Perfumers, young countrie Gentlemen and Fooles. In whofe fhip whileft they are fayling, let us obferve what other abufes the Verdimotes Inqueft doe prefent on the lande, albeit they bee never reformed, till a fecond Chaos is to bee refined. In the meane time, *In nova fert animus.*

SHAVING:

OR

THE SIXT DAYES TRIUMPH.

How? Shaving! Methinkes Barbers ſhould crie to their cuſtomers *winck hard,* and come running out of their ſhoppes into the open ſtreetes, throwing all their ſuddes out of their learned Latin baſons into my face for preſuming to name the myſterie of Shaving in ſo villanous a companie as theſe ſeven are. Is that trade (ſay they) that for ſo many yeares hath beene held up by ſo many heades, and has out-bearded the ſtowteſt in England to their faces—is that trade, that becauſe it is evermore trimming the Citie, hath beene for ſo many yeers paſt made up into a ſocietie, and have their Guild, and their Priviledges with as much freedome as the beſt, muſt that nowe be counted a ſinne (nay, and one of the Deadly Sinnes) of the Cittie? No, no: be not angry with me (Oh you that bandie away none but ſweete waſhing balles, and caſt none other then roſe waters for any mans pleaſure) for there is ſhaving within the walles of this great metropolis which you never dreamed of—a ſhaving that takes not only away the rebellious haires, but brings the fleſh with it too; and if that cannot ſuffice, the very bones muſt follow. If therefore you and five Companies greater then yours ſhould chuſe a Colonel to lead you againſt this mightie Tamburlaine, you are too weake to make him retire, and if you ſhould come to a battell, you would looſe the day.

For behold, what troopes forſake the ſtandard of the

citie, and flie to him! Neither are they bafe and common fouldiers, but even thofe that have borne armes a long time. Be filent, therfore, and be patient; and fince there is no remedie but that (this combatant that is fo cunning at the sharp) wil come in, mark in what triumphant and proud manner he is marshalled through Newgate: at which bulwarke (and none other) did he (in policy) defire to shew himfelfe. Firft, becaufe he knew if the citie should play with him as they did with Wiat: Newgate held a number that, though they were falfe to all the world, would be true to him. Couragioufly, therfore, does he enter: all of them that had once ferved under his colors (and were now to fuffer for the truth which they had abufed) leaping up to the iron lattaces to beholde their general, and making fuch a ratling and shaking their chaines for joy, as if Cerberus had bin come from hell to live and die amongft them. Shaving is now lodged in the heart of the citie, but by whom? and at whofe charges? Mary, at a common purfe to which many are tributaries, and therfore no marvell if he be feafted royally. The firft that paid their mony towards it are cruel and covetous land-lords, who for the building of a chimny, which ftands them not above 30s., and for whiting the wals of a tenement which is fcarce worth the daubing, raife the rent prefently (as if it were new put into the Subfidy book) affeffing it at 3*li.* a yeer more then ever it went for before: filthy widemouthed bandogs they are, that for a quarters rent will pull out their minifters throte, as if he were their tenant; and (though it turn to the utter undoing of a man) being rubd with quickfilver, which they love becaufe they have mangy confciences, they will let to a drunken Flemming a houfe over his own country-mans head, thinking hees fafe enough from the thunderbolts of their wives and children, and from curfes, and the very vengeance of heaven, if he get by the bargaine but fo many angels as will cover the crowne of his head.

The next that laide downe his share was no sharer among the Players, but a shaver of yong gentlemen before ever a haire dare peepe out of their chinnes; and these are ufurers, who for a little money and a great deale of trash (as fire shovels, browne paper, motley cloake-bags, &c.) bring yong novices into a fooles paradife till they have fealed the mortgage of their landes, and then like pedlers goe they (or fome familiar fpirit, for them raizde by the ufurer) up and downe to cry commodities which fcarce yeeld the third part of the fum for which they take them up.

There are likewife other barbers who are fo well cuftomed that they shave a whole cittie fometymes in three dayes, and they doe it (as Bankes his horfe did his tricks) onely by the eye and the eare: for if they either of them fee no magiftrate comming towardes them (as being called back by the common-weale for more ferious imployments) or doe but heare that hee lyes ficke upon whom the health of a citie is put in hazard, they prefently (like prentices upon Shrove-tuefday) take the lawe into their owne handes and doe what they lift. And this legion confifts of marketfolkes, bakers, brewers, all that weigh their confciences in fcales. And, laftly, of the two degrees of colliers, viz., thofe of char-coles and thofe Newcaftle. Then have you the fhaving of fatherleffe children, and of widowes, and thats done by executors: the fhaving of poore clients especially by the atturneyes clearkes of your courts, and thats done by writing their billes of cofts upon cheverell: the fhaving of prifoners by extortion, firft taken by their keepers; for a prifon is builded on fuch ranke and fertil ground that if a poore wretches fow it with hand-fulles of fmall debts when they come in, if they lie thee but a while to fee the comming up of them, the charges of the houfe will bee treble the demaund of the creditor. Then have you brokers that fhave poor men by moft jewifh intereft: marry, the divils trimme them fo foone as they have wafhed others. I will not tell how vintners fhave their gueftes with a little peece of paper not above three fingers broade; for their roomes are like barbars chaires: men come into them willingly to be shaven. Onely (which is worft) bee it knowne to thee (O thou Queene of Cities) thy inhabitants shave their confciences fo clofe, that in the ende they growe balde, and bring foorth no goodneffe.

Wee have beene quicke (you fee) in trimming this Cutter of Queene Hith, becaufe tis his propertie to handle others fo: let us bee as nymble in prayfing his houfhold-ftuffe; the beft part of which is his chariot richly adorned. It is drawn by foure beafts, the 2 formoft are a wolfe (which will eate till he be readie to burft) and he is coache fellow to a fhe-beare, who is cruell even to women great with childe: behinde them are a couple of blood-houndes: the coachman is an informer. Two pettifoggers who have beene turned over the barre are his lackies: his houfhold fervants are Wit (who is his fteward), Audacitie, Shifting, Inexorabilitie, and Difquietneffe of mind. The meanie are (befides fome perfons beforenamed) fkeldring foldiers and begging fchollers.

CRUELTIE,

OR

THE SEVENTH AND LAST DAYES TRIUMPH.

What a weeke of finfull reveling hath heere bin with thefe fixe proud Lords of Mifrule! To which of your hundred parifhes (O you citizens!) have not fome one of thefe (if not all) removed their courts, and feafted you with them? Your percullifes are not ftrong enough to keepe them out by day, your watchmen are too fleepy to fpie their ftealing in by night. There is yet another to enter, as great in power as his fellowes, as fubtill, as full of mifchiefe. If I fhoulde but name him to you, you would laugh mee to fcorne, becaufe you cannot bee perfwaded that fuch a one fhould ever bee fuffered to live within the freedome; yet if I name him not to you, you may in time by him (as by the reft) bee undone. It is Crueltie. O ftrange! mee thinkes London fhould ftart up out of her follid foundation, and in anger bee ready to fall uppon him, and grinde him to duft, that durft fay fhee is poffeft with fuch a devill. Cruelty! The verie found of it fhewes that it is no English word: it is a fury fent out of hel, not to inhabit within fuch beautifull walles, but amongft Turkes and Tartars. The other fixe monfters transforme themfelves into amiable shapes, and fet golden, enticing charmes to winne men to their Circæan love: they have angelical faces to allure, and bewitching tongues to inchaunt; but Cruelty is a hag, horred in forme, terrible in voice, formidable in threates, a tyrant in his very lookes, and a murderer in all his actions.

How, then, commeth it to paſſe that heere he ſeekes entertainment? For what cittie in the world does more drie up the teares of the widdowe, and gives more warmth to the fatherleſſe than this anciend and reverend Grandam of Cities? When hath the orphan (that is to receive great portions) leſs cauſe to mourne the loſſe of parents? He findes foure and twentie grave Senators to bee his fathers inſtead of one; the Cittie it ſelfe to bee his mother; her officers to bee his ſervants who ſee that hee want nothing; her lawes to ſuffer none to doe him wrong; and though he be never ſo ſimple in wit, or ſo tender in yeares, ſhee lookes as warily to that welth which is left him, as to the apple of her owne eye. Where have the leaper and the lunatick ſurgery and phiſicke ſo good cheape as heere? their payment is onely thankes. Large Hoſpitalls are erected (of purpoſe to make them lodgings), and the rent is moſt eaſie —onely their prayers. Yet for all this that Charitie hath her armes full of her children, and that tender-breſted compaſſion is ſtill in one ſtreet or other dooing good workes: off from the hindges are one of the 7 gates readie to bee lifted to make roome for this giant: the Whiflers of your inferior and chiefe companies cleere the wayes before him; men of all trades, with ſhoutes and acclamations, followed in throngs behinde him; yea, even the ſilver-bearded and ſeveareſt lookt citizens have given him welcomes in their parlors.

There are in Lond. and within the buildings that round about touch her ſides, and ſtand within her reach, thirteene ſtrong Houſes of Sorrow, where the priſoner hath his heart waſting away ſometimes a whole prentiſhip of yeres in cares. They are moſt of them built of free-ftone, but none are free within them: cold are their imbracements, unwholfom is their cheare, difpaireful their lodgings, uncomfortable their focieties, miferable their inhabitants. O, what a deal of wretchednes can make fhift to lye in a little roome! If thofe 13 houfes were built al together, how rich would griefe be, having fuch large inclofures! Doth Cruelty challenge a freemans roome in the city becaufe of thefe places? no, the politicke body of the Republike wold be infected if fuch houfes as thefe were not maintained to keep up thofe that are unfound. Claimes he then an inheritance here becaufe you have whipping poftes in your ftreetes for the vagabond? the ftocks and the cage for the unruely beggar? or becaufe you have carts for the bawde and the harlot, and beadles for the leacher? Neither. Or is it becaufe fo many monthly feffions are held? fo many men, women and children cald to a reconing at the bar of death for their lives; and fo many lamentable hempen tragedies acted at Tiburne? Nor for this: Juftice fhould have wrong to have it fo reported. No (you inhabitants of this little world of people); Crueltie is a large tree, and <small>Againft forced</small> you all ftand under it: you are cruell in com-<small>marriages.</small> pelling your children (for wealth) to goe into loathed beds, for therby you make them bond flaves. What ploughman is fo foolifh to youke young hecfars and old bullocks together? Yet fuch is your husbandry. In fitting your coaches with horfes you are very curious to have them (fo neere as you can) both of a colour, both of a height, of an age, of proportion; and will you bee careleffe in coupling your children? He into whofe bofome three fcore winters have thruft their frozen fingers, if he bee rich (though his breath bee rancker then a muck-hill, his bodye more drye than mummi, and his minde more lame than ignorance itfelfe), fhall have offered unto him (but it is offered as a facrifice) the tender boffome of a virgin upon whofe fore-head was never written fixteene yeares: if fhe refufe this living death (for lefs than a death it cannot be unto her) fhe is threatned to be left an out-caft, curfd for difobedience, raild at daily and revilde howerlye: to fave her felfe from which bafenes fhe defprately runnes into a bondage and goes to church to be married as if fhe went to be buried. But what glorye atcheive you in thefe conquefts? You doe wrong to time, inforcing May to embrace December: you difhonour age in bringing it into fcorne for infufficiency, into a loathing for dotage, into all mens laughter for jealoufie. You make your daughters looke wrinckled with forrowes before they be olde, and your fonnes by riot to be beggars midft of their youth. Hence comes it that murders are often contrived, and as often acted: our countrie is woful in frefh examples. Hence comes it that the courtier gives you an open fcoffe, the clown a fecret mock, the citizen that dwels at your threfhold a leery frump. Hence it is that if you goe by water in the calmeft day, you are driven by fome fatall ftorme into the unlucky and dangerous haven betweene Greenewich and London.

You have another Cruelty in keeping men in prifon fo long til ficknes and death deale mildely with them, and (in _{Againft cruel} defpite of al tyranny) baile them out of all _{creditors.} executions. When you fee a poore wretch that to keep life in a loathed body hath not a houfe left to cover his head from the tempeftes, nor a bed (but the common bedde which our mother, the earth, allowes him) for his cares to fleepe uppon, when you have (by keeping or locking him up) robd him of all meanes to get, what feeke you to have him loofe but his life? The miferable prifoner is ready to famifh, yet that cannot moove you: the more miferable wife is ready to runne mad with difpaire, yet that cannot melt you: the mofte of all miferable, his children lye crying at your dores, yet nothing can awaken in you compaffion. If his debts be heavie, the greater and more glorious is your pitie to worke his freedome: if they be light the fharper to the vengeance that will be heaped upon your heades for your hardnes of heart. Wee are mofte like to God that made us when we fhew love one to another, and doe mofte looke like the divell that would deftroy us when wee are one anothers tormentors. If any have fo much flint growing about his bofome that he will needes make dice of mens bones, I would there were a lawe to compell him to make drinking bowles of their fculs too, and that everie miferable debter that fo dyes might be buried at his creditors doore, that when hee ftrides over him he might thinke he ftill rifes up (like the Ghoft in *Jeronimo*) crying Revenge!

Againft unconfionable Maifters.
Crueltie hath yet another part to play: it is acted (like the old Morrals at Maningtree) by tradefmen: marrye, feverall companies in the cittie have it in ftudy, and they are never perfect in it till the end of feaven yeares at leaft, at which time they come off with it roundly. And this it is: when your fervants have made themfelves bondmen to injoy your fruitefull hand-maides; thats to fay, to have an honeft and thriving art to live by; when they have fared hardly with you by

indenture, and, like your beafts which carry you, have patiently borne al labours and all wrongs you could lay upon them.

When you have gathered the bloffomes of their youth, and reaped the fruites of their ftrength, and that you can no longer (for fhame) hold them in captivitie, but that by the lawes of your country and of confcience, you muft undoe their fetters, then, even then, do you hang mofte weightes at their heeles to make them fincke downe for ever: when you are bound to fend them into the world to live, you fend them into the world to beg : they ferv'd you feven yeeres to picke up a poore living, and there in you are juft, for you will be fure it fhall be a poore living indeed they fhall pick up : for what do the rich cubs? Like foxes they lay their heads together in confpiracy, burying their leaden confciences under the earth, to the intent that all waters that are wholefome in tafte, and have the fweetnes of gaine in going downe may be drawne through them only, being the great pipes of their company, becaufe they fee tis the cuftome of the citty to have all waters that come thither conveyed by fuch large veffels, and they will not breake the cuftomes of the citty. When they have the fullneffe of welth to the brim, that it runs over, they fcarce will fuffer their poore fervant to take that which runs at wafte, nor to gather up the wind-fals when all the great trees, as if they grew in the garden of the Hefperides, are laden with golden apples: no, they would not have them gleane the fcattered eares of corne, though they themfelves cary away the full fheafes : as if trades that were ordaind to be communities, had loft their firft priviledges, and were now turnd to monopolyes. But remember (ô you richman) that your servants are your adopted children; they are naturalized into your bloud, and if you hurt them, you are guilty of letting out your owne, than which what cruelty can be greater?

What Gallenist or Paracelsian in the world, by all his water-casting, and mineral extractions, would judge that this fairest-fac'de daughter of Brute (and good daughter to King Lud, who gave her her name) should have so much corruption in her body, and unlesse (that beeing now two thousand and seven hundred yeeres old) extreme age should fill her full of diseases? Who durst not have sworne for her that of all loathsome sinnes that ever bred within her she had never toucht the sinne of cruelty? It had wont to be a Spanish sicknes, and hang long (incurably) upon the body of their Inquisition; or else a French disease, running all over the kingdome in a massacre; but that it had infected the English, especially the people of this now once-againe new-reard Troy, it was beyond beliefe. But is she cleerely purg'd of it by those pills that have before bin given to her? Is she now found? Are there no dregs of this thick and pestilenciall poyson eating still through her bowels? Yes: the ugliest serpent hath not uncurld himselfe: she hath sharper and more black invenomed stings within her, than yet have bin shot forth.

<small>2700 and odde yeeres since London was first builded by Brute.</small>

There is a cruelty within thee (faire Troynovant) worse and more barbarous then all the rest, because it is halfe against thy owne selfe, and halfe against thy dead sonnes and daughters. Against thy dead children wert thou cruell in that dreadfull, horrid, and tragicall yeere, when 30000 of them

<small>Against want of places for burial in extremity of sicknes. 1602.</small>

(ftruck with plagues from heaven) dropt downe in winding-fheets at thy feet. Thou didft then take away all ceremonies due unto them, and haledft them rudely to their laft beds (like drunkards) without the dead mans mufick (his bell). Alack! this was nothing; but thou tumbledft them into their everlafting lodgings (ten in one heape and twenty in another) as if all the roomes upon earth had bin full. The gallant and the begger lay together; the fcholler and the carter in one bed; the husband faw his wife and his deadly enemy, whom he hated, within a paire of fheetes. Sad and unfeemely are fuch funeralls. So felons that are cut downe from the tree of fhame and difhonor, are covered in the earth: fo fouldiers after a mercileffe battaile receeve unhanfome buriall. But fuppofe the peftiferous deluge fhould againe drowne this little world of thine, and thou muft be compeld to breake open thofe caves of horror and gaftlineffe to hide more of thy dead houfhold in them, what rotten ftenches, and contagious damps would ftrike up into thy nofthrills! Thou couldft not lift thy head into the aire, for that (with her condenfed finnes) would ftifle thee: thou couldft not dive into the waters, for that they being teinted by the ayre would poifon thee. Art thou not cruell againft thy felfe in not providing (before the land-waters of affliction come downe againe upon thee) more and more convenient cabins to lay thofe in that are to goe into fuch farre countries, who never looke to come back againe? If thou shouldft deny it, the graves when they open will be witneffes againft thee.

Nay, thou haft yet another cruelty gnawing in thy bofome; for what hope is there that thou shouldft have pitty over others, when thou art unmercifull to thy felf? Looke over thy walls into the orchards and gardens, and thou shalt fee thy fervants and apprentices fent out cunningly by their mafters at noone day upon deadly errands, when they perceive that the armed man hath ftruck them, yea, even when they fee they have tokens delivered them from heaven to haften thither, then fend they them forth to walk upon their graves, and to gather the flowers themfelves that shall ftick their own herfe. And this thy inhabitants do becaufe they are loth and ashamd to have a writing over their dores to tell that God hath bin there: they had rather all their enemies in the world should put them to trouble then that he should vifit them.

<small>Againft want of provifion for thofe that dye in the fields.</small>

Looke againe over thy walls into thy fields, and thou fhalt heare poore and forfaken wretches lye groaning in ditches, and travailing to feeke out Death upon the common hye wayes. Having found him, he there throwes downe their infected carcafes, towards which all that paffe by looke, but (till common fhame and common neceffity compell) none ftop to give them buriall. Thou fetft up pofts to whip them when they are alive: fet up an Hofpitall to comfort them being fick, or purchafe ground for them to dwell in when they be well—and that is when they be dead.

<small>The conclufion.</small>

It is now hye time to found a retreate, after fo terrible a battaile fought betweene the feven Electors of the Low Infernall Countryes and one little citty. What armyes come marching along with them! What bloudy cullors do they fpread! What artillery do they mount to batter thĕ walls! How valiant are their feven Generalls! How expert! How full of fortune to conquer! Yet nothing fooner overthrowes them than to bid them battaile firſt, and to give them defiance.

Who can denye now but that Sinne (like the feven-headed Nilus) hath overflowed thy banks and thy buildings (ô thou glory of Great Brittaine), and made thee fertile (for many yeeres together) in all kindes of vices? Volga, that hath fifty ſtreames falling one into another, never ranne with ſo ſwift and unreſiſtable a current as theſe black-waters do to bring upon thee an inundation. If thou (as thou haſt done) kneeleſt to worſhip the Beaſt with feven crowned heads, and the Whore that ſits upon it, the fall of thee (that haſt out-ſtood ſo many citties) will be greater then that of Babylon. She is now gotten within thy walls: ſhe rides up and downe thy ſtreetes making thee drunke out of her cup, and marking thee in the forhead with peſtilence for her owne. She cauſes violls of wrath to be powred upon thee, and goes in triumph away when ſhe fees thee falling. If thou wilt be ſafe, therefore, and recover health, rife up in armes againſt her, and drive her (and the Monſter that beares her) out of thy gates. Thou feeſt how prowdly and impetuouſly fixe of theſe Centaures (that are halfe man, halfe beaſt and halfe devill) come thundring alongſt thy habitations, and what rabbles they bring at their heeles: take now but note of the laſt, and marke how the feventh rides; for if thou findeſt but the leaſt worthy quality in any one of them to make thee love him, I will write a Retractation of what is inveyd againſt them before, and polliſh ſuch an Apology in their defence, that thou ſhalt be enamored of them all.

The body and face of this tyrannous Commander that leades thus the reareward are already drawne: his chariot is framed all of ragged flint, so artificially bestowed that as it runnes they strike one another, and beate out fire that is able to consume citties: the wheeles are many and swift: the spokes of the wheeles are the shin-bones of wretches that have bin eaten by misery out of prison. A couple of unruly, fierce and untamed tygers (cald Murder and Rash-nes) draw the chariot: Ignorance holds the reynes of the one, and Obduration of the other: Selfe-will is the coach-man. In the upper end of the coach sits Cruelty alone upon a bench made of dead mens sculls. All the way that he rides he sucks the hearts of widdowes and fatherlesse children. He keepes neither foote-men nor pages, for none will stay long with him. He hath onely one attendant that ever followes him, called Repentance; but the beast that drawes him runnes away with his good Lord and Master so fast before, that Repentance, being lame (and therefore slow) tis always very late ere he comes to him. It is to be feared that Cruelty is of great authority where he is knowne, for few or none dare stand against him: Law only now and then beards him, and stayes him in contempt of those that so terribly gallop before him: but out of the Lawes hands if he can but snatch a sheathed sword (as oftentimes hee does) presently hee whips it out, smiting and wounding with it every one that gives him the least crosse word. He comes into the Citty commonly at All-gate, beeing drawne that way by the smell of bloud about the Barres (for by his good will he drinks no other liquor); but when hee findes it to be the bloud of beasts (amongst the butchers) and not of men, he flyes like lightning along the causey in a madnes, threatning to over-runne all whom he meetes; but spying the brokers of

Hownsditch shuffling themselves so long together (like a false paire of cards) till the knaves be uppermost, onely to doe homage to him, he stops, kissing all their cheekes, calling them all his deereft sonnes; and bestowing a damnable deale of his blessing upon them, they cry Roome for Cruelty! and are the onely men that bring him into the Citty: To follow whom up and downe, so farre as they meane to goe with him,

———— *Dii me terrent & Jupiter hostis.*

FINIS.

Tho. Dekker.

INTRODUCTION.

THE name of this author, Humphrey Crowch, is included in no list, and the production here reprinted is mentioned in no bibliographical catalogue that we have met with. Nevertheless, he was a voluminous ballad-writer of the period in which Martin Parker, Guy, Price and Climsell flourished; and it will be seen that his verse flows easily, though not very correctly. Crowch's grammar is also not unfrequently at fault, although we cannot say for how many of his false concords he was indebted to the printer. However, as is well known, our ancestors, especially if popular poets, were sometimes not very scrupulous about such matters. The misprints (which we have necessarily preserved) show that the old compositor was far from careful, and the curious blunder on p. 17 of "heart" for *art*, makes nonsense of a material passage, unless the word be cokainically read without the aspirate.

After reprinting it, we almost doubt its fitness for the present series: it rather belongs to the class of popular, than of general literature; and it was published in a shape (sm. 8vo. or 12mo.) and at a price which rendered it attainable by readers of a humbler class, than those ordinarily appealed to by authors of a higher grade and of loftier pretensions. The introduced ballad of " Dido and Æneas" was clearly the style of writing which Crowch preferred, and to which, as far as we know, he usually confined himself. His "Love's Court of Conscience" is in some respects a meritorious work; and as it is characteristic of the time and of the man, we have thought it right to place the unique copy of it beyond the possibility of destruction.

It bears abundant internal evidence of the haste with which it was put together; and one of the speakers of an important part of the introduction is not even mentioned. It was published in Smithfield, perhaps, for sale during Bartholomew fair. In 1607, a person of the name of West (avowedly a Bartholomew-fair poet) had composed a tract called "The Court of Conscience," and although it is of a more satirical turn than that we now reproduce, it seems to have served Crowch for an example both in title and substance. There is no indication of conclusion, by the insertion of the word *Finis*, or of any equivalent; but the writer had probably arrived, not at the end of his subject, but at the end of so much of it as could be afforded for the money required by the publisher from the purchaser.

J. P. C.

LOVES COURT

OF

CONSCIENCE,

Written upon two several Occasions,
with new Lessons for Lovers

*Whereunto is annexed a kinde Husband's advice
to his Wife.*

By Humfrey Crowch.

LONDON,
Printed for *Richard Harper*, and are to be fold
at his fhop in Smithfield, at the Hofpitall
Gate 1637.

Loves Court of Conscience,
Wherein doth fit *Reafon, Difcretion, Grace, Truth,* and *Wit.*

The Cryer of the Court.

LOVERS, ftand by, and give your *Judges* place,
Reafon, Difcretion, Wifdome, Truth, and *Grace,*
Which here is come your caufes for to try,
Where *Juftice* fits imbracing equity.

Intelligence.

My lords, here is a Lover newly flaine,
Whofe corps within this coffin doth remain;
I come to give you notice that this elfe,
Unjuftly wrong'd, unjuftly hang'd himfelfe:
A wretched woman was the caufe of all
His fad laments, and his untimely fall.

Grace fpeaks.

I can not fee, though fhe have him abufed,
How he can from the murder be excufed.

Reafon fpeaks.

Tis true, my lord: had he been rul'd by mee,
From this *fame bloudy* fact he had been free.

Truth fpeaks.

And had the woman tain me for her guide,
The man had *liv'd, and fhe* had bin his bride.

Wifdome fpeaks.

And had they both my precepts wel obferv'd,
From *Reafon, Grace,* and *Truth,* they had not fwerv'd.

Discretion speaks.
And had they not refus'd me to imbrace,
Grace, Reason, Wisdom, Truth, had taken place.
How divine *Wisdom* will of them dispose,
We cannot say, no man this secret knows;
But cause that lovers should not be so doting,
Ile read some lessons to them worth the noting.

THE FIRST LESSON.

Such whose hands with heart agree,
In true loves sweet sympathy;
Such whose loves and true affection
Doth to others give direction
How to love, and love indeed,
If in love they mean to speed;
Such that can no rivall brook,
Or suspicious of a look,
Or be angry for a kisse,
Or can wink at all amisse;
Such whose jealous friends can never
From their hearts true love dissever;
Such who, when they play and toy,
Do not work themselves annoy;
Love fixt on each others hearts,
Not upon the outward parts,
Left that when those parts decay,
Love with glory passe away;
Such that do not love to range;
Such that cannot brook a change;
Such that with a roving eye

Give no caufe of jealoufie;
Such who, when their friends would part them,
Neither friends nor foes can ftart them;
Such who, like the cammamile,
Thrive and flourifh all the while,
And the more they are oppreft,
They the more in love are bleft;
Such as hate fo foule a fact
As to break a true contract,
Or a true contract to make
Falfe when once they do forfake
Love, and friend, and honeftie,
In the twinkling of an eye;
Such as when contract they are,
Think a minute a whole yeare,
Till they do enjoy their mates,
Such fhall live in happy ftates.
Such as nought but death can fever,
Happy be their fortunes ever!
This is love, and worth commending,
Ever living, never ending:
Thefe to marry need not feare
Caufe they honeft minds do beare,
Whilft the reft, that break their faith,
Live in fear of Heavens wrath.

THE SECOND LESSON.

The turtle dove, when fhe hath loft her mate,
Being expos'd to good or evill fate,
Refufes comfort, and her mate being loft,

Matches no more, her firſt love being croſt.
Contrariwiſe, made of another nature,
Do loſe themſelves contrary to this creature;
For when their lovers conſtant do expect them,
Others do ſue for love that do affect them,
And ſteals away their hearts, wins them and weds them,
Unknowne to their firſt lovers, bords and beds them.
This is a hell, a torture to the minde
Of him that ſuch diſcourteſie doth finde,
Offerd by her whoſe credit lyes a bleeding:
No good can come wher is ſuch bad proceeding.
And ſuch a comedy moſt commonly
Ends, for the moſt part, with a tragedie:
Wofull experience manifeſtly proves
The wofull ends of ſuch falſe-hearted loves.
This ſhould teach men to have a ſpeciall care,
Whom they affect, to whom they love do bear,
Since women are ſo fickle minded grown,
That, when men think them ſure, they finde them flown.
Juſt like a boy, that finding in a hedge
A ſparrowes neſt, the yong birds hardly fledge,
Goes home with mirth, with melody and laughter,
And thinks to come again a fortnight after,
Then findes them gone: juſt ſo it is with men
That ſets their mindes on women now and then;
But ſhould they ſet a thouſand watchfull eyes
Over theſe winged birds, theſe butter-flies,
Twere all in vain, if they intend to flie,
They'l have their wills in ſpite of thee and I.
As ſoon hedge in the cuckow, as conſtrain
A woman to be true, to[o] wilfull vain:

But yet I pitty them in such a case,
That love such women, so much void of grace,
Because I know the greater is the love,
If truly plac'd, the harder to remove.

THE THIRD LESSON.

Concerning contract twixt a couple, now,
Without their friends consents I not alow;
But if the thing be done, I cannot see
Why friends should part friends that so well agree.
To hurt the tender conscience of a maid,
Who ere thou art that shalt her so perswade,
To break her faith she plighted to her love,
Shalt understand there is a God above
That knowes the thoughts and secrets of the heart,
Will be reveng'd of thee, though they two part.
Nor is shee free from Heavens punishment,
Though it be done without her friends consent;
For though rash vowes, in heat of loves affection,
Are better broke then kept by wits direction,
Yet how can this the conscience satisfie,
Corrupted with the sin of perjury?
As, for example: I do vow a thing,
I vow performance this to passe to bring,
Which if I break, and say 'twas rashly done,
Will this excuse me from presumption?
Besides, their words are very dirt and trash,
That would affirme that lovers vowes are rash,
That love is surely too too hot to last,
That at the first sight is so firmely plac'd,

To move a contract in two lovers so,
To knit the knot, and after it undo.
Children and inconsiderate fooles do use,
To do and undo and themselves abuse;
But lovers should be wiser, and so wise,
Not to do any thing without advice.

THE FOURTH LESSON.

The conscience being stretched, God offended,
The maid suborned, and the man suspended,
Closely she marries, and he shall not know
The time when he receives his mortall blow.
She that ne're thought to do him so much harme,
Now keeps anothers bed and bosome warme,
And all upon perswasion of some friend,
Whose counsell proves as poyson in the end.
The guilty conscience never can rest,
But night and day the offender doth molest:
Strange apparitions sometimes doth appeare
Unto the party, filling her with feare:
With strange aspects she is perplext a nights,
In dreames and visions, which she termeth sprites.
Sometimes shee thinks shee sees him whom shee wrongs,
Comming to her with fiery burning tongs,
To pull that tongue out that did falsifie
A spotlesse faith with foulest purgery.
Sometimes she thinks men in white sheets she sees,
Covered with white from head below the knees,
And then she thinks, although the sight be fained,
How white her conscience was before 'twas stained!

And though between her husbands arms she reft,
The thought of her firft love doth her moleft,
Her confcience ftings, her troubled heart doth fmite her,
And dreadful dreams doth night by night affright her.

THE FIFTH LESSON.

The news being brought to the forfaken lover,
As time will at the length all things difcover,
His love, fo truly plac'd, muft be removed,
From her which heretofore fo well he loved :
That which he did muft be again undone,
The hardeft tafke thats underneath the fun ;
A man affoone a mountain may difplace,
As remove that his inward thoughts imbrace ;
Or fay that he will ftraightway take in hand
To feparate the ocean from the fand ;
For nature will be nature, fenfe be fenfe,
And weakneffe unto both hath reference.
Poor man ! take Reafon ; fhe muft be thy bride,
And in this matter let her be thy guide.
But O ! why do I talk of reafon fo ?
Lovers have no fuch bride, nor none fuch know ;
For if they ruled were by her directions,
Then might they learn to rule their own affections.
I wifh diftreffed lovers fuch a bliffe,
To underftand and know what reafon is ;
But all in vain : love, in another kinde,
By violence thrufts reafon from the minde.
A grief to think : you heavenly powers above,
Shew us the way but how to rule this love !

Or if it be a thing muſt govern us,
Why are we brought to inconvenience thus?
Pittie him, O his friends! in ſuch a fit,
In whoſe behalf theſe lines of grief I writ,
And let his ſufferings in a cauſe ſo right,
Be thought upon when he is out of ſight;
Who, being croſt, himſelfe engaged hath,
To croſſe the ſeas from her that broke her faith;
That being gone he might not ſee the ſhame,
Thats drawing on upon ſo falſe a dame.
Three yeares a faithfull friend to her he was,
Three yeers contract before this came to paſſe,
And now a three yeers voyage is he going,
And all becauſe he will not ſee her ruine.
Maidens, be faithfull; yongmen, he that can
Bridle affection, he's the wifeſt man.

THE SONET OF *DIDO* AND *ENEAS*.

After the Vertues they had playd their parts,
Errour came in to alter lovers hearts.

> *Dido was a* Carthage *queen,*
> *That lov'd a* Trojan *knight,*
> *Which wandring many a coaſt had ſeen,*
> *And many a dreadfull fight.*
> *As they a hunting rode, a ſhowre*
> *Drove them in a luckleſſe houre*

*Into a darksome cave;
Where Æneas with his charms
Lockt Queen Dido in his arms,
And had what he did crave.*

*Dido Hymens rites forgot,
Her love was wing'd with haste:
Her honour shee consider'd not,
But in her brest him plac't:
And when her love was new begun,
Jove sent down his winged sonne
To fright Æneas sleeping,
Who bad him by break of day
From Queen Dido steale away;
Which made her fall a weeping.*

*Dido wept, but what of this?
The gods would have it so:
Æneas nothing did amisse,
For he was forc't to go.
Learn, lordlings, then, no vows to keep
With false loves, but let them weep;
Tis folly to be true.
Let this lesson serve your turn,
And let twenty Didoes mourn,
So you get daily new.*

He, or she, that fancies wrong,
May be ruled by this song.

A KINDE HUSBANDS ADVICE TO HIS WIFE.

My love, my bofom friend, to whom I owe
My beft refpects, if you but this did know,
That your curft and unadvifed words
Doth pierce my heart, like daggers, knives, and darts:
The reafon is, becaufe I well refpect you;
It would not be fo, did not I affect you.
My Lord my God provides all needfull things,
As well for me as for the greateft kings,
And under God I carefully provide
Meat for my children, and my wife befide.
If you or they for whom I pains do take
Deny obedience, caufe my eftate is weak,
It is [a] figne fmall love to me you beare,
As by your disobedience may appeare:
For if you will not love me for my felf,
You fhall not love me, for I have no wealth.
If you on wealth fo much did caft your eye,
Why did you marry one fo poor as I?
I had fmall wealth when firft with thee I married,
Nor do I wifh that I unwed had tarried,
Since I am richer then I was before,
And who can juftly fay that I am poor,
Since God fome children unto me hath given,
That may, for ought I know, be faints in heaven:
Thefe are my riches and my chief content.
Glory to God that mee fuch riches fent!
Many a rich man that goes fine and brave,

Would give a thousand pound for one child to have.
Gold cannot get a child, O! if it could,
Then rich men would have children made of gold.
If gold be counted riches, then have I
Many good things that gold can never buy.
Then, I am richer far then some that have
Gold in their purses, lands and livings brave;
Yet I enjoy these blessings but in vain,
Because I love, and am not lov'd again.
O! would I did not love thee half so well,
I'de nere regard that firebrand of hell,
I mean your tongue, that doth afflict my heart;
For if a stranger should but act thy part,
I would not care: I am of this belief,
Where is great love, the greater is the grief;
If that it be repulst by evill speeches,
By a curst dame that strives to weare the breeches.
Consider what I say, and be advis'd:
Silence in women kinde is highly pris'd.
How canst thou say thou lov'st me with thy hart?
Thy tongue doth shew thou lov'st me but in part:
It will be so, unlesse you rule your tongue,
That member that hath done me so much wrong.
Those women love their husbands well indeed,
That to their humours are so well agreed,
That though their husbands ne'r so crosse appear,
They silent are, because they love them deare.
I do not wish, I, such a wife embrac't,
But wish that such a tongue in thee were plac't;
For such as they may have worse faults then thee,
And such as they are sure no wives for me.

Onely, I wish thee silent as they are,
And then none of them shall with thee compare.
So well I do esteem of thee, sweet heart,
That nothing but thy tongue shall us two part.
Nor can I say that I in haste did chuse
One that good counsell scorn'd, and did refuse;
For I did never finde thee obstinate,
That I should think my words are out of date,
Or that I speak now out of time or place,
Unto a woman wanting wit and grace:
For wit I know thou hast, and that is this,
To know what should be done, and what's amisse:
And if this wit with grace together joyn,
Thou art more dearer, and more neerer mine;
For though for wit we both may go to schoole,
Yet I do know thou art not such a foole,
But that this thing thou well doth understand,
That thou dost know th' art under my command:
Unlesse you 'l say, the priest in vain did say,
That you must cherish, honour, and obey;
Which if you do deny, you do herein
Against your conscience, and your knowledge sin.
Should you do so, I think it not unfit,
To say that you have neither grace nor wit:
Which God forbid, for you have read, I know,
That after God on man did life bestow,
He made the woman out of *Adams* side,
Not his commander, but his loving bride.
It is not good that man should live alone;
This the Almighty said, this think upon.
So now you cannot chuse but understand,

Woman was made to comfort, not command.
They are fweet comforts both at bord and bed;
Alwayes provided they are not mifled
By evill company, or by the tongue
To do their husbands and their neighbours wrong.
But if their tongues, like thunder, trouble men,
They may be faid to be commanders then.
Sara obeyed *Abraham*, and did call
Him lord and mafter: mark this, women all.
O times, how are you changed! we, poor men,
Can hardly find one *Sara* among ten.
A fhrew that hath a fair and comely face,
Proves no decay in nature, but in grace:
If nature do decay in any part,
I wifh it in the tongue, not in the heart.
O! let the tongue decay of my fair bride,
That the more love may in the heart abide.
Dear heart, regard me, and the caufe remove,
That hinders the conjunction of our love.
O! let it not be faid, that thou haft bin
One that did move thy husband for to fin;
One that did move me to impatiency,
And adde affliction unto mifery.
If you do know wherin I do offend,
Tell me my fault, and I will quickly mend.
And why fhouldft thou not deale as well by mee,
Since all good women labour to be free
From all occafions that may make them ill;
Nor do they ever ftrive to have their will,
Becaufe they know the husband is the head,
Which all confeffe, but fuch as are ill bred,

And such who must to shame and ruine run,
As to my knowledge some of them have done.
O! if in thee remain true woman-hood,
Then take advise by this my counsell good.
And do not think that thou the power canst have,
To make thy bosome friend to be thy slave;
For though I scorn o're thee to tyrannize,
Because I fear the Lord that rules the skies,
Yet I will ever bear my father's minde:
I scorn as much to stoop to women kinde;
For if I should, then all men would me hate,
Because from manhood I degenerate.
And surely I should have the love of no man,
If I were such a slave unto a woman:
Which to prevent, and to avoid ill speeches,
I 'le look that thou shalt never wear the breeches.
Gall was cast out from *Junoes* sacrifice,
To shew no strife 'twixt man and wife should rise:
All bitter anger must be banished
From married folk, and from the marriage bed.
Cast out this gall, sweeten what's bitter made,
Call reason in, that long from thee hath stray'd:
Examine well thy self, and thou shalt finde
How thou hast wronged me by being unkinde.
It is reported that there is a stone
Which, if so be it in the fire be thrown,
That heat it doth receive, it will retain,
And never after will be cold again.
I am that stone, and thou the fire art,
Such heat at first to me thou didst impart,
That my affection never will be cold,

Though we should live till both of us were old;
Nay, though old time should crop thy beauty fair,
And in thy cheeks deep wrinkles should appear;
Yea, though, I say, thy beauty fair should fail,
Thy red rose cheeks by want of bloud look pale;
Yea, though I could not give, nor thou receive,
Those comforts which we being yong may have,
Yet I would love thee then, as I do now,
And thou mayst live to finde my saying true.
There is an heart, as *Aristotle* saith,
That cures and kils, such properties it hath:
Even so it lyeth in a womans will,
By kinde or unkinde words, to cure or kill.
Look on the female creatures, beasts or fowle,
Which of them do their mates crosse or controule?
O! cast thine eye upon the turtle dove:
Why should that bird out-strip thee in thy love?
Is woman worse then is the fencelesse creature,
That's onely guided by the light of nature?
Woman out-strips them all for excellence,
And should out-strip them for obedience.
It is, I say, the glory of your sexe,
To love and to obey, and not to vexe
Your husbands by ill language: 'tis unfit,
And those that do so want both grace and wit.
Rule but thy tongue, my love shall never sever,
For where I lov'd at first, I love for ever.

God is the God of order, and each creature
Is ruled by him in its proper nature:
The fun, the moon, the fea, keepeth their bounds.
The tide obferves an order on the downs:
Onely untutord men and women they,
More then all other creatures, run aftray.
Can I obedience to my Maker fhew,
That no good will unto my neighbour owe?
Can God obedience, then, from you expect,
If you your husbands counfell do reject?
If we, like children, do not know our places,
But ignorant of divine and humane graces,
Women grow mankind, men effeminate,
And the world turned upfide down by fate:
Let *Hercules*, then, keep at home and fpin,
And fend his wife to wars where he hath bin.
If women finde themfelves that they be able,
Men fhall feed chickens underneath the table:
Alwayes provided, if they go to warre,
They fhall not lofe what men fo labour for,
Or bafely yeeld that caftle of defence,
Where Chaftity hath her chiefe refidence.
Admits no entrance unto any man
But the right owner, fuch a woman can
Behave her felfe moft bravely in the wars,
Without receiving any privy fcars,
Obnoxious to her reputation,
To bring her husbands forehead out of fafhion.
O! fuch a woman's worth her weight in gold,
If it were fo that fhe were to be fold.

But I had rather thou fhould'st ftay at home,
Then with fuch *Amazons* abroad to rome,
And wifely learn, if thou to fight be prone,
To fight againft thine owne corruption.
O happy conqueft! if thou conquer thofe,
Thy ftrong temptations, home-bred, in-bred fors,
More lafting glory thou fhalt gain hereby,
Then braveft champions by their chivalry.

INTRODUCTION.

ONLY two, or at most three, perfect copies of this old, hastily written, historical romance have come down to us; and as its author, Thomas Lodge, was evidently under the pressure of necessity, we may presume that it answered the purpose of temporary relief: in 1593, as well as both earlier and later, he was a writer for his subsistence; and at one period, like many others, he coupled the professions of author and actor; but his plays are not of a degree of merit proportioned to his excellence as a lyric poet. As a novelist, it is enough to say that, he furnished Shakespeare with the story of " As You Like It;" and his popularity in this department of letters was considerable, though by no means so great as that of his contemporaries Lilly, whom he imitated, Rich, whom he aided, or Greene, whom he well knew.

Lodge was the son of a citizen who had at one time been wealthy—Sir Thomas Lodge—and how it happened that, between about 1580 and 1596, the son suffered so much from poverty, as to be driven from the university to the stage, we have no information. We may presume that early in his career he travelled; and we know that later in life, after he had been a student of Lincoln's Inn, he met with success in the medical profession (which he had taken up about 1600), and accomplished a journey upon the continent. In the work before us, and elsewhere, he shows an intimate acquaintance with Italian literature by rendering into English some varied and elegant compositions.

One of his original pieces makes melancholy reference to his want of success in different spheres of life, and especially in connexion with the stage. These interesting autobiographical stanzas have never been noticed, perhaps on account of the difficulty of procuring a sight of the small volume in which they are printed, but with which, in truth, they have no connexion.

The story of "William Longbeard," as far as it is historical, was derived by Lodge from Stow (*Annales*, p. 240, edit. 1605) and similar authorities; but he introduced some new incidents and embellishments, and enlarged upon others, in order to render his subject attractive, as well as to fill his paper. Nevertheless, he appears to have been unable to draw his matter out to a length required by his publisher, and nearly half of his small volume is made up of curious, learned (for the age), but somewhat incongruous materials. We ought, however, to be thankful for them, because we may be tolerably sure that some of the narratives were, either previously or subsequently, employed by Lodge himself, or by dramatists of his day. It was a date when all sources, ancient and modern, were ransacked for matter out of which a play could be constructed. Among the tales of pirates we might have expected to find some notice of "Bargulus the strong Illyrian Pirate" (2 Henry VI, A. IV, Sc. 1; but neither he, nor R. Greene's "Abradas, the great Macedonian Pirate," are mentioned. Abradas is introduced both into Greene's "Menaphon," 1587, and into his "Penelope's Web," printed soon afterwards.

J. P. C.

THE
𝕷𝖎𝖋𝖊 𝖆𝖓𝖉 𝕯𝖊𝖆𝖙𝖍
of William Long beard, the most
famous and witty Englifh Traitor,
borne in the Citty
of London.

Accompanied with manye other
moft pleafant and prettie hiftories, by T
L. of Lincolns Inne, Gent.

Et nugæ feria ducunt.

Printed at London by Rychard Yardley and Peter
Short, dwelling on Breadftreat hill, at the
Signe of the Starre.
1593.

To the right worshipfull sir William
Web, Knight, Tho. Lodge wisheth increase
of worship in this life, and eternall
blessing in the life to come.

THE general care which you have had in the fatherlie governement of the Cittie, and the worthy forwardnesse in establishing al vertuous councels for common good, have made me presumptuous beyond my custome, in the behalfe of my contreymen, to present your worship with this short model of histories, wherein you maye both find matter worthy the reading, and circumstances of deepe consideration. I make you patron of these rare things, who are the very pattern and true Mecenas of vertue, seeking by your wisdome to establish the estate of poore Cittizens sonnes decaied, and renew by your care which they have loste through unadvisednesse. Accept, I beseech you, my poore talent, or my widdowes mite, with as great devotion as the hart can imagine, or opinion conceit, and command me who during life am your
worships most bounden
Tho. Lodge.

TO THE GENTLEMEN READERS.

THE world is growne to that excellencie now a daies, Gentilmen, that no conceits are held worthy commendations, but fuch as have coppy of new coined words, and matter beyond all marvaile. For which caufe what fhall I expect, who have neither the ftile to indight fo high, neyther the abilitye to pleafe curious eares? Truly, my expectation fhall be anfwereable to my fkill: fo that I will expect no more then I deferve, and defire no more than the curious will afford. Taylors and Writers nowadaies are in like eftimate: if they want new fafhions they are not fanfied; and if the ftile be not of the new ftamp, tut, the author is a foole. In olde time menne ftudied to illuftrate matter with words; now we ftrive for words befide matter. Since, therefore, the time is fuch, and judgements are fo fingular; fince the manners are altred with men, and men are in thraldome to their fafhionate manners, I will with the diar prepare my felfe to wafhe out the fpots affoone as they are fpied, and borrow fome cunning of the drawer to coulour the imperfection fo well as I can, till fuch time I have cunning to cut my garment out of the whole cloath. And fo, refolved to thanke thofe that accept, and to fhake off each reproofe of the envious as lightly as it is lent me, I take my leave.

Yours in all friendfhip,
T. L.

THE LIFE AND
death of William
Long beard.

Howe Willyam Long beard betraied his elder brother unto his death; of his falling in acquaintance with the Abbot of Cadonence in Normandy, and how cunningly and coulourably they got authority from the Kinge to accomplish their ambitious pretences.

WHILST all the world was in uprore, and schismes raigned in the Church, when God by prodigious signes threatened pestilent plagues; at suche time as two sunnes appeared in our horison in England, and three moones were discovered in the west in Italie, William with the longe beard was borne in the famous cittie of London, of greater minde then of high parentage, a graff of mightie hope at the first, though (as it afterwards proved) his parents spent too much hope on so little vertue.

This free cittizen borne, tenderlie fostered in his infancie, was afterwards trained up in good letters, wherein he profited so suddenlie, that most men wondered at his capacitie, and the wisest were afraid of the conclusion: and for that the age wherein hee was bread (being the third yeare of Henrie the Second) was full of troubles, this yoong mans rare guifts were raked up in the embers, little regarded because not yet ripened: but at last, as years increased, the minde ordained for mightie thinges began to mount, the rather becaafe ambition sealed his eies, which made him with the dove foare fo hie, till his owne cunning and labour made him be overturned; for when he perceived his fathers foote alreadie prepared for the grave, his mother feafed by age, and more befotted with affection, himfelfe at mans eftate and without maintenance, he thus began the firft fruites of his impietie, the fequell whereof exceedeth all conceit, and teftifieth his devilifh and damnable nature.

He had a brother elder than himfelfe in yeares, but yoonger in pollicie, who (having by his owne frugalitie gotten great wealth) was called to be a Burgeffe of the cittie; a man beloved of all men for his upright dealing, and lamented of al men for his untimelie death. For William, little regarding the benefites he had received of him in his youth, the brotherlie kindneffe, the bountifull courtefies, fought all means poffible to betray him who had trained him up, to fuck his hart bloud who had fought his harts reft, and to that intent, feeing the opportunitie fitted him, in the raigne of Richard the firft, that noble prince of famous memorie, he fuborned certaine lewd and finifter confederates of his to accufe him of treafon: for which caufe, poore innocent man, being fuddenlie apprehended, his goods were confifcate, his body imprifoned, his wife and children left fuccourleffe, whilft wicked William, being both complotter, informer, and witnes, wrought fo cunningly with the kings Councell that the goods were his, which his brother with his long labour had gotten, and the poore innocent man, brought out before the judges, with weeping eies beheld his younger brother both revelling in his ritches, and rejoicing at his ruine. Many were the obteſtations before God, and proteſtations to the judges, manie his exhortations to his brother, and deteſtations of his periurie. But William, whoſe hart was the very harbour of all impietie, ceaſed not in his owne perſon to ſolicite, and by his companions to incenſe, the judges in ſuch ſort that his brother was at laſt by them condemned and adjudged to death, as ſome writers ſuppoſe, for coining. And being led forth to his execution, like an harmleſſe innocent, the people muſtering about the place, the curſſed brother, the occaſion and compaƈter of his confuſion, accompanie[d] him, with theſe or ſuch like words he finiſhed his life: "Thou God, that knoweſt the cauſe of my untimelie death, canſt in juſtice puniſh my unjuſt accuſers: meane while take mercie on my poore ſoule, who am forſaken of my private friends. Be thou a ſafeguard unto me, whoe am left without ſuccors, and help the deſolate widdow with hir diſtreſſed children." This ſaid, after ſome private conference, by permiſſion, between his brother and him, he ſuffered torment.

But William, having gotten wealth, began to take upon him ſtate, and underſtanding his father and mother through hartie griefe were, in their extreame age, committed to the grave, he ſeazed on their goods, carrieng ſuch a countenance in London that all men wondered at him. In wit he was pregnant, in publike affaires pollitike, in revenges conſtant, in ſpeeches affable, in countenance grave, in apparell gorgeous: yea, ſo cunning was he to inſinuate himſelfe among the commons that, as the report went, he had more prentiſes clubs at his command, then the beſt courtier had ſervants to attend him.

And as the cuſtome is, whileſt thus he behaved himſelfe,

it fortuned that he fell in companie and conference with the Abbot of Cadonence in Normandie, a man as high minded as himfelfe. and more fubtill than Sinon, by whofe advice and directions he grew fo craftilie conceited, that under a holie pretext he wrought more mifchiefe than either the Councell of England could for a long time remedie, or by induftrie reverfe; and thus it fortuned. After that the noble and warlike Richard, the firfte of that name, had to his immortall glorie recovered his rights in France, eftablifhed peace with the French king, and by the perfwafions of his mother, Dame Elianor, reconciled his brother John, who had before that time beene at deadlie feud with him, it pleafed his majeftie, partlie for his own recreation fake, partlie to remedie the discontents of his fubjects, to goe on progreffe in the eight yeare of his reigne, and in the yeare of our Lord 1197; at which time the Abbot of Cadonence and William, watching an occafion and opportunitie, fo cunninglie wrought the matter, that they had audience of his Majefties hands, and obtained under the broad feale the whole fumme of their requefts. The Abbot coulored his ftratagem under the coppie of confcience, affuring the king that the corruption[s] of his officers were the chiefeft groundes of publike contention, praieng him, in the bounty of an heroick and princelie potentate, to take fome order for the correction of them, leaft at the laft it fhould turne to his owne confufion.

His Majeftie, that had ever regard of the poore, with gracious good words thanked him for his good will, giving him warrant and authoritie to redreffe thofe inconveniences, and promising him great promotions if he tooke any profite by his pollicie. William, now that he hath the fecond subtiltie to enact, suted his lookes in all sobrietie, and stroaking his long beard, which he curiouslie fostered even from the beginning, tolde the king of the insolence and outrage of rich men, who spared their owne and pilled the poore, robbed Irus and clawed Midas, beseeching in the commons behalfe a remedie for this inconvenience: whereunto the king easilie condiscended, so that he likewise was authorized to redresse such enormities, and both he and his fellowe Abbot were with manie princelie favours dismissed.

Mounted thus upon the wheele of Fortune, which everie waie sheweth hir selfe as fickle as she is favourable, as ful of gall as she hath honie, they both of them depart for London, carrieng so high countenances as everie one were amazed at their manners. My lord Abbot first, suted in his pontificalibus, called forth divers officers, purposing to examine their accounts, taunting them with untowarde languages, and accompanieng threates with imprisonment. But as the giants that threatened the heavens were overthrowne by their most hautinesse, and as Phaeton, usurping his fathers seat, was confounded for his ambitious pride by untimelie death, so the Abbot of Cadonence, when he thoght to cavell at all accompts, was called to accompt himselfe before the tribunall justice seat of God, and died midest of his jollitie. But William, who towred with the phoenix to burne in the sunne, and adventured to crosse the troblesome seas of this world to perish with overmuch wrastling in the same, now began his pageant, exhorting and stirring the commons to love and imbrace libertie, to fight and labour for freedome; brieflie to detest and blame the excesse and outrage of ritch men, whoe, as he tolde them, reaped the sweet, whilst they, poore soules, sweat for it. Heereunto wrefted he manie ftories of antiquitie: firft the Laconian ftate, next the popular governement of Athens, wherein peace never flourifhed better, faid he, than when the commons had freedome of fpeech. With thefe and such like honie fpeech he fo animated the multitude that, like a fecond Hercules, he drew them by the eares thorow the honie of his eloquence. And to his words he annexed action, undertaking manie poore mens caufes who were overborne by the rich, handeling his matters with fuch pollicie as that he was held for a fecond God among the poore, and for a long time efteemed for a good fubject by the Prince. Yet, notwithftanding this, the mightie maligned him greatlie, for that he had informed the king that by their meanes his Majeftie loft manie forfeits and efcheats which were due unto him; and for that his detefted fubttelties may be more apparant, where through he cloked his fucceeding treacheries, I have thought good to fette downe fome one of them, which may give a tafte to thofe tragike miferies which fhall enfue.

How William with the long beard handled the caufe of Peter Nowlay, a cobler, who was injuried by Robert Befant, fometime Bailife of London.

During the time that William long beard flourifhed after this manner in all pompe and pleafure, attended dailie and hourelie by hole troops of citizens, it fortuned that one Peter Nowlay, a cobler, a man of little capacity, lived in London, whoe, having gotten uppe by his owne handie labour and endevour the fumme of fortie marks, and not knowing the meanes how to employ the fame to his beft commoditie, folicited one Robert Befaunt, fometimes Bay-life of London, to take the fame money into his hands, and to employ it to fome good ufe, to the ende that after his deceafe his poore infants, which were twoe in number, might have fome fuccour and maintenance.

This money Robert Befaunt accepted, having the ufe thereof for the fpace of ten yeares, accuftoming poore Peter, as thefe great men are wont to doo, to a Sundaies dinner and fweet words, (which in thefe our daies is the verie poifon of this world, and in that time was no fmall peftilence). At laft [it] pleafed God to call the cobler to his mercie, where through his poore wife lived diftreffed, his children complaine their miferie, and all his neighbors, confidering the honeftie of the man in his life, were compaffionate, and pittied his orphans after his death. The poore mother, feeing her neceffities increafe, and hir abilitie quite overthrowne, feparated apart from all companie, began to weepe verie tenderlie, recommending her poore babes to his mercy, who had no doubt lent them hir to a better end than famifhment.

"Ahlas (faid fhe) my God, if the leaft fparrow is not uncared for by thee, what letteth me to truft my childrens helth unto thee, who having beftowed breath upon them, mayeft likewife in favour beftow bread upon them. Thou feeft, Lord, their friend is taken from them, and the mothers neaftlings without thy helpe muft become ftarvelings. Woe is me! would God I had forgon my life or forgotten love; or would my handes were as plentifull as my heart is pittifull. Ah pellican! I muft imitate thee, and pierce mine own breaft to the end I may fofter my babes: otherwife the helpe is vaine which hope yeeldeth, fince charitie is cold which fhould feede hope. Woe is me! where fhould

I begin to mourne that have no end of mone? Shall I lament my marriage? no; the heavens ordained it. Shall I complaine of Fortune? no; for then I fuppofe an enimie where there is none. Shall I blame my fruitfulnes? How vaine were that, fince it is a felicitie to enjoy babes. What, then, fhall I doo? truelie, put my whole truft and confidence in Gods mercie, whoe, being Lord of all plentie, can beft of all relieve neceffities." Scarfly had fhe ended thefe words when as hir yoong ones, the one imbracing hir necke, cried for meate, the other kiffing hir hands moorninglie bewraied his wants; whilft fhe, like Mirrha, having teares to bewaile them, no treafure to relieve them, fung this wofull lullabie unto them, whilft the muficke of hir voice enforced them to liften hir.

Lullabie!

Ah little laddes!
    Geve ceafeleffe forow end with lullabie.
Suck up my teares,
That ftreame from out the fountaines of mine eie:
    Feed, feed on me,
Whom no good hope or Fortune glads.
    Oh! fet me free
From thofe inceffant and purfuing feares,
Which waken up my woes and kil my pleafure.

Lullabie!

Weep, weepe no more,
But let me weepe, and weeping weepe life hence,
    That whilft you want,
I may not fee falfe Fortunes proud pretence.
    When I am dead,

My God, perhaps, will fend you ftore.
   O ! fmile in need,
Poore hungry babes, let fmiles be nothing fcant :
I teares, you fmiles : both have no better treafure
To bring thefe woes, exceeding meane or meafure,
   To lullabie.

Noe fooner had fhe finifhed hir fong, but Robert Befaunt entered the houfe, who, though altogither given over to covetoufneffe, yet beholding the wofull eftate of the poore wife and children, he comforted them the beft he might, fending for fome little fuftenance to yeeld hir and hir little ones fom fuccour ; and after fome conference about hir hufbands ftate, and his maner of death, he defired colourablie to fee hir writings, to the ende he might covenablie convaie out of hir hands the bill of fortie marks, which he had paft unto Peter hir husband in his time. The fillie foule fuppofing his almes deeds was unattended with trecherie, drew out of an olde till certeine briefes which fhe had, ufing thefe or fuch like terms. "Maifter Befaunt (faith fhe), your worfhip, as I remember, ought to be a patron of thefe poore infantes ; for I have oftentimes heard my husband faye (when I had a motherlie care what fhould become of my children) that he had provided for them, charging me to remember that till ever when I needed, and to ufe you as a father for thefe infants, whofe honeftie, as he fware, he would builde his foule uppon : for which caufe (giving him the writings) I befeech your wor." quoth fhe, "to perufe all his fecrets, and to ftand my good friend in this my miferable widdowhood." Maifter Befaunt, touched to the quicke, changed coulour verie often, and receaving them at hir hands with a quivering feare (proceeding by reafon of his earneft combate betweene confcience and covetoufneffe); he at laft, after long perufing, found his own bill, which he careleflie tearing, tolde hir that all of it was but waft paper, and thereupon blufhinglie departed, giving hir but colde comfort for hir great hope.

The good woman, animated by fome divine power, and efpieng the feales of his fhame fhadowed in his blufhing browes, tooke hold of his gowne fleeve, praieng him to ftaie a little while, and not to leave hir fo fuddenly: "for (faid fhe), good fir, if you thus leave us, you fhall prove that you little love us: befides, your haft makes me to mifdoubt your honeftie (pardon, good fir, I praye you, if I miftake) for thus to wreak your felfe on paper, and to fhew by your fufpectful lookes your apparant mifdoubts, makes me imagine you have deceived my Peter's hope: befides, thefe papers which you have torne may perhaps be fome teftimonies, which I will gather as the relikes of your rage" (and therewithall fhe ftooped and tooke them up). "But above all, good maifter Befaunt, remember God," quoth fhe; "and if there be aught that concerned thefe little ones in your confcience, cloake not in that behalfe, for God, who gave them me, will not fuffer their innocencie to be unrevenged."

Maifter Befaunt, fore incenfed with thefe words, and fufpitious leaft his councell fhould be difclofed by the broken and fcattered papers, at firfte by fmooth fpeeches began to perfuade hir to reftore him them; but when reafon and intreatie injoyed no place (for the more he moved hir, the more fhe fufpected) he began to ufe violence. When as the poore children, feeing their mother injured beyond meafure, cried for helpe for hir, whom motherlie care had animated alreadie even to the triall of death, rather than to leave hir papers.

The noife in the houfe, and the crie of the chidlren called in the neighbors, whoe feeing Robert Befaunt, a man of fuch reputation as he was held, not daring to inforce, began to intreat his forbearance: who, dreading his owne difcredit beyond meafure, left hir for that time puffing, fweating, and fwearing that he would be revenged on hir whoe had in this fort wrought his difcontent: to be fhort, he never defifted till fhe were imprifoned, vowing never to graunt hir libertie, till fuche time as fhe reftored to him the torne writings.

The miferable widdowe, in this peck of troubles gathering a verie confident boldneffe unto hir, denied the reftitution. And finallie, after the councell of fome poore cittizens, put uppe a fupplication, or a fupplantation (as the fillier fort of people called it) unto William with the longe beard, prefenting him likewife with the broken and torne peeces of paper, never ceafing, in moft humble and pittifull manner, to intreat a mercifull and tender compaffion towardes the reliefe of hir felfe and hir poore children. William that pretermitted no occafion whereby he might infinuate himfelfe amongeft the poorer fort, and winne the credit of a good jufticer at his princes handes, began to examine everie circumftance, and to leave no meane unfought wherby he might get himfelfe glorie, and doo the poore widdowe good.

Firft, therefore, he joyned the papers, and conferred the manner of the injurie with the other circumftances; and at laft he evidentlie found, and therewithall certified others,

that thefe torne papers was the bill of debt for forty marks.
Finallie, comparing the eftate of the poore man with that
of Befaunts, the time the money had beene in the defendants
hands, and the corrupt intention of the riche man, whoe,
by renting the bill, thought to race out the remembrance
of his due debt, he called him before him, charging the
officiall to bring the widdow and hir children before him
in open feffions; where, after long debating and trouble
on both fides, Befaunt ftanding on his credit, the widdow
on hir innocency, William, willing to catch the cat with
his owne clawe, began thus: "Maifter Befaunt, you are
called into juftice, not that we fufpect your honeftie, or
detract from your eftimate, but for this caufe are you
called: that if you will be depofed that all allegations
that may be alledged againft you by this widdow are falfe,
you may fee hir punifhed, and juftice executed." Befaunt,
little fufpecting the fnare that was laide and the fubtiltie
intended, began with huge oathes to proteft that he neither
ftood any waie indebted to the poore cobler latelie de-
ceafed, neither was in any fort liable to the falfe fuggeftions
of the widdowe. William, perceiving evidentlie the ungodlie intent of the man to defraud, and how gratious a
deed he fhould doo to fpeak in the innocents defence, firft
commanded Befaunt's oath to be taken, and, after that, rowf-
ing himfelfe in a majefticall manner, he began thus:—

"I fee well, my countreymen, that juftice had need of a
patron, when thofe that fhould maintaine hir, feeke to
maime hir. Ah! what a world we live in when truft fhall
be betraied, when fimplicitie fhall be undermined with fubtletie, and povertie overtopped by power! Behold, faith
hee, my countreymen (and therewithall he caufed the two

children to bee placed by him) two harmleffe infants, for whom the poore father laboured in his life time, both left to begge after his death! Alas, that corruption fhould blind judgement fo farr, that where wee ought in charitie to fuccour thefe, men make no confcience to fupplant them! The cedar, though a tall tree, lets the little fhrub profper under him ; the eglantine flourifheth by the oake; the goldfinch feedeth by the griffin; but the proverb is true among us nowadaies

Homo homini Demon.

We live as we fhould know no lack ; we flourifhe as if we feare no fall; we purchafe as if life could not perifh : to win the world we make fhepwracke of our foules ; and in fuch a world, where corruptions are fo rife, juftice muft not fleepe ; for if it fhould, the weake fhould to the walles, and the peny father by his power fhould overpreffe the penileffe in their poverties. Now, therefore, countreymen, give eare, and hearing pittie, patronize thefe poore foules. This Befaunt wrongeth them, making his credit the countenance of his craft, and his goods the coulour of his ungodlineffe : behold his hand writing, wherein he, thinking to extinguifh the memorie of his debt, hath renewed the meanes of his owne deftruction" (which faid, he publikelie fhewed the papers) and after that turning to M. Befaunt, he expoftulated thus :—" Well, fir, fince your corruption is found out, and your ungodlie oathes have doubled your offence, by that authoritie which I have received from his Majefty, I condemn you to pay the fumme of fortie marks, with the ufe thereof, for ten yeares unto this widdowe and hir children : next, for your perjurie, wherein you have offended God efpeciallie, and next your countrey, I adjudge you to paie, in waie of a fine to his Majeſtie two hundreth poundes ſtirling, adviſiing you hereafter to uſe your conſcience more uprightlie, and to deale by the poorer ſort more juſtlie."

Beſaunt, who highlie ſtood on his reputation, was ſo amazed at his ſo ſudden conviction before the aſſemblie of the citie, that he knew not what to ſay: his owne hand he coulde not denie; and if he ſhould, there were ſome in the companie well acquainted therewith. To be adjudged thus of by his inferiour (as he thought) it was no ſmall diſgrace, for which cauſe, ſmothering under faire lookes his falſe hart, he appeled to the King and his Councell, aſſuring William that he would not be diſcredited in that ſort, and that it ſhould coſt him a thouſand pounds but he would be revenged. With theſe and ſuch like ſpeeches the court brake up; the widdow and the children were diſmiſſed with giftes, and William, with a thouſand cittizens at his taile, was with great triumphe convaied to his lodging. But Beſaunt, for all his braues, was committed and enforced to pay the penaltie; yea, ſo did William worke with the King and his Councell, as had not this corrupt marchant with great ſommes got himſelf free, no doubt, he had beene brought within the compas of a Premunire, ſuch ſubtill ſuggeſtions had William practiſed againſt him.

How William with the long beard behaued himſelfe to-wardes the Courtiers, and of his love to his faire Lemman Maudeline.

William (having by this means inſinuated himſelfe into the favour of the king, and by that reaſon brought the cittizens in feare of him) like the untoward childe, whoe having an inche ftealeth an elle, began to prefume above the latchet (as the proverbe is) fetting light by all men, animating the bafer fort againft the better, so that the nobilitie put up much injurie at his hands, the clergie were badlie ufed by him, and the officers of the cittie highlie offended. The Earle of Durham, then chancellor and bifhop, taking the parte of a chapleine of his, who was injuried by a meane and mechanicall townefman, was braved by him in Cheape fide, beaten of his horffe, and had not the Bailifes of the cittie refcued him, the common fpeeches went, he fhould never have courted it more. A gentleman in court, at an other time, upbraiding William of his bafe eftate and birth, told him that the worft haire in his beard was a better gentleman than hee was: for which caufe William mightilie agreeved, and watching opportunitie of revenge, at laft incountred him, bravelie mounted on his foot cloth, in Friday ftreet, where taking him forceably from his horffe, he carried him into a barbers fhop, and caufed both his beard and head to be fhaved clofe, pleafantlie gibing at him in this fort.

Gallant, now have I cut of the whole traine of the beft gentlemen you durft compare with me the laft daie, and if hereafter you bridle not your toong (as bafe a gentleman as you make me) Ile have you by the eares. The king informed heereof grew highlie offended; but William, who wanted neither money, friends, nor eloquence, fo ordered the matter, as his maligners might barke, but not bite him. But for that all his minde was planted on ambition, and his greateft feare was, leaft by over forward thrufting himfelfe into ftate, his cloaked afpiring fhoulde be difcovered, he began for a while to leave the court, to intend onelie the caufes of the poore, and complot thofe meanes whereby, labouring for mightines without fufpect, he might attaine the fame without countercheck e: and firft, to make fhewe how much his mind was altred from high climing, he craftilie pretended a new conceited love; and but pretending it at firfte, at lafte was inforced to practife it, and thus it fell out.

An honeft and well difpofed merchant of London had by his wife a faire and amiable yoong mayden to his daughter, being the onely hope of his age, and the fruit of his corage. This lovelie Mawdelin (as the leffer ftarres are in refpect of the funne, or Mercurie in regard of the orbe of Venus) amongft our London damofels was the *A perfe* for beautie, and the paragon of perfections, hir looks full of quickening puritie were able to animate love in marbel: nature could doo no more but wonder at hir own handiworke, and art had nought but fhadowes in refpect of fuch a fubftance. Al eies that beheld hir wondred; all pens that praifed hir were quickened by hir excellence: to be fhort, her leaft worth was of fo great confequence, as the beft writer might be abafhed to conceite or imagine them. With this faire damofell William Long beard traffiqued his fancies, fummoning hir yeelding affections with fo manie earneft futes and fervices, that he at laft conquered that fort wherein fancie himfelfe tooke delight to tyranize; and as the jet draweth amber, the loadftone the fteele of the compaffe, fo hir beautie affaulted his fences, that all of them had no power of their offices, but were fatallie affigned to fubfcribe to hir forceries. And whereas authoritie and countenance are wrefted, the bulwarke of chaf-

titie (though otherwife impregnable) is oftentimes impugned, and not onelye affaulted, but at lafte fubdued,
William by his friends and followers fo wrought, that what
by friends and faire words he won hir for his lemmon,
fparing no coft to trick hir out in braverie, to the end he
might by that meanes give a foile and glaffe to her beawtie. This Maudelin thus compaffed, hir paramour began
to pranke it in the braveft fafhion, wrefting his wits to
make an idoll of hir worth, whofe amorous paffions, fince
they are of fome regard, I have heer fet downe for the
courtlieft eare to cenfure of.

Amidft the maze of difcontented mind,
The royall trophey of joy-breeding love,
A happy holde and refting place did find
Within that breft which earft earthes hel did prove.

Since when my long-enfeebled eies have reard
Their drooping fight to gaze upon the funne,
Since when my thoughts in written lines appeard,
Rejoycing in that Palme my faith had wunne.

Ennobled thus by that thrife-nobled paffion,
Which hath the power all worldly cares to banifh,
I flie fweet-feeming leures of falfe occafion,
And let al thoughts but love-fweet vade and vanifh.
  The fruits I reape in fpight of Fortune froward
  Make me fuppofe no torment too untoward.

Another he made upon this occafion. Maudelin, his
miftreffe, had a faire jewell, wherein twoe Cupids of Ana-

creon were painted, wraftling the one with the other, with this motto, *Pro palma*, for which caufe he wrote this fonnet, and prefented hir therewith.

Ye braine-begotten dieties, agree you,
Nurft by tranfparant chriftall of chaft eies,
Leaft fhe that gave you life on fudden fee you,
And frowning kil you both, who caufde you rife.

From hir you came, yong Cupids, from no other,
And but for her if envious you fhal wraftle,
I feare you both wil lofe a lovely mother ;
Hir brow your bower, hir bofome is your caftle.

There gree you both, there both togither go you,
And fuck the Aprill ritches of hir breft ;
Then I, who long have ferved, and love to fhew you
How much I love the bofome where you reft,
   Will come and kiffe and bleffe you, little wantons,
   And feed you kindly, wantons, if you want once.

Another, in refpect of the occafion, I could not find in my hart to forget; for being at fupper once in hir companie, where were manie that difcourfed of love, fhewing all the idolatrie of their pens in exemplifieng that unchaft deitie, he at laft, when the table was taken up, remembring him of a fonnet in an ancient French poet, on fudden wrote this imitation.

As foone as thou doeft fee the winter, clad in colde,
Within September on the eaves in fundry formes to fold,

Sweet swallow, farre thou fliest till to our native clime,
In pleasant Aprill Phœbus raies returne the sweeter time.
But love no day forsakes the place whereas I rest,
But every houre lives in mine eies, and in my hart dooth nest.
Each minute I am thrall, and in my wounded hart
He builds his neast, he laies his egges, and thence will never
      part.
Already one hath wings, soft downe the other clads,
This breakes the skin, this newly flegd about my bosome gads.
The one hath broke the shel, the other soares on hie,
This newly laid, that quickly dead before the dam come nie.
Both day and night I heare the smal ones how they crie,
Calling for food, who by the great are fed for feare they die.
All wax and grow to proofe, and every yeare doo lay
A second neast, and sit and hatch the cause of my decay.
Ah! Maudline, what reliefe have I for to remove
These crooked cares that thus pursue my hart in harboring
      love?
But helpelesse of reliefe, since I by care am stung,
To wound my hart, thereby to slaie both mother and hir yong.

At another time, being absent from his mistresse, by reason he had a poore mans cause in Essex to be heard, he wrote this briefe fancie to her, after the manner of the Italian rimes.

    Oh faire of fairest, dolphin like,
    Within the rivers of my plaint
    With labouring finnes the wave I strike,
    Whose flouds are honored by my saint.
      Withouten heart or gall I spring,

And swim to heare thee sweetly sing,
All like the fish, when natures art
Hath reft of hate and tender hart.

And in the sea for love I burne,
As for Arion did the fish;
At everie note I skip and turne,
I harke, I praise, I like, I wish.
  But out alas! with better chaunce
  The friendly fish did him advance:
  He bare Arion on his back,
  Where I thy sweet imbracements lack.

These other twoe, for their shortnesse and strangenesse, I could not finde in my hart to pretermit, knowing that the better sort, that are privie to the imitation and method, will have their due estimate.

My mistresse, when she goes
To pull the pinke and rose,
Along the river bounds,
And trippeth on the grounds,
And runnes from rocks to rocks,
With lovely scattered locks,
Whilst amarous wind doth play
With haires so golden gay,
The water waxeth cleere,
The fishes draw hir neere,
The sirens sing her praise,
Sweet flowers perfume hir waies,
And Neptune, glad and faine,
Yeelds up to hir his raigne.

ANOTHER.

*When I admire the rose
That nature makes repose
In you, the best of many,
More faire and blest than any,
And see how curious art
Hath decked every part,
I thinke, with doubtfull view,
Whether you be the rose, or the rose is you.*

An ode he wrote, amongst the rest, I dare not forget, in that the poesie is appertinent to this time, and hath no lesse life in it than those of the ancient; and the rather because hereby the learned may see how, even in those daies, poecy had hir impugners and industrie could not be free from detraction.

HIS OADE.

*Since that I must repose
Beyond th' infernal Lake,
What vailes me to compose
As many verses as Homer did make?*

*Choice numbers cannot keepe
Me from my pointed grave,
But after lasting sleepe,
The doomb of dreadful Judge I needs must have.*

*I put the case my verse,
In lieu of all my paine,
Ten yeares my praise rehearse,
Or somewhat longer time some glorie gaine;*

What wants there to confume,
Or take my lines from light,
But flame or fierie fume,
Or threatning noice of war or bloudy fight?

Excell I Anacrion,
Steficores, Simonides,
Antimachus, or Bion,
Philetes, or the grave Bacchilides:

All thefe, though Greekes they were,
And ufde that fluent toong,
In courfe of many a yeare
Their workes are loft, and have no biding long.

Then I, who want wits fap,
And write but baftard rime,
May I expect the hap
That my endevors may ore-come the time?

No, no: tis farre more meet
To follow marchants life,
Or at the judges feet
To fell my toong for bribes to maintaine ftrife;

Then haunt the idle traine
Of poore Calliope,
Which leaves, for hunger flaine,
The choiceft men that hir attendants be.

Thefe and fuch like fruits of his fancie may fufficientlie teftifie unto you both the high fpirite and deepe invention

of this craftie citizen, who, flourifhing thus in the verie ful-
neffe of loves joy, and revelling in the chiefeft pallaces of
pleafure, at laft recalled to mind the ambitious defires that
were wont to accompanie him, which having the nature of
fire (which no fooner catcheth hold of drie matter but
prefentlie it confumeth it), from a light fmoke at laft fell to
fo huge a flame that himfelfe was confounded therewith,
and all his hopes made fruftrate : and thus it fell out.

The kings majeftie hearing of his continual affemblies,
and comparing his purpofes with his practife, began, under
no fmall grounds, to conceive his curffed intention : for,
confidering with himfelfe the manner of his life, the bufi-
neffe of his braine, the tifing eloquence of his toong, and
the mightineffe of his mind, he imagined (as afterward it
fell out) that fo great meanes of quick and capeable fuell
would at laft breake out to an unquenchable flame ; where
upon the K. with confiderate judgement called him to
court, commanding him to ceafe his difordred affemblies,
leaft, in feeking to exterminate the injuries of the rich, he
fhuld revive the infolence of the poore. For (faid he),
William, whoe feeth not whereto thefe routes tend ? whoe
thinketh not that riot will follow them ? The labouring
men, that were kept from innovations by their worke, are
now capable of all chang and novelties in their idleneffe.
In living as they doo they rather are drawne to deteft labor
then to follow it ; wherthrugh the offices and mechanicall
crafts in the cittie doo ceafe, and by the omiffion of induftrie rifeth the pretermiffion of dutie. For this caufe, as
you have care of my love, incite them not to too much
libertie. Further than what you may, if they be wronged,
but let not juftice be a colour to winne them to wickednes.

With thefe, or fuch like admonitions, kinge Richarde attempted him, and fo wrought him, that for a while the commotions and motives of trouble were laide apart, fo that he walked London ftreets with leffer troops, and whollie adicted himfelfe to play with his faire Maudeline, whofe unchaft life was a bi-word in the cittie.

How William with the long beard flew Arth::r Brown, who deceived him of his Maudline.

Whilft William was converfant in the affaires of ftate, intending everie waie to inlarge his owne power, and attending daielie uppon the kinges pleafure, it fortuned that one Arthur Browne, furthered by his youth, and fitted by occation, fell in with Maudline, Williams wanton concubine; and having welth fufficient and wit no leffe fubtill, he fo craftilie handled the caufe that he won the yoong woman to ftoope to a feconde lure and to accept his love. Manie and often times had they entercourfe, fo that at laft, the rumor paffing in everie place, it coulde not choofe but light at lafte in Williams hearing; who moved beyond meafure to fee himfelfe outfaced by one, who had fo long time beene feared by all, he frowningly prepared revenge, refolving with himfelfe that no means were too meane to give a tragicall fauce to his corrupt meaning. Whereupon, breaking his mind with certaine of his faction, he agreed to watch an oportunitie to revenge impietie; and for that caufe, watching verie craftilie when Arthur, his rivall, fhould repaire unto his lawleffe lemman, he at lafte furprifed and encountered him; and caufing fome of his train to muffle him in his cloake, and to ftopp his mouth for feare of crieng, he ſtabbed him with a dagger in divers places, and in the laſt wound left the ſame ſticking, faſtening the poor caitifes owne hande with his owne dagger, which he had purpoſelie (to avoid all mens ſuſpition, and to raiſe an opinion that he had murthered himſelfe) ſheathed in Arthurs owne bodie. This doone, he departed uneſpied and unſuſpected; and the bodie being founde, according to the cenſure and verdict of the jurie which behelde the ſame, was thruſt thorowe with a ſtake, and ſo buried, as if he had beene guiltie of his owne murther. William thus delivered of a ſupplanter of his pleaſure (after ſome unkindneſſe paſt and calmed betweene him and his Maudline), finallie fell to an accord, accuſtoming hir as he was wont under promiſe of more conſtancie in affection, and to the intent ſhe ſhould remember hir of the injuries offered, he wrot this with a pointed diamond in hir glaſſe:—

Thinke what I ſuffred (wanton) through thy wildeneſſe,
When, traitor to my faith, thy loſeneſſe led thee:
Thinke how my moodie wrath was turnde to mildneſſe,
When I bad beſt, yet baſer groomes did bed thee.

Thinke that the ſtaine of bewtie then is ſtained,
When lewd deſires doe alienate the hart:
Thinke that the love that will not be contained,
At laſt will grow to hate in ſpight of art.

Thinke that thoſe wanton lookes will have their wrinkles,
And but by faith olde age can merit nothing,
When time thy pale with purple over-ſprinkles,
Faith is thy beſt, thy beautie is a woe thing.
  In youth be true, and then in age-reſolve thee,
  Friends wil be friends, till time with them diſſolve thee.

But leaving thofe his effeminate follies of youth, wherin he ungratiouflie paffed his time, let us draw to the confideration of his traiterous practifes, and finallie, as the fruits of fuch finifter follies, conclude with his tragicall end. After he had for a time, untill the princes minde were otherwife withdrawne with more waightie matters, ceafed both his routs and riots, the old ranckled venome of his ambition began more freelie to breake forth, fo that what before time he colored under confcience, now at laft he manifefted with audacious confidence. The mightie in court that maligned him he overmaiftered by his attendants, fwafhing out in open ftreats uppon everie light occafion: for himfelfe hee thought no man fufficient to fuppreffe him, nor of fufficiencie to brave him; for at a beck coblers, tinkers, tailors and all fortes of the hare-brainde multitude attended him, fought for him, fupported him, and made him lorde of their factions: where-through, the better forts neither were lords of themfelves, neither commanders of their owne liveliehoods. From fome he extorted wealth by corrupt witneffes, fparing no meanes to inrich his followers by racking and wrefting the kinges authoritie: and no fooner did he heare that the kinge had given order to his councell to feafure on his bad demeanors, but gathering to himfelfe a huge multitude, he openlie ufed this difcourfe unto them, beginning his exhortation with this place of Scripture,

Haurietis aquas in gaudio de fontibus falvatoris;
Which is as much to fay as "You fhall draw waters with joy out of the fountaines of our Saviour." For, quoth he, my worthie and faithfull friends, whoe have more courage than coine, and abilitie in armes then poffibilities of wealth, I am the faviour of you that are poore, and the foveraigne

of fuch as are penileffe : you that have affaied the hard hand of the rich, fhall be fuccoured by the happie hande of the righteous.

Now, therefore, draw your happie fountaines of councell out of my wordes, and turne the troubles you have to affured triumphs; for the daies of your vifitation is at hande. I fhall depart waters from waters; I mean the proud from the poore, the mercileffe from the mercifull, the good from the evill, and the light from the darkneffe. I will oppofe my felfe againft all dangers to prevent your domage, and loofe my life but you fhall have living. Be confident, therefore, and bolde; for fuch as have courage are fildome conquered. Let the greateft upbraid, they fhall not bite : we have weapons to withftand, as well as wordes to perfwade : we are as couragious as our enimies are craftie. Stick, therefore, unto me, who will ftrive for you : let me be fuppreft, you are fubdued : let me flourifh, you are fortunate ; but if finifter chance threaten, whie,

Alea jaƈta eft :
Una falus viƈtis nullam fperare falutem.

Thus dailie and hourelie animated he the ill minded forte ; and although the king did oftentimes fummon him, and by letters difuaded him from his ill demeanour, yet was hee enforced to ufe violence, or otherwife that ftrife, which at firft feemed to be but a fillip, would at laft have growne unto a fiftula. For which caufe Hubert, then Bifhop of Canterburie, foundlie refolving in his thoughts that forbearance would be the meanes of further mifchiefe, by the advife of others of the privie councell, called him in queftion, fummoning him againft an appointed day to come and yeelde a reafon of thofe his faƈtious tumults.

William, that faw the iron readie to waxe hot, and the hammers readie to ftrike, began to remember himfelfe; and his guiltie confcience (which, as the wife man faieth, is a hundreth witneffes) would not fuffer him to walk with fo great confidence: yet leaft feare fhould be fufpected in him, whofe good fortunes and life wholie depended on his courage, hee oftentimes lookt abroad, but attended by fuch a band of bafe companions, as if he had beene the proude Changuis leading his legions of Tartars thorow Europe. But, when the day of his appearance came, he was backt with fuch a number of mechanicall rebels, that Hubert, in ftead of attempting him with upbraids, was faine to temper him with flattering perfuafions: yea, the ftouteft councellor[s], though never fo confiderate, were faine to intreat him whom they had refolved to threaten and imprifon. William, feeing them abafht, waxed bold, and in thefe wordds faluted them:—Honorable fathers and grave councellors, according to your honourable fummons, and the dutie of a fubject, I prefent my felf before you attended in this fort, as you fee, not to violate lawes by lewd infurrections, but both to prefent my fervice to my prince and your honors, and to drawe my friendes and well willers to that dutie, where unto in foule I am devoted to this ftate. If, therefore, you have ought to command me, or if my fervices in times paft be any waie fufpected, I ftand readie to fatisfie you in the one, or anfwre to the other. Hubert, that knew well that foft drops in time pierce harde ftones, and that the diamond, though not tainted by the hammer, is tempered in ftrong vineger, began to coulour where he might not command, and flatter where he coulde not inforce, and thus he faid:

Being aſſured, William, that good ſubjects, tied by no bountie to their prince, yet yeelde him all obſervance, wee cannot perſuade our ſelves that you, who have beene authoriſed by your prince to counterchecke injuſtice, will be the pattern of injurious inſolence: for which cauſe we have called you, not as condemners of your faith, but commenders of your forwardneſſe: neither have we ſo bad an opinion of theſe good men that follow you, that either they would be drawne to violate juſtice, or you could be induced to violate and alter their honeſt and chriſtianlike duties. Our onelie requeſt to you in the kings behalfe is to caſt off this lordlie traine, and ſuffer theſe poore men to follow their profeſſions, leaſt being unawares aſſailed by want, they ſhall at laſte deſperatelie attempt wickednes. As for theſe good fellows, who in their lookes promiſe no loſeneſſe, I beſeech them in his majeſties name to keepe their houſes, promiſing them in generall, that if any one of them be wronged they ſhall have remedie. Nay, we will have remedie in ſpight of you, ſaid they, as long as William lives. And this ſaid, without all reverence they departed the place, carrieng with them their captaine commander, ſcoffing at the fainthartednes of the archbiſhop: for full well was he aſſured that greater ſeveritie was concluded upon then he there would inſinuate: for which cauſe he continuallie ſtood on his guard, ſpoiling all ſuch men as hee thought were abettors of the biſhop.

The Bailifes of London, according to their authoritie, ſeeing matters were growne to ſuch extremitie, kept diligent and ſtrong watch, drawing ſome of the commons from him by faire words, and ſome by guifts: this notwithſtanding, William was never unattended. The Councell, who everie waies were vigilant to roote out this viper from the common weale, what they could not by proves, they adventured by pollicie, animating divers valiant men with huge promifes to marke his manners, and when the occafion was offered, to apprehend him at fuch time as he little fufpected. But long was it yer they either could finde opportunitie, or catche the foxe in his forme: yet at laft, when he leaft fufpected, they caught him tardee in Breadftreat attended onlie by ten or twelve; at which time they, drawing their fwordes, affailed him valiantlie.

But he, who in conflicts of Fortune was both confident and courageous, firft animated his retinue to the fight, and after that, wrefting himfelfe by maine force out of their hands, he tooke him to flight towards the hart of the cittie, and ranne into Cheapfide. They who were bufied againft his poore followers, feeing him fled, gave over fight, and earneftlie purfued him. By this time the cittie was in an uprore: the poorer fort laboured to refcue William: the Bailifs with the beft cittizens armed them to back the kings officers; fo that the cittie was altogither up in armes. William long beard, feeing himfelfe hotlie purfued, and knowing no mean to efcape, ftept to a poore carpenter, who ftaid in Cheape for worke, and taking his axe from him, defperatlie affailed his purfuers, and with his owne hands valiantlie flue fome of them: but when he perceived the factions of his enimies to be great, and his friends wel nigh tired, he betooke himfelfe at laft into Bow church, not for his fanctuarie, but for a bulwarke of his fafetie.

Thither repaired all the poore commons, fome with bats, fome with fpittes, and fuch weapons as they had, driving awaie all the kings officers in defpight of their friendes, and determining with themselves rather to dy than to lose their William Longbeard : amongst the rest Maudline, his minion, knowing that his wracke was hir ruine, came unto him, where, weeping mild teares from hir immodest eies, shee so mollified his marbell heart, that (as some testifie) he was more moved therewith then with the threats and terrors of his greatest enimies : but see impietie, where it prevaileth, how it worketh! That church which was sacred to praiers was now made a den of rebels : those places that were reserved to holie uses were now soiled with dishonest abuses : where be fore our Ladie was praied to, lewdnesse was plaid withall. But to bring these causes to their catastrophe, sufficeth it that darknes for this time ended the discention, and the comming on of the night wrought also the conclusion of the fight.

How William with the long beard, after long trouble, was taken by the kings officers, and executed for his misdemeanors.

No sooner gan the howers draw forth the burnisht chariot of the sun, and the star that beautifieth the morninges breake shut uppe her beames in the bowels of the hidden hemisphere, but Richard and his councell assertained that which was happened, comanded the Bailifes of the citie by expresse letters to ferret him out of his hole, and cease the tumultes by their authorities ; for which cause the Bailifes, attended by a bolde troope of men in harnesse, came into Cheape. The eldest of whom, being called Gerard de Antiloche, handled himselfe with such gravitie, and used so effectuall persuasions, that the commons, for the most parte, withdrew them to their owne houfes, and after affurance of pardon from his Majeftie, betooke them to their labour. As for the reft in the church, when neyther perfuations could allure them, nor threats intenerate their harts, the Bailifes fell to armes, and for the fpace of foure houres continued a bloudie and defperate fight. But when they perceived the traitors were defperate, and the church was fufficientlie ftrong to keep them out, they at laft found out this worthie pollicie.

They caufed fome chiefe men to bring them great ftore of ftraw, which they fiered in divers places about the church, and in everie corner whereas the wind might worke the fmoake anie entrance; which fo smothered and ftifeled them in the church, that they were all of them, for the libertie of a fhorte time of life [brought] to fubmit themfelves to the judgement of fucceeding death. Hereupon, after manie wofull plaints powered out on everie fide by William, his Maudline, and other malefactors, they were all inforced to leave the church and fubmit themfelves to the hands of the Bailifes; who, according to the kings command, picking out William with nine other his confederats, committed them unto warde for that time, difmiffing the reft under the kings generall pardon, whoe, certified thereof, was not a little folaced. For which caufe he fent fome of his Councel and Judges the next day, who afcending the judgment feat, called forth William with the long beard with his confederates, arraigning them of high treafon againft God, the king and countrey.

Among all the reft William fhewed himfelfe moft confident; for neither did the taunts of the Judges extennuate his courage, neither could the bonds he was laden withall abaſh him any waies, but that with a manlie looke, and inticing eloquence he thus attempted the juſtices. You lords and honorable judges, though I knowe it a hard thing to ſtrive againſt the obſtinate, or to extort pittie there where all compaſſion is extinguiſhed, yet will I ſpeake, uſing the officer of nature to worke you, although I know I ſhall not win you. I am here called and indighted before you for hie treaſon: a hainous crime, I confeſſe it, and worthie puniſhement, I denie it not; but may it pleaſe you with patience to examine circumſtances. I have imboldened the poorer ſort to innovation, to fight for libertie, to impugne the rich; a matter in the common weales of Greece highlie commended, but heere accounted factious, and whie? there ſubjects made kings, here kings maiſter ſubjectes: and why not ſay you, and whie not think I? Yet am I faultie under a good preſident, and the ambition which hath intangled mee hath not beene without his profit. To offend of obſtinate will were brutiſh; but under ſome limits of reaſon to defaulte, can you (my lords) but thinke it pardonable? I have raiſed one or two aſſemblies, and what of this? peace was not broken, onelie my ſafetie was aſſured: and were it not that the law had beene injured, might not the righting of a hundred poore mens cauſes merit pardon for two unlawfull aſſemblies? But you will ſaie, I have animated ſubjects againſt their prince. I confeſſe it, but under a milder title: I have councelled them to compaſſe libertie, which (if nature might be equall judge betweene us) I knowe ſhould not be ſo hainouſlie misconſtred.

For my laſt tumult, I did nòthing but in mine owne defence; and what is lawfull if it be not permitted us *veni vi repellere?* But whie pleade I excufes, knowing the lawes of this realme admit no one of my conftructions? If it be refolved I muft die, doo me this favour, my lords, to protract no time: execute your juftice on my bodie, and let it not pine long time in feare thorowe fuppofall of extreames. For my foule, fince it is derived from a more immortall effence, I dare boaft the libertie thereof, knowing that eternitie is prepared for it, and mercie may attend it. But for thefe poore ones, who have defaulted thorough no malice, but have been mifled through vaine fuggeftions, howe gratious a deede fhould your honnors do to exemplifie your mercie on them! Poore foules, they have offended in not offending, and but to enthrone me have overthrowne themfelves: for which caufe, if confideration of innocent guiltines, and guiltie innocence may any waies move you, grant them life, and let me folie enact the tragedie, who am confirmed againft all Fortunes tyrannies.

Thefe latter words were delivered with fo great vehemencie of fpirit, and attended with fo quickening motions and actions of the bodie, that everie one pittied that fo rare vertues fhould be ravifhed by untimelie death, or accuftomed with fo manie ungodlie practifes. The judges, whoe were Socratical in all their fpeeches, fhewing their rhetorique in their upright judgements, not quaint difcourfes, after the examinations, indictments, verdicts of the jurie, and fuch like, at laft gave finall and fatall judgement, that William with the long beard, with his confederates, fhould the nexte daie be hanged, drawne and quartered: and fo, after fome other worthie exhortations to the people to mainteine peace, and that they fhould fhew themfelves more dutifull, and after thanks to the bailifes and good cittizen for their faithful and good fervice to his majeftie, the affemblie broke up, and the prifoners till the next daye were committed to the dungeon.

No fooner was the gaie miftreffe of the daie break prepared in her rofeat coatch, powdering the heavens with purple, but the Bailifes repaired to the prifon, leading foorthe William and thofe his other confederates to their execution. Then flocked about them divers forts of people, fome to fee thofe who were fo much fearched after, others to lament him whom they had fo loved, at lafte arrived at the place where they fhould finifh their daies, and all ftood to beholde their death. William, as principall in his life time of feditious practife, was to enact the firft and fatall part in the tragedie: for which caufe, boldlie climing up the ladder, and having the rope fitlie caft about his neck, after fome private praiers, he fpake after this manner unto the people: My good countreymen, you are repaired hither to fee a forie fpectacle, to beholde the follie of life paid with the fruits of death, to marke how finifter treafons ende with condigne torments: if you applie what you here fee and beholde to your owne profits, I fhall be glad whoe now, even at this my laft hower, defire rather you fhuld reconcile your felves from all wickednes, then be difmaied or moved with my wretchedneffe.

Oh, my deare friends! I now proteft before God, and vowe before men, that mine owne prefumptuous climing hath beene the juft caufe of my confufion: I have had more defire of glorie then refpect of God, more regard of dignitie then of dutie, deeming it better to be a famous traitor then a faithfull and true fubject. For which my ineftimable finnes I crie God hartilie mercie: I befeech his majeſtie to forgive me, and praie you all by your praiers to implore Gods grace for me. Neither deſerve I death only for the offence I have made the king; but my conſcience accuſeth me, and I heere doo openlie confeſſe it, that I was he who murthered Anthonie Browne, in that he was a rivall to my moſt lewde love. This, this, if nought elſe, my countreymen, ſufficeth to condemne me: for this and al I am hartelie ſorie. My God! I repent from my ſoule, my God. Which ſaid, lifting up his eies to heaven, he praied a long time verie vehementlie, and after manie fruitfull exhortations, finiſhed his life to the comfort of thoſe who wiſhed his ſoules health. The reſte, his confederates, after their ſeverall confeſſions, were ſerved with the ſame ſauce, and thus ended the troubles with their tragedies.

Their bodies, cut downe, were buried by their friends, and happie was he, among the poorer ſort, that had any thing to inritch the funerall of William Long beard: and notwithſtanding the confeſſion at his death, and divers other evidences at his condemnation, yet were there divers whoe after his death held him for a ſaint, caſting out ſlanderous libels againſt the archbiſhop, terming him the bloudſucker of good men. There were manie ſuperſtitious women, who in their devotion were wont to pray to him, and after his death digged up the ground about the gallowes tree, affirming that manie had been healed of ſondrie ſickneſſes by the touch thereof. All this, their idolatrous conſtructions, at firſt began by reaſon of a prieſt, a neere alie to William, who openlie preached that by vertue of a chaine, wherewith William was bound during the time of his impriſonment, ther were divers men healed of hot feavers the bloud that fell from him at fuch time as he was quartered they cleerelie fcraped up, leaving nothing that could yeeld any memorie of him, either unfought or ungotten. But at laft the Archbifhop of Canturburie remedied all thefe thinges, who firft accurfed the prieft that brought up the fables, and after that caufed the place to be watched ; where through fuch idolatrie ceafed and the people were no more feduced. But for that William wrote many notable poems and tranflations in the prifon, which if you perufe will notifie unto you his fingular wit, I have thought good to fubfcribe them, defiring your favourable cenfure of them.

WILLIAM LONG BEARDS EPITAPH.

Untimely death and my found fruits of Treafon,
My lawleffe luft, my murthers long concealed,
Have fhipwract life amids my Aprill feafon :
Thus couerd things at laft will be revealed.
  A fhamefull death my finfull life fucceedeth,
  And feare of heavenly judge great terror breedeth.

My mangled members, in this grave included,
Have anfwered lawes extreames to my confufion.
Oh God ! let not my murthers be obtruded
Againft my foule, wrongd through my earthes illufion ;
  And as the grave my liveleffe limmes containeth,
  So take my foule to thee where reft remaineth.

Thou travailer that treadeft on my toombe
Remembreth thee of my untimely fall :
Prevent the time, forethinke what may become ;
See that thy will be to thy reafon thrall.
Scorne worlds delights, efteeme vaine honor fmall.

So maiſt yu die with fame, where men of conſcience foule
Periſh with ſhame and hazard of their ſoule.

I have herewith annexed likewiſe ſome other of his ſpirituall hymnes and ſongs, whereby the vertuous may gather how ſweet the fruits be of a reconciled and penitent ſoule.

THE FIRST.

That pitty, Lord, that firſt thy hart inflamed
To entertaine a voluntarie death,
To ranſome man, by lothed ſinnes defamed,
From hel, and thoſe infernal paines beneath;

Vouchſafe, my God, thoſe ſnares it may unloſe
Wherin this blinded world hath me intrapped;
That whilſt I traffique in this world of woes,
My ſoule no more in luſts may be in[w]rapped.

Great are my faults, Oh me moſt wilfull witted!
But if each one were juſt, there were no place
To ſhew thy power, that ſinnes might be remitted.
Let then, O Lord! thy mercy quite diſplace
The lewd and endleſſe ſinnes I have committed,
Through thine unſpeakable and endleſſe grace.

THE SECOND.

Such darke obſcured clouds at once incombred
My mind, my hart, my thoughts from grace retired,
With ſwarmes of ſinnes that never may be numbred,
That hope of vertue quite in me expired.

When as the Lord of hosts, my gratious father,
Bent on my dulled powers his beames of brightnesse,
And my confused spirits in one did gather,
Too long ensnard by vanitie and lightnesse.

A perfect zeale (not office of my sences)
So seazde my judgement smothered in his misse,
That heaven I wisht, and loathd this earthly gaile:
My heart disclaimd vile thoughts and vaine pretences,
And my desires were shut in seemely vaile,
So that I said, Lord, what a world is this!

After such time as he had received his judgement, he grew into this meditation of the miseries of life, which, I dare avow, is both worthie the reading and noting, yea even among the learnedst.

THE THIRD.

A shop of shame, a gaine of live-long griefe,
A heaven for fooles, a hel to perfect wise,
A theater of blames, where death is chiefe,
A golden cup, where poison hidden lies.

A storme of woes without one calme of quiet,
A hive that yeeldeth hemlock and no hony,
A boothe of sinne, a death to those that trie it,
A faire where cares are sold withouten mony:

A fleshlie joy, a grave of rotten bones,
A spring of teares, a let of true delight,
A losse of time, a laborinth of mones,

A pleasing paine, a prison of the sprite,
  Is this my life: why cease I, then, resolved
  To pray with Paule, and wish to be dissolved?

Thus endeth the life of William Long beard, a glasse for all sorts to looke into, wherein the high minded may learne to know the meane, and corrupt consciences may reade the conclusion of their wickednes: let this example serve to withdraw the bad minded from Bedlem insolence, and incorage the good to follow godlinesse. So have I that fruit of my labour which I desire, and God shall have the glory; to whom be all praise.

FINIS.

Of manie famous pirats, who in times
paſt were Lordes of the Sea.

THERE were manie worthie pirates in our forefathers daies, but among all of greateſt reckoning Dionides was not leaſt, who exerciſed his larcenies in the Levant ſeas in the time of Alexander the great and Darius, diſdaining either to ſerve the one or to ſubmit himſelfe to the other: yea, ſo reſolute was he in his robberies, and diſſolute in his life, that he neither ſpared friend nor favoured foe, but robd all in generall. Againſt this man Alexander levied a great armie, and by ſtrong hand ſubdued him; and afterward calling him into his preſence, he ſaid thus unto him. Tell me, Dionides, whie thou haſt troubled all the ſeas? to whome he thus replied: Tell me, Alexander, whie haſt thou overrun the whole worlde, and robbed the whole ſea? Alexander anſwered him: becauſe I am a king and thou art a pirat: trulie (replied Dionides), O Alexander! both thou and I are of one nature, and the ſelfe ſame office; the onelie difference is that I am called a pyrat, for that I aſſault other men with a little armie, and thou art called a prince, becauſe thou ſubdueſt and ſignioreſt with a mightie hoaſt. But if the gods would be at peace with me, and Fortune ſhould ſhew her ſelfe perverſe towards thee, in ſuch ſort as Dionides mighte be Alexander, and Alexander Dionides, perhaps I ſhould be a better prince than thou art, and thou a worſer pyrat than I am.

Stilcon for fixteene yeeres fpace was a pirat in the Carpathean Sea, and executed manie great robberies upon the Bactrians, and highlie infefted Rhodes. Againft whom king Demetrius levied an armie, and finallie tooke him; and, calling him to his prefence, faide unto him: Tell me, Stilcon, what harme the Rhodians have done thee, that thou fo muche indemnifieft them? and wherein have the Bactrians defaulted that thou hafte ruinated their realmes? Stilcon anfwered, I woulde thou wouldeft tell me, Demetrius, what harme my father did unto thee, that thou commandedft him to be beheaded? or wherein have I injured thee, that I am exiled by thy judgement? I councell thee in this my laft hower, and not with the leaft confideration, that thou perfecute not, neither purfue any man as much as thou maieft, becaufe it is a matter verie dangerous to deliberate with them of peace, who are defperate both of life and honnor.

Cleonides was a pirat in the daies of king Ptolomey, and fcowred the feas for the fpace of twenty and two yeares, and for feven of them never fet foot on land from out his gallie. This Cleonides was fquint eied and crup fhouldred, not unworthelie in that manner marked by nature, becaufe every waie he was moft tyranouflie minded againft everie prifoner he tooke: he never obferved promife, or pittied prifoner; but thofe enimies he tooke (amongeft other millions of torments wherewith he tyrannized over them) he powred hot fcalding oile into their fundaments, and fet their feete in boiling oile, till they were burnte and fcorched. Againft him Ptolomey fent out an armie; and having taken him called him before his judgement feat, and fpake unto him after this manner: Tell me, Cleonides, what barbarous inhumanitie or infernall furie have inftigated thee to inflict fuch infufferable torments on those who, as thy felfe, are men, and being as thy felfe ought to be pittied by thy felfe? To whom Cleonides gave this churlifh anfwer: It fufficeth not me, thou king, to execute my envie upon the bodies of thofe I hate, and whoe have perfecuted me in their life times; but alfo I refolve to burne their bowels up, and fcalde out their harts wherewith they hated me. Ptolomey, wondring at his defperate inhumanitie, gave him this judgement: that he fhould likewife, by little and little, be dipped in fcalding oile, to the ende hee might taft the felfe fame torment wherewith he had attempted manie others.

Chipanda, the pirat, was a Theban borne, and flourifhed in the time of Cyrus, a man of high minde, great valour, generous hart, and vertues hardineffe; for he had under his conduct 130 fhippes, with which he brought under his fubjection all the kingdomes of the Levant, and ftruck continuall feare into all the heartes of the princes in the Weft. Againft him Cyrus rigged out an armie, by whome his fhips were conquered and himfelfe taken captive; who, comming into Cyrus prefence, was by him faluted in this manner: Tell me, Chipanda, whie forfookeft thou my paie, and afterwards fubmitteft thy felfe to the fervice of the Parthian? To whom he thus anfwered: The lawes which are made on land binde not thofe that ferve by fea; and thofe alfo which we capitulate at fea are not accuftomed or ufed on lande: and I tell you this, O king, becaufe it is an ancient cuftome amongeft pirats, fo often to alter and change our patrons, as often as you fhall fee the windes alter and change at the fea.

Millia, the pirat, lived in the daies of Dionifius, the firft tyrant in Syracufa, and both of them were highlie at oddes, the one with the other; yet in fuch fort enimies, as they contended not which fhoulde exceede one another in goodneffe, but which of them fhould have the palme for ungodlineffe; for Dionifius ruinated all Sicily, and Milia facked all Afia: he ufed this exercife of pyracie more then thirtie yeares, and at laft the Rhodians, arming themfelves againft him, took him: and afterwards, they bringing him to the place of his execution, he lifted uppe his eies to heaven, and faid thus: O Neptune, god and lorde of the feas! whie wilt thou not helpe mee at this houre, who have facrificed and drowned five hundred men in thy waves, and peecemeale cut them in gobbets before thy majeftie? Fortie thoufand have I fent into the bowels of the floud, to the end they fhould inrich the bottome, and thirtie thoufand have died in my fhippes thorowe fickneffe: twentie thoufande have perifhed in my gallies manfullie fighting; and fhall it now fuffice in that heere I die alone, whoe have glutted thy vaft waters with fo many carcafes?

Alcomonius was a pirat at fuch time as Scilla and Marius flourifhed (and following the faction of Scilla) was he that tooke Caius Cæfar when he fled from Scilla; whom Cæfar very often, after a pleafant manner, affured that he had deliberated to hang him and all his confederates by the neck, and according to his words accomplifhed his promife at fuch time as he came to the governement of the Romaine commonweale. This Alcamonius being readie to die, faid: I am little grieved for that I lofe, and leffe afflicted for the maner of death by which I die; but this is it which urgeth me, that I [am] fallen into his hands who was once my prifoner, whome I might have hanged then, as he now hangeth me.

There were likewife manie other ancient and moderne pirats, whom, for that I am ftudious of brevitie, I in this place willinglie pretermit: It onely fufficeth you, that you confider that no one of them died in his bed, neither made teftament of his goodes, but as foone as the fatall houre of their deftinies was arrived, they died both defamed unto the world, and detefted for their wickednes.

The Agifincts were famous pirats in the time of Themofticles, who turned out a hundred gallies amongft them, and tooke all of them: and after he had imprifoned and difarmed them, hanged them up: which act of his caufed him to be favoured in Greece and feared on the fea.

Frauncis Enterolles, a famous pirat, was borne in Valentia of noble parents and a princelie ftocke: This man committed mightie and manie robberies at fea, and in the river of Genova; and finallie when, in the yeare 1491, he had longe time followed the chace, he was by tempeft and Fortune driven upon the Ilande of Corfica; and thofe whoe by chance efcaped the daunger and the fury of the feas, incountred death on the land, and were all of them with their capteine Francis hanged by the neck for their piracies: the reft that were left were made gallie flaves, being by the ilanders furprifed in their gallie: and this was the end of this noble Valentinian.

Monaldo Guecca, a famous pirat, borne in Navar, flourifhed in the yeare 1496. This manne, having occupied and ftrengthened himfelfe upon the rocke of Hoftia, hindered all the convey of victuals to Rome after fuch manner, that neither wine nor corne, neither any other marchandife could be brought either from the kingdome of Naples, from Corfica, or the river of Genua unto the cittie. Againſt him Pope Alexander ſent the great Confalvo, who tooke the rocke and brought Menaldo bound to Rome upon a leane jade in maner of triumph. And it is reported that he went with ſo confident a countenance, that he inforced terror in all thoſe that beheld him. Confalvo, for that he was a Spaniard, got him his pardon, and wrought the Pope to be very bountifull unto him.

A true and famous Hiſtory of Partaritus, King of Lombardie, who being purſued by Grimaldo, fled firſt of all to Cucano, King of the Avarior Huns, and then into France, and finallie, after manie travailes, was reſtored to his kingdom with much majeſtie; wherein the worthy memorie of two faithfull ſervants is happilie regiſtred.

PARTARITUS was the ſonne of Albert, Kinge of Lombardie, who after the death of his father raigned himſelfe in Millan, and Gundibert, his brother, in Pavia. Betwixt theſe twoe there grew a mortall difcention, for which cauſe Gundibert ſent Garibald, Duke of Turinge, to Grimoald, Duke of Benivent, a moſt worthy and valiant capteine, requeſting his aſſiſtance in armes againſt his brother, and promiſing him in rewarde thereof to beſtowe his ſiſter upon him in mariage. But Garibald uſed treaſon againſt his lord, animating Grimoald to the enterpriſe, not as an abettor, but a conqueror. For (ſaid he) you may eaſilie occupie the kingdome, by reafon of the twoe brethren, whoe, through their diſſentions, have almoſte ruinated the ſame. Grimoald, aſſerteined herof, made his ſonne Duke of Benevent, and levieng a mightie power ſet onwards on his way to Pavia ; and through everie cittie that he paſſed he drewe friends unto him, and won the better ſort with benefites, to the end they ſhould aſſiſt him toward the attainment of the kingdome: and comming to parlie with Gundibert, who (little ſuſpecting the trecheries which Garibald had complotted) came ſlenderlie and courtlie accompanied to entertaine him, he on ſudden ſlue him, and occupied the kingdome. Partaritus aſſertained hereof abandoned Rhodeline, his wife, and his little ſonn, and fled to Cucano, king of the Avarior Huns : Grimoald confirmed in the kingdome of Pavia, underſtanding that Partharithus was entertained by Cucano, ſent ambaſſadors unto him, threatning him, that if he retained Partharithus, his enimie, in his kingdome, he ſhoulde be aſſured to purchaſe of him a mightie enimie, and more, to occaſion a preſent and dangerous warre.

The king of the Hunns, aſſertained heereof, called Partarithus unto him, and ſaid thus : I pray thee, gentle friende, depart into ſome other place ; for if thou be heere reſident, my good will towards thee will occaſion great warres againſte my ſelfe. Partharitus underſtanding the kings mind, returning into Italie, went and ſought out Grimoald, repoſing his life upon the good diſpoſitions of his enimie. And drawing neere the cittie of Lodi, he ſent before him one of his faithfull ſervants called Unulfe, who might make manifeſt to Grimoald, both how much he truſted him, and what he required at his hands. Unulfe preſenting himſelfe before the kinges Majeſtie, told him that Partaritus, his maiſter, had recourſe unto his clemencie, and ſought ſuccour in his court. Grimoald admiring his confidence, faithfullie promifed him that he might repaire unto him, uppon the faith of a prince affuring him that before he fhould be harmed, he would hazard his owne hart.

A little while after, when Partharitus prefented himfelfe before Grimoald, and humblie kneeling upon his knees, befought his favour, the king pitiouflie and gratiouflie entertained and kiffed him, whome in humble manner Partharitus faluted thus: Mightie Soveraigne, I am thy fervant, who, knowing thou art a Chriftian, doubt not of thy compaffion. I might (as thou knoweft, O king!) have lived among Pagans; but what life were that? and howe bafe confidence were I in, rather to truft the faithleffe, then humble my felfe to the faithfull? I befeech thee of mercie, and kiffing thy feet crave maintenance. The king according to his maner fwering a folemne oath, promifed him, faieng: By him that begat me, fince thou haft recourfe unto my faith, I will never forfake thee; but I will take order for thee in fuche manner, that thou maieft both honeftlie and honourablie live in this countrey. Whereupon he commanded him to be worthilie lodged, giving charge that he fhould be furnifhed of all neceffaries whatfoever upon his treafurie.

It chanced that Partaritus, departing from the king and repairing to his lodging, was fuddenlie encountered with a whole troope of cittizens of Pavia, who came to fee him and falute him as their foreftemed friend. But fee what great mifchiefe proceedeth from an evill and detracting toong! For fome malignant flatterers, beholding the fame, fought out the king, and gave him to underftande, that if he made not Partaritus fuddenlie out of the waie, himfelfe, without all doubt, fhould lofe both his kingdome and life; fwearing to him that all the cittie was alreadie addicted to take his part.

Grimoald confidering thefe thoughts, and by his overmuch credulitie fufpecting more then he needed, fuddenlie refolved on the death of miferable Partharitus; and calling his councell unto him, ceafed not to contrive the meanes howe the innocent might be made awaie. They, feeing that daie far fpent, refolved the deed fhould be doone the next morrowe, animating the king by good words, who otherwife through feare was almoft out of his wits: notwithftanding thorow their perfwafions gathering to himfelfe more confidence, the better to colour his intention, hee fent unto him that night manie excellent difhes and ftrong wines, purpofing (if it were poffible) to make him drunke; affuring himfelfe that by the meanes thereof he for that night fhould have more care of his fleepe than regard of his fafetie.

But fee how God helpeth the innocent! for a certein gentleman, who before that time had beene a fervitour in Partharithus fathers court, prefenting him with a meffe of meate from the king, and leaning downwards, as if intending reverence to his Majeftie, tolde him fecretlie howe the kinge the next daie had refolved to put him to death. For which caufe Partaritus fuddenlie called his fquire, willing him that night to give him no other drink but a little water in a filver cup: knowing this, that if thofe who prefented him in the kings behalfe would requeft him to caroufe to his health, he might eafilie doo without intoxicating his braines, drinking onelie water. Thofe that ferved him at the table, feeing Partaritus take his liquor fo livelie, certified the king thereof; who with much joyfulneffe faid,

Let the drunkard drinke his fill for this night; but to morrowe, yer ever he fufpect the banquet, I meane to feaft him
with his owne bloud.

This faide, he caufed his guard to be fet in the houfe,
fearing and fufpecting leaft Partaritus fhould efcape him in
any fort. The fupper being ended, and everie one having
taken his leave, Partharitus thus left alone with Unulfe, his
truftie fervant, and the page who ordinarilie attended on
him to bed, he difcovered unto them howe the king had
refolved to kill him: for which caufe Unulfe winding him
about the necke with the fheetes of the bedde, and laieng
the coverlet and the beares fkin upon his backe, leaving
him without capp, as if he were fome rufticke or common
drudging fellowe, began to drive him out of the chamber,
dooing him manie injuries and villannies, fo that he verie
oftentimes fell to the ground.

Grunoalds guard, whoe were appointed unto the watch,
feeing al thefe outrages, afked Unulfe what he meant?
Why, faid he, my maifters, this rafcal flave hath made me
my bed in the chamber of that drunken palliard Panthari-
thus, which is fo full of wine, that he fleepeth as if he were
dead, without ftirring; and this is the caufe whie I beat
him; and I praye you dooth he not deferve it? They
hearing thefe words, and beleeving them to be true, did all
of them laugh verie hartelie to heare the tidings, and giving both of them licence to depart, Partaritus hafted to the
cittie of Hafti, and from thenfe went into France, praifing
God for his happie deliverie.

As foone as they were gotte awaie, the faithfull page
locked the door verie diligentlie, remaining all that night
alone in the chamber; and when the meffengers of the

king came with commiffion to bring Partaritus to the pal-lace the nexte daie, they knocked at the doore ; whom the page in humble maner faluted, praieng them to have patience for a while ; for (faith he) my lord, being wearie of his laft journey, fleepeth now verie foundlie. The meffengers returning to Grimoald, told him the pages anfwer, who all inraged, charged them prefentlie to bring him to his prefence : who repairing againe to the chamber doore, were in like fort once more folicited by the page to ufe forbearance ; but they, admitting no delaies, cried out haftilie and hartilie, Tut, tut, the droonkard hath now flept enough, and thereupon bearing the doore of[f] the hinges, they forceablie entered the chamber, and fought Partaritus in his bed, but found him not : whereupon they afked the page what was become of him ? who anfwered them that he was fled. The meffengers, all amazed herewith, furiouflie laieng hands on the childes bufhie lock, and buffeting him piteouflie, brought him to the pallace ; and conducting him to the prefence of the king, faide, Mightie Prince, Partharitus is fled, and this caitife boy helpt to convey him, and for that caufe meriteth death. Grimoald commanded them to laie hands off him, and willed him with a friendlie countenance to difcover unto him the manner and meanes how his maifter had efcaped awaie. The page told him everie thing as it had paft ; whofe faithfulnes when the king had confidered upon, he royallie offered him to make him one of his pages, affuring the lad that if he would be as faithfull to him, as he had fhewed himfelfe towards his old maifter, he fhould both be rewarded and regarded.

After this he made fearch for Unulfe, who being brought before his prefence, was pardoned by him, and not only pardoned but commended. But as where affection is rooted there no favors can fupplant it, nor promifes fuppreffe it, fo thefe two loving their maifter Partarithus verie deerelie, took no delight but onelie in defire they had to fee and ferve him; for which caufe in a few daies after they repaired to Grimoald, befeeching him of licenfe to feeke out their mafter. Whie, my friends (quoth he), had you rather feeke out your neceffities, then live with me heere in all pleafures? By God, replied Unulfe, I had rather die with Partharithus than live in all other worldlie contents and delights. What (faid the king to the page) wilt thou alfo rather feeke out a banifhed man, then ferve a king? I, my lorde, faide he; for they are bad fervants that will leave their maifters in miferie. Grimoald, wondering at their confidence, and praifing both their faithes, difmiffed both of them with all favour, giving them both horffe and money to furnifh and further them on theyr journey.

The two faithfull fervants, humblie thanking the kinge, tooke their waie into France, hoping to finde their maifter in that place according as was appointed. But Partaritus, fearing leaft, by reafon of a peace latlie capitulated betwixt Dogobert kinge of France and Grimoald, he fhould be there furprised fuddenlie by fome finifter fubtletie, tooke fhipping for England; and having alreadie failed from the fhore, the voice of a man was heard among the rocks, which afked for Partaritus, and whither he were in that fhip? Whereto when anfwer was made that there he was, the voice replied, Then will him prefently repaire into his countrey, for Grimoald, a three daies hence, is departed this life. Partaritus fuddenly returned backe, commanding the marriners to reenter the harbour; and as foon as he was landed, he diligently fought out the meffenger that had thus informed him: but finding him by no meanes poffible, he fuppofed it to be fome meffuage fent from God. For which caufe, poafting towards his countrey, and arriving amongft the confines of Italie, hee found there a great number of Lombards, who expected him, with whom he entered Pavia, and driving out a little fon of Grimoalds from the kingdome, he was by generall confent created kinge of Lombardie, three moneths after the death of Grimoald. For which caufe he prefentlie fent unto Benevent for his wife Rhodolinde and his fon Cunibert. And being a godlie Catholike and juft man, a liberall patron of the poore, and father of the innocent, as foone as he had quiet poffeffion of the kingdome, in that place from whence he fled, which is on the other fide of Tefinus, he builded a monafterie to the honor and glorie of God, his faviour and onelie defender, wherein there were divers Nunnes inclofed, whom he alwaies enriched with many verie goodlie poffeffions.

The Queene likewife builded a church, in honour of our Ladie, without the cittie wals, adorning it with marvelous rich ornaments. His page and truftie fervant returning to his court as foon as they had tidinges of his eftablifhment, were by him favourablie intertained and richlie rewarded. Finallie, after he had reigned eighteen yeares he departed this life, not without the generall lament and teares of the whole inhabitants of Lombardie.

The wonderfull dreame of Aspatia, the daughter of Hermotimus, the Phocencian, a verie poore man, who afterwards thorow hir wonderful vertues became the wife of Cyrus, King of Percia, and was afterwards married to Artaxerxes.

ASPATIA was the daughter of Hermotimus of Phocis, who after the death of hir mother was brought up and nourished in great povertie: yet was not hir povertie so greevous as her continencie was gratious. In her infancie she had under hir chin a great swelling which disfigured hir face, and was a great disgrace to hir faireneffe: for which caufe hir father, desirous to have hir cured, carried hir to a phisitian, who promised to heale hir for a certaine summe of money. The good olde man, having no money, tolde the physitian of his little meanes, beseeching him to stand favourable unto his child; but the greedie wretch, which was too well learned in no pennie no Pater noster, told him, that then he had no medicine for him: for which caufe the poore Hermotimus and his sicklie daughter repared home without succors. Aspatia, being thus ill bested, entered hir chamber, and setting hir glasse betweene hir legges, she gased so long intentivelie on hir imperfection, and with so manie tender teares bemoned hir wants, till at last she fell asleepe, where upon a suddaine she beheld a dove changed suddenlie into a woman, which saied unto hir, Bee of good cheere, and leave these drug maisters, and goe unto the dried crowne of Roses upon Venus head, and taking some of them, beate thou them to powder, and then doo thou but strew them upon thy greevous sore.

Aſpatia, having performed no leſſe then was commanded hir in hir viſion, was healed, and became verie faire, and ſo manie were the graces wherewith ſhe flouriſhed, that no man could either compare or equall them. She had hir haires, glorious and gold-like golden, ſomwhat daintilie curled, hir eies fierie and chriſtalline, hir noſe hooked, hir eares little, and the colour of hir face like unto Roſes waſhed in milke : hir lippes crimoſin, hir teeth more white then ſnow ; hir voice was delicious ſweete and muſicall, hir delightes were eſtranged from all effeminate newfangleneſſe : ſhee ſtudied not to be rich in apparell (which is but the verie ſurfet of ſubſtance) becauſe being nouriſhed in povertie, ſhee could not, nor would not, in anie wiſe yeelde any art to her beawtie, wanting both the meanes and the manner.

It chanced that this maiden, amongeſt a great manie others, was bought by a Baron who belonged to king Cyrus, who ſeeing that ſhe was beawtifull and faire, brought hir (after a verie ſolemne and ſumptuous ſupper) into the preſence of Cyrus, accompanied with three other Grecian maids, who were tricked and attired by courtlie dames before hande, to the end they might know how to entertaine and delight the king : onlie Aſpatia would not admit anie foile for hir faire, but after many refuſals, at laſt conſented to put on a ſumptuous habit, wherein ſhe ſtoode ſo melancholie and bluſhinglie, as if ſhe thought all lookers on unworthie to beholde hir beawtie ; and fixing her fiery eies upon the ground, ſhe wept bitterlie before Cyrus, who commanded the three other Virgins to ſit downe by him, who were obſequious to his will ; but Aſpatia fained as though ſhe heard him not when he called hir, untill the

Baron who bought hir, enforced hir to fit by his majeſtie.

Cyrus dallieng and beholding the three other virgines, commended their countenances, and condemned not their behaviour; but having but touched Aſpatia with the tip of his finger, ſhe ſuddenlie cried out, telling him that ſhee ſhould be puniſhed if ſhe uſed ſuch licentiouſneſſe. This her behavior pleaſed the king, whoe afterward offered to dallie with her paps: ſhe preſentlie flung from him and offered to depart; for which cauſe Cyrus, marvelling at the great mind of Aſpatia, farre againſt the cuſtome of Percia, ſaid unto him that had brought hir, Thou haſt onelie brought this mayden unto me free, ſincere, and without ſpot: the others are but counterfeits in their cuſtomes, and their beawties are but borrowed, not naturall.

Hereupon Cyrus, affected by this meanes, and earneſtlie fixed his love upon Aſpatia, ſo that he forgat all other fancies, addicting himſelfe onlie to hir bed and beawtie. Not longe after, Aſpatia called to hir mind the doome ſhe had ſeen in hir dreame, and the ſpeeches which were uſed, and in regarde of thoſe benefits she had received, ſhe erected a ſtatue of golde in honor of Venus, and annexed thereunto a dove beawtified with coſtlie gems, offering daielie ſacrifices to remunerate the Goddeſſe kindneſſe. She likewiſe ſent unto her father manie rich jewels, and made him a man of great authoritie. A few daies after, a faire and curious carkanet was ſent out of Theſſaly in preſent to king Cyrus, who rejoicing greatlie at the ſame, and finding his Aſpatia one daie aſleepe laid him downe by hir, and (after ſome amorous embracings) drewe the carkanet out of a caſket, and ſaied unto hir, How ſaieſt thou, my love, dooth not this jewell become either a daughter or mother of a king? Yes, my liege, faide fhe: whie then, my love, it fhall be thine, quoth he: difcover therefore thy neck, and put it on.

Afpatia, little refpecting the rich guift, reverentlie and fagelie replied thus: How fhould I be fo bold to fubmit my necke unto that gift, which is a prefent more convenient for Parifatides, thy mother? Give it hir, my lorde, and I am readie to fhew you my neck without any fuch ornaments. Cyrus, rejoyfing at hir anfwer, kiffed hir, and having written all the manner of difcourfe which had paft twixt him and Afpatia, he fent the fame with the carcanet unto his mother. Parifatide, no leffe delighted with the letter than the carcanet, remunerated Afpatia with rich gifts and royall prefents, and conceiving a gratious opinion in that Afpatia gave hir place, fhee ever after loved her, and prefented hir both with the carcanet and much other treafure. Afpatia, humblie receiving hir ineftimable curtefies, fent both the jewell and treafure to Cyrus with this meffage: Thefe for a time will helpe thee, and for that thou art mine ornament, mefeemeth I have obtayned a great gift, if, as I both fhould and woulde, I heartelie love the.

Cyrus was amazed at this deed, and not without reafon, becaufe this woman had no meane minde, but the courage of a great and magnificent princeffe. But when Cyrus was flaine in the warre which he waged againfte his brother, Afpatia remained prifoner: notwithftandinge fought out and at laft found by the noble Artaxerxes, fhe was delivered of hir bonds, and fuch as had captivated hir were committed themfelves. Finallie, being richly apparailed like a princeffe (although by reafon of the deth of Cyrus she made great resistance) Artaxerxes being vehementlie enamored of her beawtie, after long intreatie and comforts, at last won her consent, and married hir: yet, as some writers testifie, the intire affection she bare her last husband was never extinguished untill she died.

A wonderous revenge executed by Megallo Lercato of Genova upon the mightie Emperour of Trabisonda.

AT such time as the Genowaies weare Lords of certeine citties in the Levāt, it chanced that, amongest other cittizens whoe traffiqued in Caffa, and were most familiar with the Emperour of Trabisond, there was one called Megollo Lercato, whoe by reason of his rare quallities was exceedinglie favoured by him: for which cause he was greevouslie envied and hated by the principall courteors, whoe ceased not continuallie to invent new meanes and waies whereby they might bring him in disgrace. It fortuned that, sporting himselfe one daie at the chaffe with a yoong noble man who was greatlie beloved by the Emperour, they fell at wordes and bitter upbraides: amongst all others, the yong Noble uttering certeine speeches in contempt of the name of Genowaies, Megollo was inforced to give him the lie; but seeing the other little moved therewith, his countrey dishonoured, and the court laughing at him, he sought his remedie at the Emperors hands, from whom he could get no redresse in repaire of his honor.

For which cause Megollo hotlie discontent (though for a purpose he smothered his displeasures a space) a fewe daies after, upon a lawfull cause, tooke occasion to crave the Emperours licence, and departing to Genua, altogither inflamed to revenge, he furnifhed himfelfe, by meanes of fome parents and friends, and rigging out two warlike gallies, he failed with them into the great fea, and there indevored himfelfe to fpoile all the coaft and ranfacke everie fhippe belonging to the Emperour: whomefoever he tooke, in the waie of great difdaine, he cut off their nofes and eares, and though there were manie fhips fet out againft him, yet in fpight of all he never defifted from endangering him: and this might he the better performe in that his fhips were verie fwifte; and when he found himfelfe at any difadvantage, he could both leave and take how and when it pleafed him. It chanced, amongft manie other preparations that were fet out to intrap him, foure ftout gallies were rigged, who upon confultation, as foone as they had difcovered him, devided themfelves apart, thinking to inclofe him in the midft of them, and fo all at once to affaile him. Megollo, that quicklie perceived their pollicie, fuddenlie fained to flie; whom when their fwifteft gallie had long time purfued, and over-wrought all hir conforts, Megollo made head againfte them, and flewe them, and ferved them all after the fame fauce, to the woonderfull amaze and difcontent of the Emperor.

Amongeft one of thefe gallies there was an olde man with his two fonnes, whoe, fearing the like fortune which had befalne others fhould light on him and his fonnes, humblie proftrating himfelfe at Megollos feet, he humblie intreated him for mercie. The old mannes teares were gratious, and had fuch power over the generous mind of Megollo, that he forgave both him and his fonns with the reft that were alive in his gallie, and fent him back unto the Emperor with a veffell full of eares and nofes, willing the olde man to let the Emperor underftand that he would never ceafe to indemnifie him, untill fuch time as he hadde fent unto him the man who had fo difdainfullie and difhonorablie injured him in his court.

The Emperor afferteined hereof determined with himfelfe, as the leffer evill, to go himfelfe in perfon unto the fea, and carrie with him (as he did) the yong man who had occafioned all this trouble. Megollo, hearing thereof, thruft his gallies neerer the fhore, when as the Emperor prefently in a light boat fent him the yoong noble with a rope about his necke; whoe, having his eies proude with teares, humbled himfelfe at Megollos feet, befeeching mercy. Megollo, compaffionate therewith, bad him get him thence, telling him that it was not the fafhion of the Genowaies to tirannize over effeminate milkfops.

The parents of the yong man, feeing him returne againe beyond their expectation, received him with great joye: divers offers were made by the Emperor to Megollo, who, refufing them all, returned this anfwer:—That he came thither not for defire of riches but for honors fake, and to eternife the name of the Genowaies, admitting no other covenantes but this; that in memorie of thofe his actions, a pallace fhould be reared in Trabifond for the commodity of the Genowaies, wherein he would, by a curious hand and cunning workman, thofe his actions fhould be eternized: which being afterwards fullie obferved by the Emperor, they whoe traffiqued there followe their marchandize with more honor then they were accuftomed. Megollo after this worthie acte returned home to Genova, where he was received and gratified with great honors by the cittizens.

The memorable deeds of Velafca, a Lady of Bohemia, whoe, caufing all other Ladies to kill their husbands, Brethren and fonnes, raigned feven yeares in Bohemia.

I READ in the Bohemian hiftorie written by Pope Pius, that this Velafca, of whom I heere meane to intreate, was a woman of great mind, bolde in all attempts, and highlie favored by Fortune; and to the end you may the better underftand hir hiftorie, I will firft of all begin with hir caufe of hatred. You have therefore to confider that Crocus, fecond Duke of Bohemia, dieng without iffue male, his daughter Libuffa (held in thofe daies in as great account as one of the Sibils) with the favour of the people, and good liking of the better fort, was placed in hir fathers feate, and governed that Province manie yeeres, with the generall good liking of all men. Finallie, having given a juft fentence in right of certeine poffeffions againft a mightie man in that countrey, he being therewith incenfed, provoked up the people againft hir, faieng it was an opprobrious and fcandalous thing for fuch a people as they were, and fo great a Nobilitie as was refident in that place, to fuffer the kingdom and caufes of juftice to be under a woman.

Libuffa, having intreated filence at their hands for a time, faid unto them that fhe knew their new defire, and was not ignorant of their firme determination, difabling her felfe to fatisfie their expectations, praieng them to affemble the next daie; which according as she willed them they perfourmed. The morning began noe fooner to pufhe forth his blushinge beawties, but the people repaired to the judgment feat in great multitudes; and as foone as the pallace was filled everie waies by them, Libuffa began to fpeake unto them on this maner: You know (Bohemians) that to this prefent day I have beene your peaceable and bountifull Ladie, according to womens cuftome, whoe are audatious in nothing but in offering curtefies. Hitherto have I not beene offenfive to any of you, either chargeable by reafon of Pompe, fhewing my felfe rather a mother unto you then a miftreffe: but ingratefullie, unkind men as you are, requite you my government. But at thefe your actions woonder not I at all, becaufe you accuftome your felves to the common fashions of men, who are never content, but are more fkilfull to defire a juft and mercifull Lord, then having him they have knowledge to keepe him.

As touching mine owne title, I whollie furrender it into your hands; and as you have defired one who fhal governe you, and order your lawes as he lift, fo I am contented you shall have him. Therefore go ye and take me a white horffe, and bridle him with all his other apparell and ornamentes, and afterwards lead him to fuch a plaine, where he may take that waie which beft likes him. Which doone, let him trot as he lift, and follow you him by his footfteps: as he turnes, fo turne you; and as he returneth, fo returne you: finallie, when you fhall fee him ftaie before a man that feedeth at an iron table, then affure your felves he is the man forpointed to be my husband, and your prince.

This hir fpeeche pleafed them all; fo that taking with them the horffe as Libuffa had inftructed them, they let him freelie goe, and followed him. But fcarfelie had they travelled ten miles, when as the horfe ftaied at a river called Bieli, and arrefted himfelfe before a countrey fellow called Primiſlaus, ſhewing manie ſignes of humanitie and obſervance toward them.

The Bohemians, as well the nobles as commons, behoulding this, ran with all haſt unto him, and after their ſalutations ſaid thus unto him:—Libuſſa hath choſen thee for hir husband, and the Bohemians admit thee for their prince. Primiſlaus, although he were a poore countrey clowne, not incapeable of the generall deſire of rule which attainteth all men, gave unto them a homelie ſalutation after his manner, and tolde them that he was addreſſed to doo whatſoever pleaſed them: and underſtanding that he was to goe to Libuſſa (as if hee had a longe voiage to make) he faſtened his bottle to his ſaddle bow, and graſping his bread and cheeſe in his hand, he rode on feeding like a ruſticke king, which was a verie ſufficient evidence of that which Libuſſa before time had declared and told unto them.

As ſoone as his guttes were full and his bottle emptied, he mended his pace, and they conducted him with great pomp and honour into the cittie, where he tooke Libuſſa to wife, and during all his life time was wholie ruled and governed by hir counſels and perſwaſions. But after ſhe had ſubmitted hir ſelfe to the deſtinies, the government remained wholie in Primiſlaus hands, and the authoritie of Ladies ceaſed, which even unto that hower was both maintained and augmented by Libuſſa. After this Valaſca (which whilſt Libuſſa lived was hir ſecretarie) being a Ladie of great valour and no leſſe reſolution then an Amazon, not induring or abiding that the authoritie of women ſhould be thus annihilated, aſſembling one daie in a priuie place all thoſe that were of her faction, ſhe ſaid thus unto them:—

My ſiſters, we have loſt our good Ladie, who alwaies defended us from the outrages of men; neither could she ever endure that we should be overborne by them, so that she her selfe held the Emperie, and we with hir were in respect held and accounted for Queenes. You see now how enforced we indure a hard and miserable servitude, living under the government of our husbands after the maner of slaves, except of our selves we shall gather head and courage to recover our former liberties. Wherefore, if your thoughtes be as mine is, let us joine like heroick Ladies, and we will easily recover our estates. I (as you know) was secretarie unto Libussa, of whom I learned that which she knew: I am skilfull in inchantments, and the nature of hearbes is not unknowne unto me: if, therefore, you have any meaning, or will to followe me, assure your selves that you shall be once again lords over men.

Upon these words the whole assemblie of women condiscended to Valascas words, and mutuallie conspired against men. During this time Primislaus dreamed one night that a virgine gave him bloud to drinke; for which cause he being a notable soothsaier, and willing to prevent a mischiefe which (as he imagined) might verie easilie be impugned, hee convocated all the chiefe nobles of his Province, under intention to prohibit the over-great licence and libertie which women had in the common weale: namelie, the women were accustomed to ride and run the race on horssebacke, to tournay, shoote, and followe the chace, and brieflie to exercise themselves in all warlike discipline, which (as he thought) were matters manageable by men, and unfit tasks for women. But the Barons scoffed at him when he told them therof, and said that they rather deserved love and reverence for their agilitie and hardines, then reproofe and dishonor.

Valafca meane while defifted not neither daie nor night to exhort hir confederates, and often with drinks and inchantments turned away their affections from the love of men, and daie by daie drewe more and more into this her League of confpiracie. Finallie, when fhe perceived that fhe hadde gathered a fufficient power, both of married wives and maids, in one night fhe caufed everie one of hir faction to kill their fathers, husbands, brethren and fonnes in their beddes; and afterwards, taking armes with great expedition, they all of them marched togither to a place appointed them by Velafca, not farre diftant from Prage, and fubduing fome that had them in chace, they made a roade to Vifigrade, whereas Primiflaus aboad, intending there to furprife him: but feeing fhe could not take the fortreffe, they retired themfelves into a mountaine, a place naturallie impregnable, and there building a caftle they called it Deiuizo, that is, the place of virgines, bicaufe that in their toonge a virgine is called Deiuize.

This action of theirs feemed abhominable to all the inhabitants of the countrey, as well in refpect of the great flaughter they had made, as alfo becaufe they had a great fufpition of further mifcheefe; for which caufe they generallie gave Primiflaus to underftand that they were addreft to bidde thefe new Amazons battell, and that if it pleafed him to marche forward with his hoaft, they alfo were in readineffe to follow him. The K. certified them that at that prefent he could not come, by reafon that the Gods had admonifhed him, that all thofe who were addicted to indemnifie the virgines were to die; certifieng them that it was behovefull to go another time. But they, who fet light by his counfell, levieng by them felves a great armie, marched toward Deiuifo, and ftriking battell with Velafco were ignominiouflie overthrowne and put to flight with the flaughter of the greater part of the armie. And whereas in this fervice Malada, Nodea, Suatacia, Vorafta, Ragda, Zaftana and Triftana had behaved themfelves valiantlie, in rewarde of their fervice they had collars and chaines of golde given them: and amidft that unmeafurable pray which they had, everie one was rewarded according to their defart.

Velafca flue with hir owne hand feven of hir enimies, and after that time was held and efteemed for a goddeffe, fo that never after that time the Bohemians had the courage to troble or moleft them; but they euerie daie ranged about the confines, fpoiling, robbing and burning, and daie by day inforced greater dread and feare in the harts of their enimies; and being now Ladies and foveraignes of the better part of Bohemia, they were conftrained to have the companie of men, by reafon that otherwife by courfe of time and warres they were likelie to be reduced and brought to nothing: for which caufe, marrieng themfelves, they made a lawe that thofe maidens that were borne by them fhould with all dilligence bee tenderlie and carefullie brought uppe: as for the males, they commanded that their right eies fhould be pulled out, and their middle fingers cut off, to the ende that having attained mans eftate, they fhould be difabled to fhoote in the bowe, or to handle warlike weapons.

Finallie, Velafca, having afflicted Bohemia for the fpace of feven yeares, and made them altogither tributarie, was deceived by Primiflaus, whoe wrote hir a letter that the Barons, againft his will, had attempted hir with war, and that he was greatlie pleafed that they had received condigne punifhment for their infolence; affuring hir that he hadde alwaies held hir in place of his daughter, not onlie for that fhe had beene fecretarie to his wife, and well thought of by her, but for that fhe knew fo well to governe fo great a ftate as Bohemia was for the fpace of feven yeares. And moreover, that now, fince he felte himfelfe olde and unable to governe his fubjects, on the other fide, his fonne too yoong in yeares for fo waightie a credit, that his will was to render into her hands the fortreffes; fo that by this meanes at one time he would yeeld all Bohemia into hir hands, referring the eftate of his fonne and heire to hir kindneffe and curtefie, contenting himfelfe to returne unto his firft eftate, and live fatisfied in the towne from whence perforce they had taken him, and afterward unwillinglie crowned him. And him feemed, as he wrote that it fhould fo be, that as from a ladies hands he received the throne, so to a ladies hands he might return the title.

This letter, written and fent unto hir, wonne fuch credit with hir, that prefentlie fhe fent before hir a fquadron of hir beft Amazons to receive the fortreffes, who were brought into the lande with great folemnitie, and entertained in the Dukes owne pallace: but whilft thee were at the table, they were all flaine by a troope of armed men, whoe were hidden for that purpofe. They, having flaine thefe, ran to Deiuizo with a great armie, and Velafca having notice of the ftrange accident, iffued hir felfe, fmallie unattended, and cloafed in glittering armes, and mounted upon a verie brave and luftie courfer, that lightened fire from his noftrils, fhee was followed by fome few a farre off, whilft hir felfe folie incountred the whole hoaft that came againft hir; and without anie word fpeaking fhe laied about hir like a Lioneffe or Libian Tygre in hir great furie. Finallie, falling in the midft and thickeft of hir enimies, she died valiantlie.

Hir companions a farre off, as foone as they underftood of the death of their princeffe, not under anie hope to conquer, but ftimulated to worke revenge, fell to armes: betwixt whom and the Bohemians was a moft bloudie and defperate fight; but the Ladies at laft having the worft, were inforced to flie, whom the Viffegradians following entered, togither with them, into their Caftle, and having caufed the gates to be fhut, and being Lordes of the fortreffe, they cut all the poore women to peeces. And thus was Bohemia delivered from the tyrannie and thraldome of women. And Velafca, being worthie to be eternized amongft the Ladies of moft famous memorie, laie unburied, and ferved for a prey for birds and beafts to feed upon.

An excellent example of continence in Frauncis Sforza.

AMONGST all other, I will not pretermit a fingular example of continence in Francis Sforza, whoe deferved in this action of his to be compared with Alexander the great and Scipio the noble. Caffanova, a caftle of Luke, being forciblie furprifed by Erle Francis, there were certaine fouldiours who tooke a faire and tender yoong damofell prifoner, whoe, whilft they forceablie drew hir from out the houfe, weepingly befought them to prefent hir to the earle Francis Sforza, and to no other; fo that they whoe had outraged hir, fearing the difpleafure of the countie, fuddainlie prefented hir unto him.

At that time Francis, by reafon of his yoong yeares, and the found compleƈtion of his bodie, was verie proane and addiƈted to wanton and effeminate paftimes : and although hee were inveigled by the tender yeares and exceeding beautie of the maiden, notwithftanding he inquired of hir, whither fhe had rather confent unto everie pleafure wherein he might imploy hir, or remaine in their handes whoe had firft taken hir ? Whom fhe thus anfwered ; that fhe would be alwaies readie to obay him, fo that it might pleafe him to fet hir free from the handes of bafe injurie. Where upon Francis prefently commanded that fhe fhould be conduƈted into his pavilion. When night came, and before he entered the bed, he afked the maiden againe, if fhe were of the fame minde, or whether fhe had changed hir purpofe ? Who anfwered him that fhe continued refolved : then he willed that fhe fhoulde difrobe and uncloath hir bodie, and fo to laie hir felfe downe by him.

But no fooner was fhe entred the bed, but he efpied the piƈture of our Ladie painted after the maner, wheron turning towards the Earle fhe wept, and with all reverence and fhamfaftneffe she faied unto him, O, my Lorde, I pray thee for that unfpotted virgines fake, whofe image is in our fight, vouchfafe to be the proteƈtor of my virginitie, and thorough thy clemencie grant, that without ftain or dishonor I may returne unto my betrothed fpoufe, who liveth a defperat and defolate life amongeft the other captives. And whereas I promifed thee to fubmit my felfe to thy will, no other thinge moved me there unto, then the defire I hadde to deliver my felfe from the hands of thofe who ravished me : and not that alone, but the juftice and pietie

I have heard of thee, made me conceave a great hope to submit to him who had so great vertues to command.

Thefe words had so great power in the mercifull and generous mind of the Captaine, that they extinguished in him all heat of vaine defires, so that of his owne proper charges he refcued the husband, and redeemed him from thraldome, reftoring the yoong virgine unto him as foone as he came in to his prefence. Hir fpoufe, kneeling uppon his knees, and fighing bitterlie, faid: My Lord, thou dooeft fullie anfwere the great expectation and fame which through everie part is difperfed by thee, so that there is no land, nor no peere in the world that either may match thee for humanitie or conquer thee in clemencie. Almightie God, who may requite thee in our behalfe, yeeld thee condigne favours for thy vertue. The Countie would have given him manie thinges of that praie that he had taken, but the yong maiden would accept nothing, faieng that the neighbours, feeing fuch gifts, woulde thinke and imagine that it were the price of hir virginitie that fhe had loft; and fo by that meanes fhe fhoulde fall into verie great infamie, which fhe rather chofe to flie than death, whereupon Frauncis Sforze difmiffing them, they joyfullie returned into their countrey.

Of many learned men, ancient and moderne, who violently and infortunatelie ended their daies.

THEMOSTOCLES, the Athenian, flue himfelfe. Lucretius, the Philofopher, died the felfefame death, and Gallus (as learned as both they) was murthered by his owne handes: Pliny was fmothered by fire in the mountaine Aetna.

Of many learned men.

Befides all thefe manie other, never feconded in fcience, perifhed finifterlie. Thales, the Milefian, died for thirfte: Zeno was flaine by the commandement of the tyrant Phalaris. Anaxarchus, by the judgement of Nicocreon, finifhed his life with manie tortures. Archimedes, the Philofopher, an excellent Mathematifian, was flaine by Marcellus fouldiers: Pythagoras, with his threefcore fchollers, was put to the fworde. Anacharfis died fuddenlie. Diodorus burft thorough harts greefe, by reafon he could not anfwer a queftion which Stilpo, the Philofopher, had propounded to him. Ariftotle, after he had loft the favour of Alexander, being in Calcide, drowned himfelfe in the floud Euripus. Califtines his fcholler was caft hedlong out of a window. Marcus Tullius had his ears and hands cut off, and fet up in the publike place where the Orators declaimed.

Seneca was put to death by his fcholler Nero, whoe had firft caufed his vaines to be opened in a bathe of hot water. Johannes Scotus, reading in England, by a fudden confpiracie of his fchollers was with his beft favorites put to death: but if I fhould undertake to repeat all the hapleffe endes of thefe ancients, who were excellent in learning, it were too long for me to write, or you to read. For which caufe I will begin to let you underftand the death of fome moderne learned. Petrach died fuddenlie; Domitius Calderinus perifhed through the fickneffe of the plague. Conciliator was burned alive. Angelus Politianus finifhed his daies by having his braines dafht out againft a wall. Peter Leo of Spoletum was drowned in a ditch: the Lorde Francis Pico was flaine by his tenants. Fisher and Thomas Moore were beheded; Cranmer and Latimer burned: the

reft, fince fresh in memorie, I need not trouble you with:
I onelie fet thefe down for the learned to confider uppon,
and examine themfelves by circumftances, and cunninglie
canvafe in their confcience an argument *a comparatis.*

*Howe kinge Rodorigo, the laft of the Royall houfe of the
   Gothes, loft his kingdome and life thorough his in-
   continence.*

IN the yeare 712 Roderigo raigned in Spaine, who, earneftlie enamored of a daughter of Julians, Countie of Can-
tabre, and defirous to gather the fruite of his love, becaufe
otherwife he might not, in that the maiden was verie
honeft and vertuous, he fent hir father embaffadour into
France, and by that opportunitie enforcing hir, he fatisfied
his lewd and diffolute luft. Julian returning into Spaine,
and underftanding the heavie cafe and eftate of his daughter, made fhew before the king that he was utterlie ignorant
thereof, and after a few daies he fled into Affrica with all
his familie, taking uppe his houfe in the cittie of Lepte;
and feeking out Muca, the governour of Affrica, hee tolde
him of the outrage doone him by the king; and howe for
that caufe he was come unto him, firft to offer him a great,
rich, and faire empire; next, to profer him his fervice:
and, moreover, faid he, the time is come to revenge the
Arabians which were flaine a few yeares paft in the hoaft
of king Bamba. To the performance whereof I will backe
you with the greater part of the Lords of Spaine, whoe
will be readie to affift you in this enterprife, bycaufe the
king is deadlie hated of them, both for his crueltie and
lawleffe corruption.

Muca sent him to king Mulit in Arabia, whoe, hearing Julianos purpose, dispatched him with letters to Muca, wherin he wrote that he should favour him with all reasonable helpes. Muca gave him an hundreth horsse and foure hundreth men on foote, under the conduct of a famous captaine called Tariffe: with this power they passed the seas and landed in Spaine; and to the end they might the more securelie beard the enimie, they builded a cittie which they called by the name of Tariffe, captaine of the Barbarians; and assoone as Julio had given notice to his confederates for what occasion he was come, and what desire he had to revenge him of the injurie doone unto him by the king, many of them united themselves with the Arabians and overran al the contrey of Algazera, which the said Juliano had in governement under the said king.

The Arabians of Africa, seeing the great progresse and fortune the countie had, and assured of his faith, sent him twelve thousand horsse and a great multitude of footmen, by reason that they had intelligence that the king had sent against him his cosin Ignicus with a huge host; who fighting many times unhappilie with the Moores, at the last was himselfe slaine, and all his followers cut in peeces: whereupon the Moores, being rid of this impediment, overran and spoiled a great parte of Spaine. For which cause the king levied a greater army than the first, and comming himselfe to wage the fight with the Moores, there fell a terrible and dreadfull battell betweene both the armies, which continued eight continuall daies, save onlie the intermission of night; but by reason of the rebellion of the two late kinges sonnes, called Detisa, the king had the worst, and perished in the field with many other valiant persons, and the

Moores, like couragious victors, poffeffed the fpoiles. This defeat was on funday, being the xi of Septeber in the yeare 719. The Moores, attaining victorie, had the dominion of Spaine.

Of many famous men, whoe, leaving the governement of the Commonweale, gave themfelves over to a private life.

CATO the Cenfor was the moft vertuous and beft reputed Romaine that flourifhed in that time; for during al the daies of his life there was never man that faw him commit anie light action, neither lofe or diminifhe any one inch of his fevere gravitie. This man, after he had lived fifty and eight yeares, leaving the travailes of the common wealth, went and fpent the remnant of his life in the kingdome of Naples, in a village called at that daie Picenio, and in this time Pozzuolo, living upon his owne livelihoods and revenews. And whileft thus this good and vertuous Cato lived fequeftred from all others, fometimes reading his bookes, fome other times trimming his vines, there was one of his neibours who wrote upon his gate with a coale, "O, fortunat Cato! thou only amongft al others knowft how to live in this world." Lucullus, the Conful and Romaine captaine, remained in the Parthian warres, and continued the fame for the tearme of fixteene yeares; in which he acquired much honor to Rome, many landes for the common weale, much fame to himfelf, and as great riches for his houfe. This man, after he returned from Afia to Rome, and found the common weale altogither fwarming with diffentions, by reafon of the factions of Scilla and Marius, purposed with himselfe to leave Rome, and to build him a certaine place of pleasure neere Naples, upon the river of the sea at this daie called Castello di Lupo; in which place he reposed ten yeares, entitled to all kind of pleasures and quietnesse of mind, free from all travailes and troubles, till such time as he finished his wearied age with a contented and worthie death.

Dioclesian, after he had governed Rome and the emperie for the space of eighteene yeares, utterlie refusing all the empire, departed Rome, and repaired to Salona in Dalmatia, where he was borne. But two yeares after that he had refused the Romain empire, an honourable embassage was sent by the senate unto him, praieng him earnestlie that he would have pitie on the commons and content himselfe to returne to Rome. It chanced that at such time as the said embassadors came into his poore and homelie cottage, hee himselfe was in a little garden he had, setting of lettises and divers other hearbes; and assoone as he had heard the discourse of that they were to deliver him, he returned them this answer: Seemeth it a requisite matter unto you, my freendes, that he who hath planted, cut and watered lettice as these be, should leave them to seeke royalties, and not to eate them in repose and quiet in his owne house? Yes, my friends; it is better eating these in quiet, then governing of Rome with care.

Moreover, he said unto them: Now have I proved howe much it availeth to commande, and howe healthfull it is to plough and dig. Leave me, therefore, I pray you, in my house: for why, I rather desire to get my living in this village with my handes, than to have the charge of the Romaine empire, accompanied with hate. Porides, the

Athenian, having in great juſtice governed his common weale for the ſpace of ſixe and thirtie yeares, at laſte growing olde and ſatiate of publike affaires, departing Athens, he went unto a certein lordſhip of his, left him by his aunceſtors in a certeine village without the citie; in which, plieng his booke by night, and labouring in his fields by day, he lived fifteene yeares more. Above the doores of his houſe theſe words were written:

*In veni portum: ſpes et fortuna valete
Nil mihi vobiſcum eſt, ludite nunc alios.*

Scipio, the Affrican, was one of the beſt beloved and honored captaines that ever Rome had: for in the ſpace of ſixe and twentie yeares, wherein he continued warre in Spaine, in Affrica and Aſia, he never committed anye diſhoneſt action, neither loſt any battell: he never denied any man juſtice, neither was there ever one obſcure or baſe thought knowne in him: he ſubjugated Africa, ruinated Carthage, overcame Hannibal, deſtroied Numantia, and alſo reſtored Rome, which, after the battell of Cannas, was almoſt forſaken and abandoned. This man, in the two and fiftie yeare of his age, departed Rome and retired himſelfe unto a little farme of his which was betwixt Pozzuolo and Capua; in which (as Seneca witneſſeth) he had no other revenewes but certeine fields wherein he lived, a houſe wherein he lodged, a barne wherein he bathed, and one of his nephues who ſerved him. And with ſo great affection retired hee himſelfe to the farme houſe, that for eleven yeares ſpace which he lived, he went not once to Capua, or ſet foot towardes Rome. All theſe excellent men of whom I have ſpoken, with manie infinite others alſo, left their kingdomes, confulſhips, governments, citties, pallaces, favourites, cares and riches for no other intent but a quiet life; intending after worldlie affaires to reconcile themſelves to a more ſtraight order, having reſpect to that which in-ſueth after death.

A moſt ſubtill diſpute made in Antioch, in the preſence of king Ptolomey, by ſeven ſeverall Ambaſſadors, which of their common-weales had the beſt lawes and moſt notable cuſtomes.

PLUTARCH writeth, in his booke *De exilio*, that king Ptolomey being in Antiochus, there were, upon an appointed day at dinner with him, many embaſſadors from the Romaines, Carthagenians, Scicilians, Rhodians, Athenians, Lacedemonians and Scicilians; whoe, falling into diſputation amongſt themſelves, everie one began to praiſe and extoll their countries lawes and cuſtomes as the beſt and moſt exquiſite.

The diſpute was handled with great fervencie betweene them, and with manie reaſons each one endevoured him ſelfe to dignifie his ſtate; for which cauſe Ptolomey, deſirous to know the truth, and to bring all contentions and diſcords to an exigent, commanded them that everie one ſhould write or ſpeake their cuſtomes or perfect lawes which they had in their common weales, for by that means it might be eaſilie judged which province beſt deſerved the palme of juſtice.

The embaſſadors of Rome began, and ſaid, We hold our temples in wonderous great honor and reverence: we yeeld great obfervance to our governors and rulers: we greevouflie punifh the wicked offenders and malefactors.

The Embaffadors of Carthage faid, in the Common-weale of Carthage the nobles ceafe not to fight, the commons and mechanicall perfons to labour, the Philofofers and learned to inftruct.

They of Scicilie faid, In our lande we obferve intire juftice, we traffique with upright confcience, and generallie imbrace equalitie.

They of Rhodes faid, In our common weale the olde people are honeft, the yonger fort fhamefaft, the Ladies and women folitarie and filent.

The Athenian Embaffadors faid: In our common weal the rich are not permitted nor allowed to be partiall, the poore to be idle; neither thofe that governe are fuffered to be ignorant.

The Lacedomonians faid, In our ftate envie reigneth not becaufe all are egall; nor avarice becaufe our goods are in common; nor any fuffred to be idle, but everie one doth labour.

The Scicionians faied, In our common weale we permit nor maintaine any travailler, leaft returning home againe he fhould bring us matters of noveltie: neither admit we Phyfitians, who fpoile and kill the whole; nor Orators who maintaine publike contentions.

Affoone as Ptolomy had heard all the feven Ambaffadors, he praifed all their common weales, faieng, that they were juftlie and worthilie governed, commendinge their cuftomes, and holding their lawes praife worthie: where upon with great honors everie one returned to his lodging, glorifieng and rejoycing in their credit, and fatisfied in his jufticc.

Strange Lawes of Tirzus the Tyrant, where through he withstood Conspiracies.

TRIZUS, the Tyrant, indeavouring to prevent the conjurations and tresons which might be imagined and wrought against him by his cittizens, forbad them by an especiall and prescript law to surcease their private and publike conferences, tyranizing aswell over their toongs as their tresure. But his cittizens envieng and hating this his commandements, kept their consultations by becks, gestures and eager countenances when they were agreeved, and smiling and pleasant lookes when they were contented: if dangers threatned them, they frowned; if Fortune fawned, they were not froward: by this meanes expressing and shewing the affections of their minds, and deluding the pollicie of the tyrant.

Tirzus, seeing and beholding this varietie in the faces of his cittizens, began to feare, and for that cause forbad them such like significative and mute consult: whereupon one of his cittizens, amongst the rest, repining at his tyrannie invented a new meanes; and entering the pallace with other friends, wept and cried out verie bitterlie. The Tyrant, understanding heereof, hasted him with some of his guard to deprive the eies of their naturall libertie, in like manner as he had reduced the toong and gestures into servitude; but the people amazedlie hating his insolence, drew the weapons out of the hands of his guard, and murthered him and all his followers.

FINIS.

INTRODUCTION.

THIS singular poetical tract seems, until now, never to have been heard of in our bibliography; but it is of value as the production of a man who was, at least, joint-editor of one of the most famous miscellanies in our language, "The Gorgeous Gallery of Gallant Inventions," 4to., 1578. The name of Thomas Procter will be found, not only on the title-page, but at the end of the small work in the hands of the reader: his father, John Procter, was at one time Master of Tunbridge School; and, among other pieces, he wrote an account of Sir T. Wyat's insurrection, Wyat having been a resident in Leeds Castle.

In the Stationers' Registers, under the date of 17th August 1584, we find a hitherto unnoticed entry regarding the son; which shows that he then became free of the Company, and that John Aldee, to whom Thomas Procter (or Proctor, as it is there spelt) had been apprenticed, had paid three shillings and four pence for his admission. This fact may explain the words at the bottom of our title-page, "Published by T. P.;" and, probably, he had been both printer and publisher of his own verses. Whether they were intended for general, or only for private circulation, we cannot ascertain; but, if for the latter, it may serve to show how, and why, the work became so scarce, that it has escaped notice from about 1585 (when it probably appeared) to the present day. It may have been Thomas

Procter's first essay as a printer and stationer, though we know that he commenced as a poet some years earlier. This circumstance makes us the more confident in our opinion, that Owen Roydon was the editor of the first portion of "The Gorgeous Gallery," and that Thomas Proctor was mainly concerned in the "pretty pamphlets," which he contributed with his own name, towards the conclusion.

The poems which we now reproduce have little value in themselves, and may establish that Thomas Procter had not improved in style or originality between 1578 and 1585. His account of the siege of Troy, with Helen's lamentation, has more merit in the choice of the subject than in the execution: it was then a comparative novelty in our versification, although the story, on the authority of Dares and Dictys, had been known in our language, by the aid of Caxton, for about a century. The last piece in our reprint is curious on account of its personal relation to the writer; but out of what events it arose, we are quite ignorant. We are led to infer, from some expressions in his address of warning and reproof to young people, that Procter's own early career had not been very staid or regular, and, perhaps, his enemy had assailed him on this vantage ground. If Procter, as is likely, afterwards vindicated himself, such vindication has yet to be discovered.

In reprinting this literary curiosity, we have followed the original so exactly, that we have preserved Procter's errors of grammar, orthography and punctuation.

J. P. C.

THE TRIVMPH

of Trueth, manifesting the aduanceme[n]t
of Vertue, and the ouerthrow of Vice. Wherin
Youth is admonished to withdrawe
his affection from the
vain seducements
of Fancie.

¶ **Set down with sundry Inuentions for
modest Recreation.**

*Heerunto is added Cæsars Triumph,
the Gretians Conquest, and the
Desert of Diues.*

―――――――

Published by T. P.

Nil tam difficile quod non solertia vincat.

THE TRIVMPH
of Trueth.

WHEN God had by his mightie power
    made heauen the earth & sea:
Hee shaped Adam in his fourme
    from earthy slime and clay.
And placed him in Paradice,
    as keeper of the same:
But hee transgrest, then God was wrath.
    Who turnd him thence with shame.
Wherby, wee Children vnto him,
    and heires vnto his fall:
Are apt by Nature vnto sinne,
    and subiect vnto thrall.
Such is in vs the small regarde,
    which Nature dooth vs giue:
If Reason did not teach a mean,
    to learn vs wel to liue.
The pleasures of our pamperd Prime,
    wherin wee vse to ioy:
Are but seducements vnto sinne,
    whence springeth our annoy.
For let vs run our youthful race,
    vnto our largest lust:
If not ere Age, when yeeres comes on,
    wee finde therin no trust.

Yet wilful Youth ſo careleſſe is,
    that hee dooth rather chuſe :
Although he ſees how vain it is,
    the wayes of vice to vſe
Whence nether looue or freendly ſpeech
    may ſeem to mooue his minde :
Nor others harmes of lothſome ſhame,
    which Follies fall dooth finde,
Deceit by wiles induceth him,
    to taſte her poiſned ſap :
When Error in his tender yeeres,
    dooth lul him in her lap.
Wherewith his witleſſe wil is brought,
    vnto his owne deſire :
From ſinne to ſinne in wilful meanes,
    hee ſeeketh to aſpire.
The dayly danger of whoſe fall,
    if hee conſider well :
With feare may daunt his careleſſe minde,
    in ſeeking to rebel.
What greeuous greef is it to ſee,
    th' vntruſt of his eſtate :
What cruel horror to obtain,
    for ſinne his Parents hate.
How lamentable iſt to ſee,
    therof the lothſome ſhame ?
How greeuous to the eare to heare
    Of Follie the exclame.
Beſide what greef may greater bee,
    the[n] Parents to beholde :
A ſhamleſſe ſonne in ſhameful ſorte,
    his ruin to vnfolde.

The Trivmph of Trueth.

Wee fee by proof the truftleffe fteps
    which witleffe Youth dooth tread.
Wee fee how vain defire by wiles,
    to follie dooth him lead.
Whofe wilful paths fo plefant be,
    in foothing of his minde:
That hee forgets how vain it is,
    vntil his fall hee finde.
The tedious care his Parents had,
    in tendring of his youth:
The toyle they took in teaching him,
    to follow what is trueth.
The coft of welth they did beftowe,
    in learning vpon him:
The charge in nurifhing his Corps,
    and clothing of it trim.
Are foon forgot as things of nought.
    When hee comes vp to yeeres,
And vnregarding of him felf,
    forgets his Parents cares.
His learning left, the coft beftowed
    vpon him is in vain:
His profit quite forgot vntill
    his pleafure breeds his pain.
All things are irkfome vnto him,
    which dooth his minde perfwade:
Vnto his good, but they are fweet
    which fhameleffe finnes doo fhade.
What lothfome vice leaues hee vnvfde,
    what meanes dooth hee procure?
In feeking fondly after that,
    which Reafon prooues vnfure.

His wilful Fancie hee dooth feed,
  with follies that be vain :
His eyes delight to gaze vpon
  the troup of Venus train.
His courſie Carcaſſe hee dooth make,
  inferiour vnto luſt :
His minde is redy to receiue,
  the goods he gets vniuſt.
His harmful hart dooth bode with harme,
  his lothſome tung dooth tel :
His ſhameleſſe ſin in ſhameleſſe ſorte,
  the which contents him wel,
It greeueth him to come in place,
  where godly liuers bee :
The ſimple he derides and ſmiles
  their dealings iuſt to ſee.
Hee glories of the gotten gain,
  which wrongfully hee gets :
Hee borrowes but hee ſeeketh not,
  again to pay his dets.
Hee runnes from place to place,
  and hath no certain ſtay :
Such are the frutes of them who ſeeks,
  by ſinne their owne decay.
Whoſe greeuous end of life is ſuch,
  as may example giue :
To other viewers of their fall,
  to learn them wel to liue.
But ſhameleſſe ſinne dooth beare ſuch ſawy
  within the mindes of Youth :
That hee is careleſſe to receiue,
  the warninges tends to trueth.

And wilful led from bad to wurffe,
  as fenceleffe of refpect:
Their dutie vnto God and Man,
  doo more and more neglect:
For as hee groweth vnto yeeres,
  fo growes hee vnto fin:
Delighted with the filthie vice
  they haue been noufled in.
And fondly foothing of him felf,
  to run his retchleffe race:
Dooth finde occafion at the length,
  to mone his wretched cafe.
For proofe wee fee by dayly vieu,
  the fhameleffe fall of fuch:
Who vnregarding of their weale,
  doo truft their wits to much.
The minde of Youth is fetled fo,
  vnto his owne defire:
That hee is redy to obey,
  what filthie finnes require.
More perfect proofe hath not been feen,
  then prefent at this day:
So careleffe Youth is proued now,
  to feeke his owne decay.
And feeding of his careleffe minde,
  with fancies that be vain:
The mean eftate of quiet life,
  dooth ftoubbornly difdain:
Shall (I faith hee) inferiour bee,
  or feeme to yeeld to thofe:
Whofe counfaile to my luftie prime,
  no tafte of plefure fhowes.

What shall it need? the World is wide,
    and I for one shall shift :
In euery place where so I come,
    my learning is a gift.
My stock wil serue mee yet awhile,
    my Feends wil redy bee :
If I shall want at any time,
    with aid to succor mee.
Who ventures not, shall neuer win,
    who looks not, can not finde :
Thus carelesse youth with fond conceits,
    dooth sooth his retchlesse minde.
But when that hee hath spent his time,
    in running of his race :
And wasted what his Freends him left,
    ashamde to showe his face.
With wishes vain I would (saith hee)
    that I had been content :
To learn a trade to liue in Youth,
    which lewdly I haue spent.
The fauour which hee surely thought,
    by freendship to obtain :
Hee prooues vnsure, and hee is forst,
    to sterue or els take pain.
His former Freendes beholdes his want,
    and wish him to forsee :
The danger of his poor estate,
    wherin hee seemes to bee.
His learning nought preuaileth him,
    to help him at his need :
And profferd seruice seldome now,
    of entertainments speed.

The Trivmph of Trueth.

Thus beeing left through lewd attempt
    in danger of his fall :
To ruin, fhame and mifery,
    hee yeelds him felf a thrall.
From whence fuch careful thoughts of greef
    doo daunt his troubled breft :
That though he would yet can hee not,
    enioy his former reft.
Wherby he falls to further vice,
    vnleffe of mercy great :
God dooth withdrawe his careleffe minde,
    with filthy finne repleat
My felf hath tryed vnto my greef,
    th' vntruft of wilful youth :
My felf hath lothde the freendly fpeech,
    which tended vnto trueth,
And foothing of my felf in fin,
    as careleffe of my good :
Forgot the proffit of my prime,
    which Refons fkil withftood.
In which eftate of careleffe life,
    I often did beholde :
Such fundry fhiftes of fhameleffe finne,
    as greeues mee to vnfolde.
Such filthie follies wherwithall,
    through Fancie Youth is led :
Such boafting vaunts of vanitie,
    which rules his idle hed.
Such wilful motions of the minde,
    fuch pampering vp in pride :
Such dealings tending to deceit,
    as few can them abide.

Such fraude fuch cruel othes in vain,
    to couer his abufe:
Such redines of wit and minde,
    to put his finne in vfe.
Such trufting to his owne conceit,
    fuch bofting of his wit:
Such feeking after vain delights,
    as fure are far vnfit.
Such fmall regarde of Parents care,
    fuch little dutie showen:
To Elders, as vntil this time,
    the like hath not been knowen.
Such lewd neglecting of their good,
    fuch following what is vain:
Such shifts to put his vice in vre,
    with coullours of difdain.
Bad are the feeds which hee doth fowe,
    but wurffe he reaps again:
Hee loades him felf with heapes of harmes,
    which he cuts vp with pain.
His harveft is a lothfome greef,
    his labour tedious toyle:
And looking for a fertile ground,
    hee findes a brambled foyle.
For though a while he fondly feeds,
    his fancie with delight:
Ere long it vades as vapours doo,
    deminish from our fight.
His youthful pleafures paffe away,
    as dooth a blaft of winde:
Whofe force once paft vnto our vieu,
    no ftate dooth leaue behinde.

The Trivmph of Trueth.

And as the dreadful wallowing waues,
    which furgeffe in the feas:
Are of no force when as the calme,
    their furie dooth appeafe.
So is the ftay of youthes eftate,
    which cannot long indure,
Becaufe it hath a thoufand meanes,
    his chaunges to procure.
For as hee hath a time to liue,
    fo all things haue a time
And Time dooth vade, fo certain doo
    the pleafures of our prime.
Our time the ancient Writers haue,
    definde as wingd to flee.
With back and hed behinde all bare,
    whofe locks before her bee.
The reafon why becaufe there is,
    in her a prefent ftate,
Which paft, to call her back again,
    wee prooue it is to late.
Her wings expreffe how fwift fhee is,
    our careleffe mindes to leaue:
Efteeming not the proffit good,
    in time we might receiue.
Wherfore if Youth would haue refpect,
    vnto his prefent time:
With wifhes vain olde Age fhould not,
    bemone his idle prime.
With forrowing fighs from heuy hart,
    hee need not to lament:
The follies of his fancy fond
    if time had wel been fpent.

But when he lewdly dooth neglect,
    the time which prefent is :
To ferue his vfe when need requires,
    a time fhall furely miffe.
Then learn to vfe thy time fo wel,
    that left when time is paft :
Thou wifh thou hadft employd thy felf,
    when profferd time did laft.
Look ere thou leap haue care vpon,
    the danger of thy fall :
Remember that thy felf and thine,
    at length to cinders fhall.
What haft thou then to vaunt vpon,
    what glorie is in thee ?
Thy dayes decaies, thy pleafures paffe,
    thy carcaffe lothde fhalbee.
Be mindful how vnfure it is,
    to troft to thine eftate :
Then with thy felf of what is vain,
    thou fhalt the motions hate.
Haue care for what intent thou waft,
    appointed on the earth :
Remember that thy time is vain,
    when comes vncertain death.
Vfe heer thy talent to thee lent,
    that when thou makfte account :
How thou haft fpent the vfe therof,
    th' increafe may wel furmount.
Flee from the waies of filthie vice,
    learn wel in time to liue :
Bee mindful that vnto the Lord,
    thou fhalt a reckoning giue.

The Trivmph of Trueth.

Delay not of from day to day,
    to call thy felf from fin:
Remember how vncertain is,
    the ftate thou lieueft in.
Efchue the fnares of vain delight,
    as meanes vnto thy fall:
Learn how to leaue fuch follies fond,
    which may procure thy thrall.
And to the warnings of thy Freends,
    be redy to obey:
Left vnregarding of their woords,
    thou runft to thy decay.
Let others fall example giue,
    in teaching thee to flee:
The futtle fnares of fhamelesse finnes,
    whofe paths diftruction bee.
Thus in thy youth in Vertue liue,
    So fhall thine Age be bleft:
And when thy earthly life is paft,
    thy foule fhall liue in reft.

FINIS.

Nil tam dificile quod non folertia vincat.

THE ARGUMENT OF THE TRIUMPH.

Frō tender yeers when Youth is brought
To knowledge by the Parents care:
The gifts of good which Learning wrought
To vain attempts feduced are.

The leud defires of Fancies willes,
Withdrawes his mīde from Vertues lore :
And feeds his wit with worldly guiles,
Which retchleffe life, makes Age deplore.

His Parents woords and weeping eyes,
Can not perfwade him vnto good :
(But as vnmeet) their fpeech defies,
As though that Refon it withftood.

Yet when his youthful yeeres are fpent,
And Age with ftealing fteps drawes ny :
With triftfull teares his cheeks befprent,
To late his Fancies fhall defie.

FINIS.

Sola Virtus.

Shall hautie harts enioy ye ftately feat
Of heauēly power by their vfurping pride
Shall redy wits by learned Art intreat,
With bleffed Saints as equall to abide ?
Shall worldly men whofe riches doo aboūd
For gotten welth a heuenly place obtain ?
Is this ye mean wheron we ought to groūd
Our erneft faith ? no, thefe be vaūtes of vain
Its vertuous life, whofe hautie honor is
By Fame extolde vnto the loftie Skie :
Frō whence wee get the path to perfect blis
Which thefe vain vaūtes makes men deny.

The Trivmph of Trueth.

Shee liues exilde fmall reftīg place fhe hath
Although fhe feemes to fit in euery bower :
Her godly fear of modeft life decaith :
As vnefteemd, & vice depriues her power.

Bona vertuntur in mala.

The fhāleffe fins which fhāleffe fots doo vfe
W^tdrawes ye minde frō vertue vnto vice :
And wallowing in their owne cōceites abufe
The gifts they ought to gouern w^t advice.
Few liues content w^t their appointed ftate
Mofte enuies at their neibours good fucceffe
Mindes are corrupted w^t a deadly hate,
All are enclinde to follow wickednes.
Sin fits aloft and treads down Godlynes,
Vice conquers vertue, falfhod wrōgeth trueth
Hate hinders looue, plenty by couetoufnes
Is waxed poor, the greater is the rueth.
Freendfhip is colde & woordes efteemed wīde
Deeds few or none belonging vnto good :
Flattery dooth florifh ye fimple forte to blinde,
And fmiling lookes are redy to fpill blood.
In plefant fpeech deceitful craft is hid,
In promife fair, performaunce is not found :
Refon and right in matters are forbid,
Rich wrongs ye poor, & preffe thē to ye groūd.
Few things are doon as they apointed were,
Good gifts of God are turned to abufe :
The mindes of men to finne adicted are,
Of this vain world fuch is the common vfe.

FINIS.

THE ARGUMENT.

Among the motions of my Minde,
    mee thought I plain did fee:
How Cæfar in his armour braue,
    aduaunft his force to mee.
Which glorie when hee had pronounft,
    by reafon I did finde:
In feeking of fuch great Attempts,
    Ambition moou'd his minde.
Wherwith the honor of his deeds,
    beeing blemifht with defire
Of Lucre, vanish from my fight,
    as fmoke dooth from the fire.

FINIS.

Giue place, let Iulius Cæfar fpeak,
    whofe name Reporte dooth fou[nd
Through out the World for conquefts g[reat
    in fundry Regions found.
Whofe Rumor raifd by fuch Report
    for his victorious might:
Made Forrains feare of force of Ar[mes
    with Cæfar for to fight.
Who rulde but Iulius Cæfar then
    who bare the fway but hee
Bothe People ftout and Citties fair,
    inferiour were to mee.
I got renowme in euery place

The Trivmph of Trueth.

    if men renoum'd may bee:
And got the glorie of the Earth,
    for Marsses pollicie.
Huge Castels, Towers and Du[kes
    by mee were ouer throwen
None durst the Romains force r[esist
    defiance beeing showen.
With Rampiers huge I rased d[own
    their cities which were [strong
Bulwarks built of mightie stone
    my forces laid along
I tr]encht their Cities round about,
    and did them vndermine
I scalde their Fortes and made the men,
    in caues them selues to shrine.
My furie death, my fauor life.
    vnto the yeelding minde:
The] neighbour Regions round about,
    to tribute I did binde.
Of mine] exploits perceiuing then,
    the glorie and the gain:
I full so]on sought by leude desire,
    such honor to obtain.
But wh]at preuaileth it to gain,
    or conquer all the earth:
When] bothe the man and what he hath,
    is subiect vnto death.

FINIS.

The Argument.

Ag]ain me thought I plainly heard
    [ho]w Helen did bemone :
Her li]fe and death whofe beauty was
    inferior vnto none
To m]ee fhee breefly made difcourfe
    how Greeks huge Troy did fack :
The Troyans flew and fhee her felf
    therof did feel the wrack.
Whofe woful motions when I fcand,
    it greeued mee to fee :
So braue a Dame in Natures gifts
    of Vertue void to bee.
And as the Flower whofe beautie is,
    dride vp with fcorching heat
Mee thought the glorie of her gifts,
    fel down from Honors feat.

FINIS.

The Gretians Conqueft.

When Helen fair by Paris was,
    conueid to Troy foom Greece :
They warres begun as enuied with,
    the loffe of fuch a Peece.
Who beeing fled and kept in Troy,
    the Greeks imbaffadge fent :
To Troy to fetch their Queen again,
    if Troians would confent.

Which meffage when the Troyans fcand,
  their anfwere thus they made :
That Helen as a gueft to Troy
  did come, and her denaid.
If Paris did (quoth they) obtain
  her fauour by his fute :
The Greeks vnto vs Troyans can,
  no caufe of wrong impute.
If wee by force of Armes had fetcht
  your Helin to our Land :
And feemed when fhee was in Greece,
  the Gretians to withftand.
To win her thence, as wrongd you might,
  to Troy defiance giue :
(But beeing heer) fhee fhall remain
  in Troy while Troyans liue.
What Paris did when hee as Gueft,
  arriued in your Realm :
Wee haue not for to deal therwith,
  yet deem wee it extream
That fuch defiance fhould be fent
  to vs (Men ignorant)
How Paris did your Helin gain
  not mooued by our graunt.
And for your threats wee way them not,
  wee Troyans redy are :
As you for her, fo wee for him,
  fhall yeeld our felues to war.
This anfwere made, the Gretians ftrait,
  made hafte vnto their Land :
And told how ftout the Troyan did
  their meffage fent withftand.

Wherwith the King an armie huge,
    did prefently prepare:
And fent them vnto Troy with fpeed,
    the Troyans force to dare.
Long was the warre, great was the fight,
    and many People flain:
The Troyans kept their Citie fafe
    wherby the Greeks in vain
Did think their comming for to be,
    and with their whole affent:
Were minded to return to Greece,
    when ten yeeres war was fpent.
But Pallas bearing fpight at Troy,
    procurde the Greeks to frame:
A mightie horfe, of timber built,
    in honor of her name.
Which beeing placed neer the wall,
    the armed Greeks did lurck,
Within the horfe, til Sinon did,
    his craftie practice woork.
The Troyans deeming that the Greeks
    had left their war, and gon
To Greece again, the Gates of Troy,
    did open thereupon.
And People had delight to walk,
    ful ten yeeres kept in holde,
To vieu the place where Greeks erft lay,
    their paffage to withholde.
And alfo for to gaze vpon,
    the huge and ftately frame:
Of timber built, which they had lefte
    to Pallas endleffe fame.

The Trivmph of Trueth.

Vnminding of the fubtle wiles.
    the Greeks therin did hide:
Nor yet efteeming of the harmes,
    therby they fhould abide.
Although with furious mood,
    Laocoon loud did crye:
And wild the Troyans of the Greeks,
    the treafon to defie.
Atlength with falfe and fubtle fhowes
    of heuie penfiue breft:
His face befprent with brinifh teares,
    complaning of vnreft.
Comes Sinon foorth in fimple forte,
    brought bound vnto the vieu:
Of Troyans all, who blamde the Greeks
    as bloody beafts vntrue.
When Greeks (quoth hee) from war were bent
    in recompence of praife
To Pallas as an Offering ment,
    to end my breathing dayes.
But when I faw their furious rage,
    to mee poor wretch forlorne:
I ftole from them to faue my life,
    which long they held in fcorne.
(I fled) at length they did erect,
    this mightie frame of wood:
To pallas as a prefent great,
    for facrifice of blood.
Which if you can by any meanes
    conuey into your Town:
As iniur'd with a fpiteful wrong
    the Greeks in rage will frown.

Thus yeelding of his life to them,
　　with falling on the ground
Before the King, hee pitie took,
　　wild him to be vnbound.
On vow he would to him and Troy,
　　a faithful fubiect liue:
Wherto by othes to fhroude his craft,
　　his promife hee did giue.
But lo, ere long his time did ferue,
　　to put his guile in vre:
And opned wide the horfes paunch,
　　when Troyans thought them fure.
From whence there iffued armed men,
　　who gaue them felues to fight:
Burnt vp the houfes huge in Troy,
　　and fpoyld them in the night.
The Citie flamde, the People cryde,
　　amazed from their fleep:
No meanes they had to faue them felues,
　　their foes their force did keep.
They flung the fire from place to place,
　　the Troyans they did flea:
Theirs was the conqueft then of Troy,
　　they lookt for ten yeeres day.
The ancient Sires they ouerthrew,
　　the Matrones they did kil:
Yung men and Maides they forft to death,
　　And Infants blood did fpil.
The fonne before the Fathers face,
　　bereued was of life:
Great was the flaughter then in Troy,
　　ere ended was the ftrife,

Wherin that Helen falfe of faith,
    vnto her wedded mate:
Did lofe her life as one deferu'de,
    for caufing of the hate.
For who but Helin bare the fway,
    in Troy while Troy did reign:
And did againft the Gretians force,
    the Troyans war maintain.
Thus Troy was fackt, the People flain,
    which ftood and erft did liue:
For Helens fake who moning now
    thefe fpeeches foorth dooth giue.

Helens Complaint.

See heer by due deferued death,
    the fall of mine eftate:
And learn to fhun ambitious pride,
    whence rifeth deadly hate.
My beautie what preuoileth mee,
    or ftate of Honors feat:
The vain defire of lawleffe luft,
    my fal may wel repeat.
A peerleffe Prince of beautie braue,
    feduced with defire:
Did yeeld vnto the vain delights,
    which fancie did require.
Whome neither loue of princely fere,
    nor honors hye degree:
Might mooue to liue within the mean,
    of vertuous modeftie.

But yeelding to the plefant fpeech,
    of Paris did confent :
To leaue the glorie of my dayes,
    ere youthful yeeres were fpent.
Whofe hainous fact hath been the fpoyle,
    of many a Troyans life
And Gretians to, fince them between,
    began the deadly ftrife.
My felf pertaker of their woes,
    hath tafted of their fall :
By dint of fwoord becaufe I was,
    the vrger of their braul.
Loe, thus beholde the fall of finne,
    the ruine and the fhame :
Of fuch as look not in their liues,
    to liue in honeft fame.   *FINIS.*

Argument.

After the fight and fpeech of thefe,
    rich Diues did prefent :
His life his fall and his eftate,
    with forrowing teares befprent,
Wherin he did difclofe to mee,
    how fubiect Worldlings liue :
To ruin, as his owne eftate,
    to vs example giue.   *FINIS.*

See worldlinges fee th' ūtruft of your eftate
Beholde the pomp & glory of your time :
Look vpon mee (now dead) who liued late

(As you) on earth inferiour vnto crime,
Delighted with the plefures of my Prime.
And foothed with the follies of my minde :
The due deferts of follies pathes I finde.

No certain ftate I had to vaunt vpon,
My glorie was compared to the flower :
Vnlooked for my ftately ftrength was gon,
To faue my life it lay not in my power.
Or might prolong the minute of an houre.
Death ftrook his ftroke, I might no lōger liue
Though in my hands I thoufandes had to giue.

The worldly welth which I had leudly got
My careful cōfcience makes mee to expres :
To fhroude fuch acts my guilty hart cānot,
In life I vfde the wayes of wickednes,
Would God I had contented been with leffe
And not haue fought by leud defire yᵉ droffe,
Which dayly is inferiour vnto loffe.

What booted mee to build vp houfes braue,
To purchafe landes or keep my goods in ftore
All are depriu'd my body laid in graue,
The greedy woormes my caren carcafe gore
The worm of cōfcience prickes me more and more
The hanous fin I vs'd while I did liue :
As due deferu'd a thoufand torments giue.

Fie on the filthines of greedie gain,
Fie on the fubtle fleights of leud defire :

Fie vpon plefure, Nurifher of Pain,
Fie on vntrueth which worldly men require
Fie on yᵉ fin, which mooues our God to ire.
Wo worth yᵉ man whofe hart dooth burn wᵗ hate
Twife happy hee content with his eftate.

I loth'd to hear the needie mans requeft,
I grudg'd to giue but ioyed to retain :
No godly feare did harbour in my breft,
The Scriptures red I termed fpeech in vain
Of godly life the ftate I did difdain
To hourde vp droffe I did decline my minde :
In heaps wherof no certain ftate wee finde.

Diues I am, who fcorned Lazarus,
Whofe gotten gain of riches did furpaffe :
For which mifdeed I am tormented thus,
In flāes of fire which neuer quenched was
For worldly men a perfect looking glaffe.
Wherby they may perceiue the fall of fin :
And learn in life the ioyes of heauen to win.

FINIS.

An Inuectiue againft Enuie.

When Enuie in his furious rage,
 had fpitted forth his fpight :
Againft the falfnes of his fpeech,
 I thought it beft to write.
Wherby I might difcharge my felf,

of his vnlawful charge:
Which in my abfence (to my greef)
    hee hath put forth at large
But though falfe Enuie fought by fpight,
    to blemifh my good name:
Yet tryed trueth in tract of Time
    fhall vtter his defame.
And all the threatning bragging boafts,
    which witleffe he hath vfde:
Without controle my tung fhall tel,
    how vyle he me abus'de.
The freendly fpeech which he did vfe,
    attending to deceit:
Til hee had caught me in his fnare,
    and chokte mee with his bait.
Was fo delightful vnto mee,
    in following of his train:
That all the warnings Refon vfde,
    I deemed woords in vain.
But yeelding vnto his requeft,
    I fee I did confent:
Vnto the ruin of my felf,
    wherto his minde was bent.
For as the blinded floeworme dooth,
    in darcknes fhine like Golde:
So his falfe woords (I witleffe) thought,
    that only trueth they tolde.
But as the day light dooth withdrawe,
    the flowwormes gliftring hue:
So trueth dooth manifeft to mee,
    his deeds and woords vntrue.

Wherfore vntil the running ſtreames,
   returns from whence they flowe :
The woords of Enuie ſhall not ſpeed,
   when Trueth pronounceth (no.)

☞   FINIS.   *Thomas Procter.*

Nil tam dificile quod non ſolertia vincat.